Playing Their Part

Playing Their Part

Language and Learning in the Classroom

Nancy King

HEINEMANN Portsmouth, NH

HEINEMANN
A division of Reed Elsevier Inc.
361 Hanover Street
Portsmouth, NH 03801-3912
Offices and agents throughout the world

Every effort has been made to contact the copyright holders for
permission to reprint borrowed material where necessary. We regret
any oversights that may have occurred and would be happy to
rectify them in future printings of this work.

Some material from Chapter 2, "Stories: Shaping a Teacher's Life,"
first appeared in "My Own Beginning" in *Giving Form to
Feeling*, published in 1975 by Drama Book Specialists.

Library of Congress Cataloging-in-Publication Data
King, Nancy, 1936–
    Playing their part : language and learning in the classroom /
Nancy King.
        p.   cm.
    Includes bibliographical references.
    ISBN 0-435-08672-3
    1. Language arts (Elementary).   2. Interaction analysis in
education.   I. Title.
LB1576.K487   1995
372.6044—dc20   95-12799
                                                              CIP

Editor: Lisa Barnett
Production: Melissa L. Inglis
Cover and interior art: Kyra Teis
Cover design: Barbara Whitehead
Printed in the United States of America on acid-free paper
99 98 97 96 95 EB 1 2 3 4 5 6 7 8 9

....

This book is for
Anita Grünbaum and Karin Gustafsson

and in memory of
Grethe Eller

friends and colleagues for all times

Contents

ACKNOWLEDGMENTS *xi*

INTRODUCTION: Origins *1*

LAYING THE FOUNDATION

ONE: Questioning *7*
            Why Use the Arts in Education? *8*
            What Place Do Feelings Have in the Classroom? *9*
            How Might Giving Expression to Feeling Facilitate
                Learning? *11*
            What Formal Preparation Is Required of Teachers? *13*

TWO: Stories: Shaping a Teacher's Life *17*
            Maria *18*
            The Baseball Players *19*
            Catchers and Throwers *21*
            The Woman Who Was a Mountain *22*
            The Seven Boys *23*
            Cinderella *27*
            Resonance *33*

GROUNDWORK

THREE: Teacher Preparation *37*
            Observing Patterns *38*
            Describing Patterns *39*
            Designing a Study *40*
            Discovering Possibilities *40*
            Choosing a Solution *42*
            Reflecting on Choice and Process *42*

Regaining Access to Imagination *43*
Regaining Access to Creativity *44*
    Suggestions *45*
Ideas for Exploring Imagination and Creativity *45*

FOUR: Tools for Teaching Language Arts *49*
Imagemaking *50*
Storymaking *52*
Movement *55*
Drama *58*
Soundmaking and Music *61*
Ideas for Exploring Imagemaking, Storymaking, Movement, and
    Drama *64*

FIVE: Classroom Management *67*
Engagement *72*
Discipline *76*
Imagination, Creativity, and Expression *80*
Creating Community *84*
Collaborative Learning *91*
Components of Learning *96*
Process-Centered Learning *98*
    Suggestions *103*
Response-Tasks *104*

SOURCEWORK

SIX: Framework for Designing Classroom Activity *109*
Components of Program Design *109*
Organization of Activities *109*
Participation *110*
    Self-consciousness *110*
    Disruption *112*
    Suggestions for Planning Tasks *112*
Warming Up *114*
    Warm-Up Suggestions *114*
Relaxation *116*

SEVEN: Exploring Nonverbal Communication *119*
Exploration of Imagemaking *119*
Exploration of Movement *129*
Exploration of Soundmaking and Music *145*

CONTENTS

.... ix

EIGHT: Exploring Oral Language *159*
         Exploration of Storytelling   *159*
            The Buddy Business   *160*
            Sharing Stories in the Classroom   *168*
            Connecting the Story to the Storyteller   *169*
         Exploration of Drama   *170*

NINE: Exploring Written Language *185*
         Exploration of Poetry   *187*
         Exploration of Storymaking   *200*
            Choosing the Story   *200*
            Sharing the Story   *201*
         Exploration of Drama   *211*
            Creating a Framework for Writing Drama   *215*
            Writing Drama   *221*
            Selected Theatre Vocabulary   *234*
            Some Questions to Consider When Looking at a Script   *235*
            Playing the Play: Script in Hand   *236*

TEN: Reflection and Assessment *241*
         Establishing Priorities   *242*
         A Framework with Which to Begin   *244*
         Assessment Strategies to Encourage Learning   *247*
            Making Space for Children to Share in Planning   *247*
            Motivation   *250*
            Image Journals   *251*
            Reading Logs   *252*
            Learning Journals   *253*
            Student Portfolios   *254*
         Assessing Creative Work   *256*
            Love of Learning   *259*
            Educational Development   *259*
            Incentives and Rewards   *260*
            Exploring Connections Between Teaching Methods and
               Assessment   *260*
            Lifelong Development   *261*
            Questions Which Empower Children to Become Active
               Learners   *261*

AFTERWORD   *263*
REFERENCES   *265*
INDEX   *273*

Acknowledgments

I wish to thank the many teachers and children who have given of their time and energy, collaborating with me to explore and develop language arts programs in schools.

I especially grateful that my tireless readers, Claudia Reder, Julie Van Dyne, Ann Brown, Chris King, Glover Jones, Leveina Washington, and Phyllis Conner were willing to continue to read despite confusing organization and the many drafts that kept filling their mailboxes. My colleagues in Europe, Anita Grünbaum, Karin Gustafsson, Stig Starrsjö, Fiddeli Persson, Marianne Nikolov, and Lidia Doba'nyne, continue to share ideas that cross cultures and contexts.

It is a particular pleasure to have Kyra Teis design the cover and interior art. I first met her when she was twelve, a student in a course I designed to enable university students and area children to work together to create theatre from myth. Later, as her senior thesis advisor, I watched her transform from student to artist. Now we are colleagues.

I am deeply appreciative of the support of my editor Lisa Barnett and the staff of Heinemann who are a joy to work with.

Playing Their Part

Origins

Playing Their Part: Language and Learning in the Classroom, based on principles and ideas originating from my experiences in classrooms and workshops with children and teachers, evolved out of the Stories Project, a language arts program I developed to help children who were having difficulty reading, writing, and/or speaking. The Stories Project was developed as part of the service-learning component of the Honors Program at the University of Delaware. Students enrolled in the Stories Project course selected myths and tales from around the world to develop oral and written expression in children having difficulty reading, writing, and/or speaking in the classroom. University students working one-on-one with a child aged six to fourteen shared a story, and painted and sculpted images to evoke and enhance meaning. Each child then told or wrote a story, either made up or based on the child's real-life experience. The original images and stories were bound and given to the children to keep.

The program grew out of my love of stories, a desire to use the UNICEF collection of books at the University of Delaware, and a compelling belief that stories have a magical way of living inside us as a source of nourishment, hope, and wisdom, connecting us with other cultures and times.

For years, as consultant and teacher, I have used the arts (drama, poetry, imagemaking, movement, storymaking, and music) as the core of all my work in the classroom because the process of "making" (painting, sculpting, writing, moving, etc.) helps us connect who we are with what we think, feel, and know. Not only do we benefit from making, we also derive pleasure and self-esteem from ownership, from being able to say, "I made this." Children who make books from their stories, see their plays enacted, or keep learning journals, are more likely to feel they are persons of substance because they have tangible evidence of what they can do.

The actual writing of this book was fueled by a request from a

1

teacher who was participating in a workshop I was leading. With more than a hint of embarrassment and frustration in her voice, she told me she was disturbed by her anger in the classroom and disconcerted by her inability to respond creatively to her students. She said, "I enjoy teaching. I like my kids. But some days all I do is scream. Today, everything they did set my teeth on edge. I yelled. I warned. I threatened. Nothing worked. I'm tired of feeling stuck. I'm tired of being the bad guy. There's got to be a better way to help kids learn. What can I do?"

All teachers have days when nothing works. No teacher makes the right decision every time. When we are tired, harassed, feeling inadequate, or not up to the demands placed on us, it is even less likely that we will react as we might under easier circumstances. No teacher teaches every student equally well. Every teacher who has been teaching for more than a few days has met students she didn't like, couldn't reach, or wished would leave the classroom. As teachers, all we can do is develop a variety of activities and responses so that we are more likely to be able to use what is happening to and with our students to facilitate learning and growing.

Since beginning the Stories Project, I have become even more convinced not only that stories and the arts have a central place in education, but that their use is crucial if we want children to become active learners. Telling or writing stories is a superb way to synthesize disparate bits of information to create a new understanding of what one has been learning. It is also an excellent way to test both intelligence and competence because we are forced to make a whole narrative from isolated pieces of knowledge. Repeatedly, I have seen children who initially couldn't or didn't want to read, write, or speak, create stories, make plays, enter into discussions, and become interested in learning as a result of their experience with the arts. Perhaps this is because we all learn best when we are engaged, when what we are struggling to discover is personally important and meaningful.

Tragically for too many children, much of what goes on in classrooms and passes as education is based on memorization for its own sake in curricula designed by people who may not have set foot in a classroom since finishing their own education. All too often teachers are not helped to discover their own connection to learning. The specter of state and local testing shapes what is taught as does political, parental, and administrative pressure. Fear becomes a part of and partner to educational planning. Although children and teachers often start the new school year hopeful and excited, filled with energy and ready to begin learning, before much time has passed school becomes drudgery for many, a place to which one has to go. This does not have to continue.

We can make the classroom a place of excitement, challenge, discovery, and creativity if we are willing to pay close attention to the children in our classrooms.

Playing Their Part: Language and Learning in the Classroom is a book fueled by hope, curiosity, and an unwavering belief in the power of human beings to shape their identity, their knowledge, and their capacity to achieve wisdom if given the opportunity. It is a book of stories—old stories, new stories, personal stories, and stories about children and their teachers. I have recounted stories to share ideas, stimulate questions, nourish psyches, explore experiences, and impart wisdom which has been handed down from generations of storytellers. Telling stories has not only been the most effective way for me to communicate feelings, ideas, and experience in the classroom, it has also proven to be a powerful method to help people appreciate and honor the knowledge, insights, and experiences of people from other cultures and countries. Every time I tell a story to my students, each hears the story in her or his own way, taking from it what seems most important. Others have the same experience. As a small Japanese-American child, author Lydia Minatoya was told the Japanese tale of "Momotaro the Peach Boy," about a childless couple who find a small boy inside a peach and lovingly raise him until he grows up and leaves his foster parents to defeat cruel ogres. As an adult, Ms. Minatoya recognizes that her mother told the story to help her, so that she would travel under the protection of love, finding friendship when she most needed it. Reflecting on the experience, the author writes, "But a child listens to the fable and hears a siren's song. I loved, not the soothing security of the tale in its entirety, but the uncertainty in its progress. Proceed to Ogre Island! To the place where your hopes meet your fears! Bring on the cast of comical characters! Now, let the adventure unfold!" (123–24). I have learned through experience that moralizing or telling what the story means (to me) depotentizes the story and prevents students from exploring what the story means to them. For this reason I tell stories and let my students find their own meaning.

In this book, teachers and those working with children will find ways to use imagemaking, movement, drama, storymaking, poetry, and music to teach language arts to children. The activities are designed to help teachers consciously and deliberately discover ways to connect what we are asked to learn with who we are as human beings in ways that best facilitate our learning. The book is divided into six sections: "Laying the Foundation" introduces the techniques used in the book and describes the powerful experiences which formed me as student and teacher. "Groundwork" explores how teachers can develop their own capabilities, describes the tools for teaching language arts in an interactive manner, and examines useful approaches to classroom management. "Sourcework" begins by describing ways to design interactive classroom activity and then explores ideas for developing nonverbal communication, oral language, and written language as part of a comprehensive language arts experience. In "Reflection and Assessment," questions and suggestions focus on ways to rethink the place of evaluation in the educational process. The two final sections, the Afterword and the Bibliography, provide resources for the reader.

Whether studying fine arts, language, or science, the process of making learning a growing experience is essentially the same—engaging the hearts and minds of students, and helping them connect who they are with what they are learning. Although some teaches have no educational or practical experience with the arts and collaborative learning, it is possible for teachers to learn on the job. What is absolutely essential is the willingness and openness to explore a variety of responses and to investigate new possibilities. Once teachers feel comfortable examining and practicing innovative approaches to learning, they will be able to generate their own activities based on individual and group needs. This practice will nurture an increased awareness of the importance of meaningful curricula, critical thinking, authentic expression, group and individual reflection, collaborative learning, and effective procedures in reflection and assessment.

I welcome letters from readers who wish to share their experiences using this book. Please send letters to:

Nancy King
University Honors Program
University of Delaware
Newark, DE 19716

Laying the
Foundation

CHAPTER ONE

Questioning

Children have fertile imaginations, yet at a remarkably early age their creative and imaginative impulses as well as their ability to express ideas and feelings with authenticity and authority are often stifled. This is the result, in part, of an educational experience that discourages questioning, multiple solutions, diverse practice, meaningful personal and collaborative exploration, and creative expression. The material in this book is written to help teachers and students regain access to their imagination and creativity as a way of learning so that it becomes possible not only to look at something and describe what it is, but also to give expression to what it could be.

Optimal conditions for learning require that each student is valued and allowed to study in an environment where inquiry, open discussion, exploration, and reflection routinely take place before solutions are chosen. Such circumstances do not happen automatically despite good intentions or desirable equipment. What is needed are human beings with ideas, techniques, and practices designed to stimulate, support, and create effective educational pedagogy. When teachers and students share ideas and feelings without fear of premature criticism and judgment, all learning is enhanced.

It is impossible to teach what we don't know or haven't experienced, yet teachers generally find it difficult to practice new methods before trying them on their students. This book provides ideas, techniques, and activities that have been safely and effectively used with children of differing ages and capabilities in a variety of classrooms with teachers of varying educational and experiential backgrounds. Activities using various forms of art and media are designed to help teachers begin in ways that are manageable, practical, and easy to assess.

The following questions are those which are most commonly asked of me. I briefly answer them here so that teachers can use the questions and answers as a reference when they are asked similar questions.

However, the questions are examined in greater depth throughout the book.

Why Use the Arts in Education?

The arts provide a variety of means by which we explore and express our inner-life experience using techniques which are not only necessary in the classroom, but useful and important for our whole lives. Primitive visual media such as clay, pastels, fingerpaints, and paper sculpture allow us to discover our thoughts and feelings with little or no concern for technique, rules, or talent. The generation of images evokes words, which further our awareness of who we are, what we know, and how we think and feel, regardless of what we do or how we do it. When we make music, movement, drama, sound, poetry, storymaking, and/or collage, we extend our knowing. Artistic expertise is not necessary for us to have powerful learning experiences and could get in the way if we focus on product rather than on process. Knowledge is not the same as wisdom, and artistry is not synonymous with making, whether that making involves words, images, sounds, or motion.

When we participate in an arts activity to explore our knowing, we are forced to make many decisions: What color paints shall we use? What amount of clay do we want? Do we choose soft rounded forms or sharp acute angles? Do we use words or movement, or both, to establish how the environment feels? Do we work by ourselves or with others? In our collaboration do we criticize or merely reflect? Do we work for the purity of form, or are we guided by a sense of wanting that which has no perceptible form? Do we use essential words to form a poem, or do we want to take the time to describe setting, circumstance, and character in a story or a play? Each decision prompts new choices, elicits new opportunities, and increases possibilities. Even without frames, applause, pedestals, and praise, using the arts to express our inner knowing in outward forms enables us to reap rich rewards, discovering the pleasures of working and playing according to our own authentic selves. Martha Graham is only too aware of the power of premature self judgment and censorship when she says:

> There is a vitality, a life force that is translated through you into action. And because there is only one of you in all time, this expression is unique, and if you block it, it will never exist through any other medium and be lost. (Kornfield, 211)

When we explore our lives through the arts to uncover meaning and discover knowledge, common definitions of success and failure have no relevance; there are many solutions to any given problem. What initially appears as chaos is often an ordered search for clarity. When the arts are a primary basis for knowing, those who participate experience their own uniqueness, seeing the best and worst inside themselves without being forced to defend, explain, justify, or attack. As one student said, "When I put what's inside me out there, I'm amazed. I didn't know I had so much inside me."

When the arts are central to education, the experiences provide students with a myriad of opportunities for the development of oral and written language, spatial awareness, computation and perception, interpersonal negotiation and compromise. Perhaps most important of all, the use of the arts in education allows administrators, teachers, and students to understand that who we are matters. We can collaborate to create an environment where personal worth is fundamental to what we learn and how we develop. The knowledge, release, and satisfaction we achieve by working with various art forms can become a source of lifelong pleasure and learning.

What Place Do Feelings Have in the Classroom?

One reason some educators shun the use of the arts as a central part of teaching is that they are afraid students' feelings will be evoked, and teachers will lose control of their class. But our feelings, attitudes, and ideas are part of who we are, which affects both our learning and our participation in the classroom. Our feelings may interfere with or even transform what we want to happen, thereby creating difficult and/or unanticipated situations, problems, or opportunities, but when we give voice to our feelings we identify, explore, and express what it is that makes us who we are. We learn how our feelings affect what and how we think and we learn to deal with our feelings in personally rewarding and socially acceptable ways.

Acknowledging feelings is dismissed by some people as "touchy-feely" stuff with no place in any institution devoted to learning. But what constitutes "touchy-feely" to some is simply good educational practice to others. Modern science acknowledges that the observer affects what is being observed. Similarly, we fool ourselves when we assert that it is possible to separate our thinking from our feeling. Such belief leads to sterile practice. Rather, what we need to do as teachers is design classroom practice which expressly integrates thinking and feeling so that we consciously connect who we are to what we are asked to learn and do. When students and teachers are helped to learn about their biases, they are enabled to move past them to critical observation, considered action, and thoughtful reflection and assessment.

For example, when we deny an angry person's right to be angry we do not help the person who is angry; the energy of the anger remains. Often, an angry person lets this energy out by hitting, shouting, cursing, or provoking further, uncontrollable action and reaction which generally provides inadequate release. Even young children suffer from stress, developing ulcers, rashes, muscle tension, or uncontrollable bouts of hitting. Ideally, when an angry person is helped to acknowledge the anger and find constructive ways to explore the energy and meaning of the anger, the person learns not only how to deal with a difficult feeling but is also helped to shape self-identity positively. Unfortunately, the classroom is often perceived as a place to engage solely in objective and intellectual activity, not as a place to express feelings, positive or negative. As human beings, our feelings are always part of our thinking and acting; our emotions create energy which we must learn to use to our advantage, particularly in the classroom, the place to learn how to integrate thinking and feeling conciously.

Teachers can help children to identify their feelings as part of the process of becoming aware of other people's feelings. Who we are and what we feel are affected to some extent by the feelings of those around us, and these in turn shape our ideas, responses, and ability to act appropriately. It is impossible to make a decision purely on the basis of thought even when we try to ignore, suppress, or avoid awareness of our feelings. Ultimately, our best decisions and judgments are made when our feelings and thoughts are consciously connected to create a total response.

The consideration of people's feelings can play an important part in traditional academic inquiry. For example, when studying the role of immigration in the development of the United States, students might benefit from attention to the following questions:

> What feelings might encourage a person to leave the known for the unknown, one culture for another? What consequences could this choice have?
>
> How might these feelings have been developed? What heritage will the person leave behind? At what cost?
>
> How might it feel to be a person living in a strange country where no one speaks your language, eats the same foods, celebrates the same holidays, sings the same songs, or shares the same values? What effects might these have on family life? On the relationships between generations in the same family?

> How might parents feel when their children speak in a language
> they do not understand? How might this influence
> family choices regarding where to live, jobs, educational
> choices, friends?
> How might feelings about oneself be affected by a poor economic
> climate, community prejudice, lack of or different
> education, misunderstanding of culture, fear of difference?
> What consequences might flow from these experiences?
> What resources might the family need to develop in order
> to survive the initial transition from the previous to
> the current culture?

In the classroom, questions such as these help students to become aware that feeling influences thought, which subsequently affects action. The result is an enriched educational experience.

How Might Giving Expression to Feeling Facilitate Learning?

Who we are affects what we hear, how we process information, how we think, and how we act. We know that children who are treated with respect often respond more spontaneously and authentically than children who feel disliked. This is especially true in the classroom because teachers have so much power to influence their young students. When teachers encourage children to express their ideas and feelings in connection with what is being learned, knowledge is amplified beyond the moment. Children who are encouraged to ask for help from their teacher and classmates do not suffer ridicule when they are stuck or puzzled. An atmosphere of open inquiry where multiple solutions are routinely explored and even the seemingly ridiculous is valued, is a place where students' self-esteem is enhanced and nourished.

I have often observed students who were so bothered by a personal problem that they read a text as if the material in the book were only about their issue, unaware they were doing so. They usually got poor grades on written papers because they could not differentiate between their personal concerns and those discussed by the author. Working with imagemaking, storymaking, and drama eventually enabled these students to become aware of the nature and place of the particular issue in their lives so that they could separate what was happening inside themselves from what they were reading, and could write with a clearer perspective. The value of working with imagemaking, storymaking, and drama lies in the process of self-discovery. The student is never forced to confront issues he or she may not be ready to acknowledge; rather, students in their own time, and in their own way, begin to notice that every image, story, and/or drama serves to deal with the same issue regardless of text. This observation is the beginning of concious differentiation that often leads to healthier perspectives.

In one instance, an eight-year-old boy who was enrolled in the Stories Project kept making stories about male heroes being killed. The university student who was working with him became troubled and sought advice as to how to help the child move beyond stories where the hero is murdered. After consulting with the classroom teacher we discovered that the child's father, a policeman, recently had been severely injured during an attempt to arrest a burglary suspect. The student and I searched for stories where the hero is involved in precarious adventures for the good of his people. We didn't want to suggest that everything would be all right because we didn't know whether the child's father would survive, or, if he did, what his condition would be. Instead, we enlarged the frame to include the power a person acquires when he or she is willing to take the consequences for doing what is personally important. This seemed to comfort the boy. His second-to-last story was about the momentous funeral given to the hero who died to save his family. His last story was about a hero who faced great danger and survived.

In another instance, a formerly well-behaved seven-year-old boy began to disrupt classroom activity on a regular basis. Because this was happening during the Gulf War in 1990, I suspected there might be a connection between the war and the boy's sudden change of behavior. When the classroom teacher contacted the mother, she said her son never mentioned his uncle who was fighting in the war. Yet when the boy began working with a university student in the Stories Project, the first story he wrote was about his uncle fighting in the war. One story led to another, and the disruptive classroom behavior occurred less frequently. As the boy began to take an active interest in reading and writing, his behavior and his skills improved dramatically. He began to demand time in school to write more stories and to make these stories into books.

In a third instance, a nine-year-old child working below grade level wrote a story based on an experience of finding her mother's lost pocketbook. Sharing her story with the rest of the class allowed the girl to feel good about herself, as a person as well as an author with something to say that was worth hearing. Her interest in reading and writing improved slowly and steadily until one day she told her teacher, "I'm not so dumb after all."

Teaching students to give expression to their feelings is not a magical cure for learning difficulties, although sometimes it may seem to be so. Rather, it is an opportunity for teachers to enable their students to connect personal experience with academic skill development in a public forum. In the process, students often become excited about reading, writing, and speaking because suddenly this knowledge matters, not only to them but to others who are important in their lives.

Yet it is not only reading, writing, and speaking that improve when students are helped to give form to their feelings. Teachers can also use this process to pique the interest of their class in mathematics and science by constructing story problems based on student concerns and worries. For example, students in a science class were asked to imagine what substance could be liquid, gas, and solid and then to write a story about how these transformations occurred. In another class, as part of their work in math, children reading a story about Snow White were asked to figure out how much flour, sugar, butter, vanilla, raisins, and milk it would take to make cookies for the seven dwarfs, assuming each dwarf would eat three cookies.

What Formal Preparation Is Required of Teachers?

Where you are is where you start. What teachers do need is a commitment to the process of creative dialogue in the classroom, of designing and implementing an environment where it is okay not to know, where the class is expected and willing to help any member who is stuck or in need of assistance. When the emphasis is on sharing ideas, on extending and deepening work, and on respect for the diverse nature of who we are and how we learn, real and meaningful learning happens. This is no small task, especially when teachers are trained to be the sole source of expertise in the classroom, when administrators have their own agenda, when curriculum is derived from teaching for a test, or when public officials use children as their private footballs.

What does it take for teachers to start using the arts in education, to give expression to feeling as well as thinking in the classroom? The impetus might come from a teacher's sense that she can devise new ways to reach her students more effectively. Perhaps he wants students to have more fun while learning. Maybe you want to make a significant difference in the way your students perceive themselves.

Whatever the initial impulse to make changes in pedagogy, the first step is always *observation*—of self, techniques, responses, choices during crisis situations, attitudes toward students and education, the sense of support for change from students, and administrators and parents, combined with the willingness to be a bit uncomfortable as we learn to replace old habits and reactions with new techniques and responses. Not easy!

The second step involves what we do as human beings in *prepara-*

tion for working with our students. We need to learn to note our own reactions as we struggle to confront personal inadequacies, develop new skills, and begin to make order from chaos. We remember teachers and adults from our past who said in so many different ways, "Not good enough! You can't draw! You can't write! Who do you think you are?" We probably still feel the shame and pain and embarrassment of being told we weren't good enough. Yet, if we do nothing to address the deficit within ourselves, we are likely to pass on our personal sense of inadequacy to our students.

Become aware of your own tensions so you can discover helpful ways to cope with them. Listen to the ways you communicate with yourself and with others. Observe what is going on inside you, and notice what you choose not to say. Explore ways to refresh yourself and to deepen sensory awareness by stretching tired muscles, yawning, breathing more deeply, or washing your face. Notice the weather, object shapes, light, smells, and sounds.

The third step, in some ways the hardest, is *restructuring classroom practice* to encourage collaborative learning, creative participation, and to make time and space for our students to imagine. We become aware that even as we take the first, small steps necessary to reconfigure lesson plans, we evoke a sense of personal inadequacy and anxiety. We may feel separated from what we know and not yet knowledgeable about what we want to achieve.

Although I suggest a variety of activities that teachers can use to develop new skills in "Groundwork," some initial consideration may help to effect subsequent work. Consider whether there are other teachers with whom you could share ideas and processes. Are there modest ways you could begin to work with your class, such as with small reading groups? Is your principal or supervisor amenable to working with you? If not, what have you tried to enlist their support? Even if you perceive there are no others with whom to share ideas, the act of beginning often attracts interest from unexpected people and places. Develop sound educational principles on which to base any changes you make in your teaching so that you can explain your goals even as you struggle to develop the new practice.

I suggest that you buy a set of fingerpaints containing at least six colors: black, brown, red, blue, green, and yellow. I use regular white copy paper with no water, only paper towels to wipe my fingers. Fingerpaints are a primitive medium which makes representation difficult. People like myself, who are not painters, can still express ideas and feelings just by plopping fingers in the little pots of paint and smearing various colors on the paper with no planning or skill. Notice that when you play with color and form, the imagery evokes ideas and feelings. Pay attention to your response. Do you immediately condemn your work, or do you allow yourself to appreciate what emerges? Play with clay and allow your fingers to explore connections between your inner and outer self.

Just as painting and sculpting help to expand our sense of self, so can preparing or eating unfamiliar food, listening to music you might not normally choose, and paying attention to your responses. Notice the people you encounter on your way to work, while shopping, at the post office, when getting your car fixed, or while visiting the dentist. Become sensitive to what habitually attracts your attention and to what has hitherto gone unnoticed.

Decide to banish "I can't" from your vocabulary for a specific period of time. Stay focused on the present, on what you are doing/feeling/thinking at the moment. What, if anything, makes this difficult or easy? What, if anything, happens when you do this? Experiment with how you worry. Can you decide to focus on something else if there is nothing you can do about the issue at the moment? In difficult situations, how might you explore alternatives? Are you able to ask yourself what choices you have? Think about the worst thing that could happen as a way of achieving perspective. Can you set aside past practice to make new decisions? What happens, if anything, when you pay attention to your feelings and inner thoughts in the moment?

Considered thinking and exploration are useful because they foment new thinking and feeling and generate valuable questions and opportunities. If we conceive of change as happening on a continuum rather than as an either-or situation, we give ourselves time and space to practice. What helps me most in a time of change is to ask, "Is this in my best interest?" If my answer is no, I focus on my objectives, consider why I am making changes, and try to keep my eye on my goals. Even if I weaken and revert to old patterns, I don't lapse completely. I use what happens to strengthen my convictions about what I am doing and why I am doing it. Always, internal changes bring new people and valuable experiences into my life, which more than compensate for the difficulty of making new choices and establishing new and healthier habits.

CHAPTER TWO

Stories: Shaping a Teacher's Life

In the beginning were stories. Mostly I made them up. Sometimes I read them. Occasionally I could find a lap and hear a story. When the world was more than I could manage, there was always the library. What I looked for in books were strong girls who overcame great odds to win the day. They were hard to find. So I allowed my curiosity to guide me and wandered through the stacks reading whatever caught my attention. Books and stories were life support, nurturance, comfort, and magic.

When I was in the fourth grade, I read a book about an experiment in education in a Springfield, Massachusetts, public school. The book described how teachers, working together, had developed a curriculum based on the *children's* ideas and questions, which impressed me as an exciting and new kind of education. When my teacher assigned book reports, I prepared an oral presentation on this book, including pictures, anecdotes, and questions of my own regarding my school and classroom. I was about halfway through my narrative when the teacher stopped me, asking in a puzzled and angry tone if I had found my book in the children's section of the library. I said, "No, I have 'adult privilege.' I found the book in the section on education."

She chastised me, "Sit down! This is not a suitable book. We are only interested in books that fourth graders want to read." Crushed and embarrassed, I returned to my seat, not hearing her say that I could have another chance. I pretended not to hear the titters and snickers of the other children.

I think this was when I first decided I would be a teacher and protect kids like me who made the mistake of wandering outside boundaries I neither saw nor understood, even after I learned of my transgression. Still, this painful memory has its use—I remember how I felt then when, as a teacher, I comment on a child's work. It is all too easy for a teacher to destroy confidence, enthusiasm, and interest, sometimes without even realizing the *child's sense of self is shattered*.

As I began to write this book I thought about events which shaped me as a teacher. Originally I intended to share recent stories of my life in the classroom but I came to realize as I traced each story to its beginning, that every story had its roots in one of six experiences that happened just before and after I became a teacher. These events so shaped my philosophy that I decided to include them as a way of talking about how I learned what matters most to me as a teacher.

Maria

In my experience, good methods of teaching often evolve while I'm worrying about solving a problem and not thinking about pedagogy. In my third year of college, I was enrolled in a course to become a water safety instructor, and one of the requirements involved teaching a young child to swim. I eagerly set off for the locker room full of confidence, prepared to teach my assigned child to float quickly, as I had many other children and adults. My student was a thin, frightened seven-year-old girl named Maria who walked with a severe limp from polio. She was the only one not wearing a bathing suit; her deformed leg, encased in a thick brace, was tucked behind her. She had "lost" her suit. After a fruitless search, I asked her to go to the pool and put her feet in the water, but she remained silent and tense, refusing to move. We sat on a hard bench in the locker room as I passed the time by telling her stories about how much fun it was to swim.

When the session finally ended, as she was leaving, she said, "I'll take better care of my suit next time." I felt reassured until I noticed a swimsuit sticking out of the bag she clutched in her hand, hiding it as best she could. I consoled myself; the next session would be more productive.

Wrong! The next four sessions ended as they began, with us still in the locker room. Desperate, I continued to tell her stories about people overcoming great odds to learn to swim. By the end of the sixth week, although I had gotten her to put on her suit, I could not get her to walk to the pool. I thought about asking my instructor for advice and help, but my self-pity and embarrassment stopped me. Instead of being aware of and dealing with her fear, I focused on my bad luck.

On the last day of class all the students, except Maria, went to the pool to be tested. While the other teachers and students greeted each other eagerly, Maria and I were quiet. Resigned, I told her, "There's no point in putting on your suit. I'll tell my teacher I couldn't help you and then we'll go for a soda." Even at this point I was thinking only of myself, my failure, my F.

Maria asked, "What happens if you don't teach me to swim?"

Too miserable to lie I said, "I take the course again next year."

"You mean you fail the course because I can't swim?"

"No. I fail because I didn't teach you to swim." In the long silence that followed I really looked at her; I saw the fear and sadness in her eyes. I hugged her, suddenly feeling better, "It's okay. Failing's not the end of the world. Next time I'll know more."

"No! It's not okay. You shouldn't fail because of me. You told me all those stories, I should do something for you. Let's go to the pool."

Switching roles, Maria led me to the pool and found a quiet corner in the shallow end. "What do I do?" Looking at her small, trembling body I was overcome by misery. I promised myself I would be less self-concerned the next time. She followed me into the pool and I held her hand, her teeth chattering uncontrollably. We had ten minutes in which to accomplish what we had been unable to do in seven sessions.

Holding tightly to my hand, Maria put her face in the water and blew some bubbles, floating for a few seconds. My instructor, surprised to see us both in the water, asked Maria, "Show me what you can do by yourself." I watched, awestruck, as she managed a couple of strokes with her feet off the pool floor, propelling herself like a desperate puppy.

As we were getting dressed she said, "I didn't want you to fail because of me. You tried. You told me all those stories."

Later, I understood that although I told her stories in order to pass time, she saw them as my way of caring about her, that I was not angry or disappointed when she refused to do what I asked her to do. I had helped her in spite of myself.

The Baseball Players

In my early days as a teacher I sometimes lost perspective and had trouble achieving a balance between helping a group achieve what mattered to them and what I thought was most important. A particularly painful example of this occurred during the summer before my senior year in college when I worked as a recreational therapist in a large state mental hospital. Although the drug thorazine (supposed to make patients feel "better") was just beginning to be used, many patients suffered from unrelieved stress, a sense of isolation, and endless time. To ameliorate some of these symptoms I developed opportunities for my patients to become involved in hard physical activity such as baseball, soccer, running, walking, and dance. I hoped they would learn to cooperate, talk with each other, and develop a sense of camaraderie. Although the men's sports program involved teams which regularly competed against teams in other mental hospitals, allowing the men the rare privilege of leaving the hospital grounds, there were no teams for the women. I decided to form a women's team knowing they would benefit from being on a team just as much as the men. I recruited women on the basis of personal desire, in contrast to the men's teams which required special training and selection.

In order for the women to play on the team they had to behave in the wards; if they were unruly or disruptive their attendants would not let them leave the wards. As the women's interest in playing grew, their behavior in the ward began to change. Because they wanted to get out they obeyed orders, whether or not they approved of them, and wasted less time doing assigned tasks. Feeling that cooperation was extremely important, I had them play all positions, each one taking a turn, even as referee and coach. I finally convinced the director to allow the women's team to travel with the men on the bus the next time the men played off the grounds. My elation was tempered by the director's words, "If you win I might consider making this a regular event." The director used team scores as proof of therapeutic value—a team who lost had no use and received no attention or funds.

Most of the women on the team had been inside the hospital for more than ten years and none had been allowed off the grounds since being hospitalized. On the bus, they didn't know where or what to look at first; everything interested them. As guests rather than patients, they were given a lovely lunch, a spacious room with clean showers in which to change their clothes, and the freedom to roam over a large area. Their joy made me determined to help them win their game; this would not be a one-time experience.

Full of confidence, the women threw themselves wholeheartedly into the game, and at the top of the fifth inning, the score was 4 to 0 in our favor. But by the eighth inning, our opponents were ahead, having scored five runs. I called a time out to talk with my team, who were enjoying themselves, totally confident they would pull ahead in the next inning. Unconvinced, I asked them to send me in as a relief pitcher. Very reluctantly, they agreed. Taking the pitcher's place in the lineup, I hit a long hard drive with two women on base and we won the game, 6 to 5.

None of the women cheered. None of them looked at me. When I asked what was wrong they were silent. Finally, after repeatedly asking, one of them told me, "It was nice of you to help. We know you meant well. It's just that we wanted to do it by ourselves." In the hospital they were forced to be dependent on the good will and care of others yet they yearned to be independent. This one time they felt they had a chance to accomplish something by themselves. I made them pay too high a price for winning the game even though they understood that losing probably would have meant no further opportunities to play other hospital teams. I promised myself I would never again make my needs for a group more important than theirs. I would not help people until they exhausted their own resources and asked for my help.

Catchers and Throwers

Another experience at the mental hospital also made an indelible impression on me, teaching me to make my own decisions about the power of teaching based on active student participation. Each day, as I picked up my patients, I had to pass a closed ward which housed thirty women who had been hospitalized for more than twenty-five years. Labeled unresponsive and unreachable, no one ever visited them. I began to wonder what their lives were like and how they passed their time. One day, out of curiosity, I decided to take a large rubber ball and "play catch" with them. In reality it meant I gently threw a ball at a woman, waited until it rolled to her, then retrieved it, and threw the ball to another woman. I did this for about half an hour, three times a week, for most of the summer, with no response from the women.

Working without expectations, I viewed it as a break from the active and intense interactions I had with patients who were more in touch with reality. On the day before I was scheduled to leave, I went to their ward and began, as usual, by saying, "Good morning. Let's play catch." I threw the ball to a woman and it gently bounced against her. She picked up the ball while I stared, open-mouthed. She giggled, pushing it back to me. Stunned, I threw it back to her, just to make sure I wasn't "seeing things." She returned it. How could this be? I threw it to all the other women. Two others responded as the first had done. Toward the end of the session, my joy turned to despair. I was leaving. Who would take my place? What would happen now?

I shared my experience with the other therapists during our end-of-the-summer meeting, but none of them believed me. They assured me that they had all tried to work with these women for many years and knew the patients were incapable of responding. I began to wonder if I had imagined their response, but I knew that three women had returned the ball. I could do nothing more for the women—except to remember that three had broken through the barriers that kept them isolated from the world.

I assuaged my pain by making a promise to the three women. I would follow my instincts and trust my experience. I would remember that until I explored an idea, neither I nor anyone else could know what might ensue.

The Woman Who Was a Mountain

After a year of teaching, I became a resource teacher for about thirty elementary schools, helping teachers design classroom programs in physical education and drama. Conducting lessons with an aim to give teachers ideas, I noticed how often teachers lost control, screaming and threatening students to make them behave. I also couldn't help observing how miserable many children looked, so I designed drama activities to pique the children's interest and to help them express their ideas and feelings. Most of the teachers were not receptive. I was discouraged and depressed.

Then I met Miss H., a huge mountain of a woman, teaching first graders in a school which served very poor urban children. Walking into her classroom was like being in an oasis of calm and quiet. The room, painted off-white and unlike the other classrooms which were bilious green, was spare. On a back shelf was a vase with a single flower. Lots of books were neatly arranged on specially designed shelves, so children could easily reach them. On one side was a bulletin board with one notice. The blackboard was clean. When I entered the classroom at the beginning of the school year I was amazed. The children, working in groups, quickly returned to their desks and sat quietly while their teacher introduced me. I explained what we would be doing and that is what we did. I had never worked with such a responsive group.

At first I thought these first-grade youngsters were specially chosen but this was not so—students were assigned randomly. And, it was no fluke. Week after week, her students were quietly responsive, unlike the other first graders from the same neighborhood, who kicked and screamed and made me use every disciplinary trick I ever knew or thought up.

What was her secret? She told me that her first order of business was to teach the children to enjoy being still. This took about two months. In the process she helped them learn to focus, to pay attention to each other, and to enjoy listening to stories. Only after they could sit and listen comfortably did she begin to teach traditional subject matter though she never taught it traditionally. When a student caused a problem she was likely to gather the child up in her arms and take him outside to "have a little chat." She helped the children to love learning for its own sake and to enjoy asking questions. Although she took a lot of grief from her principal because her students did not score well on tests in the middle of the year, by the end of the year their grades always improved considerably, and every second-grade teacher wanted her students. Unbelievably calm and focused, her students were always a joy to teach. I began to understand and appreciate the power of simplicity, serenity, and clear focus. Even today, when I enter a room where chaos reigns, I think of her standing quiet and calm. I take a deep breath and begin.

The Seven Boys

Soon after I began traveling to various schools I volunteered to work in an enrichment program for children in an inner-city school. The program's goals were to improve the children's self-esteem and reading, and to give them opportunities to express their ideas through play making, writing, and crafts.

I was assigned to a teacher with an excellent reputation, who was particularly noted for being a strict disciplinarian and a hard worker. The children in her class spoke of her respectfully, parents of her students seldom complained about her methods, and her students scored relatively high on national achievement tests. That particular year she had seven boys in her class who she claimed would not pay attention, were often in trouble, and spent most of their time in disciplinary programs. While I was in the principal's office, I overheard the teacher recommend that the principal exclude the seven boys from the program because she was sure they would ruin the other children's experience. Without thinking, I offered to work with the boys by themselves. Despite the teacher's disapproval, the principal allowed me to do so, warning me that they were very difficult, "You'll really have to sit on them if you don't want things to get out of hand."

Because no one trusted the boys to come by themselves, I went to their classroom a few minutes before class was over to pick them up. Invited in, I noticed that every child who was not writing was sitting with hands folded, facing front, books neatly piled, all waiting for the final bell to ring. The seven boys were seated in the back of the room, heads down, busy writing. To my embarrassment, the teacher began telling me, in front of the whole class, why each of the boys was bad, and that I really should not work with them because they did not deserve special privileges. I tried to stop her but she interrupted and said, "Anyway, they can't work with you today because they haven't finished their work. All they do is fool around."

Feeling defeated, I moved toward the door but I caught the eyes of one who dared to look up. Turning to the teacher I said, "I'm supposed to have these boys now. If you intended to detain them you should have left word with my office. They'll have to make up their work another time; I haven't come all this way for nothing." Anger made me sound more confident than I felt. The teacher silently acquiesced.

I had intended to begin with some stretching, just to ease the strain of sitting for so long, but the boys were too tense to listen to any directions, no matter how well intended. Desperately looking for a way to help them relax, I told them to go to the courtyard and run back and forth until they were tired. They looked at me as if I were crazy but quickly took off. I sat on the floor wondering if they would return.

Not only did they reappear, but after they got over the shock of seeing me sitting on the floor, they proudly reported how many laps each had run. I wrote the numbers on a piece of paper and suggested that before working with me they should run laps. We spent the rest of the allotted time and an additional half hour exchanging ideas about what to do in the coming weeks. Obviously, it is easier to deal with seven boys than with twenty-seven, but I was immediately struck by the difference between their teacher's description of them, and my observation of their willingness to participate.

Our sessions followed a pattern. After dismissal, each boy ran as long as necessary, entering the amount of time and number of laps on a chart. Each boy competed against himself to improve his number of laps. One day, instead of running, the boys came directly to my room. I asked what was wrong but no one spoke. One boy finally burst out, "Our class be doin' a play and the teacher say we can't be in it 'cause we too bad." Furious, I told the boys I would complain to the head of the program but they were horrified, begging me to calm down. I asked, "Well, what do you want me to do?" They had already decided.

"We want to do a play and show that dumb teacher!" Amazed, I asked what kind of play they wanted to make up.

One of them retorted, "Make up a play? You know we can't make up a play. You know we don't read good. You just want us to be dumb."

Angrily I retorted, "You're talking about yourselves the way your teacher talks about you. I know you can make up a play. You all have lots of ideas. What's more, you'll like your own play a hundred times better than any play someone else wrote. You might even like it so much you write down the lines and make a real script. You might even put it in the library."

Although full of disbelief, they agreed to try; the idea of no play was worse than making up their own. We spent the rest of the afternoon exploring ideas. The boys wanted it to be scary, "real," and about them. I suggested they each write a short incident fitting this description and bring it to the next session. This provoked a new outburst, "Why you keep asking us to do stuff we can't do? You is mean, mean, mean."

"You'll never know what you can do unless you try." I promised not to keep what they wrote or correct spelling and punctuation. Refusing to take no for an answer I overruled their objections, "You will do it. I don't want to hear one more word about can't, won't, don't, or ain't!" They stormed out of the room.

The next week, the principal stopped me. "What is this play the boys are writing? Those boys are troublemakers. They shouldn't be getting special attention. They'll ruin the festival. Why don't you work with some nice children?"

"The boys are not troublemakers. They're working very hard. But if you're worried about them spoiling the presentation let them do their play in the evening, for parents and friends. I'm tired of everyone talking about them as if they were monsters."

"We'll see," she said coldly. I suddenly realized I had put the boys in a terrible position. I wished, not for the first time, that diplomacy was one of my virtues.

I was thinking about my talk with the principal when the boys came running into the room, shouting out their ideas. I could not resist a few "told you so's," which they accepted good-naturedly. We put together the outlines of a play using some of everyone's ideas, so absorbed we lost all track of time. When the custodian knocked on the door to tell us it was closing time we all jumped. As he threw us out the janitor grinned at me, "Sure is nice to see them kids so happy."

Everything did not go smoothly. The boys had trouble putting their thoughts down on paper, and even more difficulty deciding which events to include. Although I was willing to act as director, I compounded their frustration by refusing to create the contents of the play. They changed their mind so many times about which scenes to include that they memorized words which no longer fit but which the boys couldn't forget. The biggest crisis came when no one could think of an ending acceptable to all of them. Bitter words and accusations achieved no results and they took their anger out on me. "You s'posed to tell us how it ends. You the teacher. You s'pposed to be helping, not just sittin' there!"

"If I tell you how to end the play you'll have to say we wrote it together and then everyone will think I did most of it. You'll be even madder at me." They were not convinced.

When I asked them why they couldn't find an ending they responded as before, "'Cause we dumb and you know it." I was tempted to make suggestions but I remembered the baseball players at the hospital. I knew the only way to really help the boys was to continue to insist they would find their ending by trying each other's ideas. It was a long seven days.

Something worked. The next week they danced in, "How'd you like to see a play with the greatest ending in the world?" I sat entranced as they performed their finished script, a play about five boys who are punished and have to stay after school. By mistake, they are locked in a closet and have to break out. Lost, they end up in the basement where they come upon a man with a broken leg who had given up all hope of being rescued. The boys discover a way to carry the man out, saving his life. For their help, they are rewarded with medals and honored at a dinner sponsored by the mayor.

I asked the boys how they found their ending but my question provoked peals of laughter. Once again I learned that there is wisdom in the group if they are helped to tap into it. The boys drew lots as to who would perform what role. The sixth boy played the injured man and the seventh boy played the teacher and the mayor. The latter role was his compensation for having to act as the teacher. We spent the whole time shaping their performance until each boy felt satisfied.

The principal finally allowed the boys to perform their play for the rest of the class. No one commented on why theirs was the only original play. The teacher and principal never talked to me about their work, the playwright/performers, or the playbook which the boys made. Soon after, I was informed that the school did not wish me to return when the next term began.

Had I been less involved in proving my point I would have made an effort to enlist the interest and support of the teacher and principal. Years of teaching remind me that no teacher works effectively in isolation; children are part of a system and have to be helped to maintain their place within it. The seven boys were capable students but they had been labeled as troublemakers and no matter what they did, they were unable to change how people saw them. I could have better helped the boys by teaching them how to work more effectively with their teacher, within the matrix of the school's expectations. I should have told the teacher that the boys were eager and ready to be part of her class. Although I provided the boys with a powerful learning experience, my own rebelliousness distorted my vision. I judged the teacher as rigidly as she judged the boys, and this judgment negatively affected the boys' subsequent interaction with their teacher. My experience convinced me that a primary goal of education has to be to teach students how to function capably and independently, given the realities of their school situation.

Cinderella

"We're developing a language arts program for at-risk children based on the story of Cinderella. Will you join us?" Absolutely! I was given nine fourth-grade girls who could not read or write, seldom spoke, and had very poor social skills. They attended a badly maintained school where everything screamed failure. The room in which we were to work had peeling paint, dirty locked windows, broken desks, and chairs with missing legs.

The girls entered, refusing to look at me, even when I asked their names. They spoke so softly I could barely understand their words when they ventured to speak. My suggestion that they speak louder produced lower voices. The children acted as if they were worthless as human beings. Before I could teach them to read, I was going to have to convince them they had value, but I also knew it would take more than a few encouraging words to change years of educational deprivation.

I have learned that when ideas come to me, I need to honor them. So, without further ado I began telling them the story of Cinderella. The children slowly raised their heads and began to listen raptly. Pleased and grateful to have their full attention, I elaborated on the loneliness of Cinderella, the misery in which she lived, the despair she felt, and her inability to make her stepmother and stepsisters love her or be kind to her. Heads nodded when I recounted how hard she tried to be good so they would like her. They murmured approvingly when I described how the fairy godmother helped Cinderella because she was kind and worked hard. As the story worked its way into the children's hearts I could feel the beginning of a powerful connection between us. After I finished telling the story there was a contented silence, as if we had all eaten a very good meal.

One girl, with thick black braids and piercing eyes, said, "That's a good story." The others murmured their agreement. More silence. She spoke again, "Yes ma'am, that's a real good story." Heads nodded.

"We could make the story into a play if you like," I said. Nine pairs of incredulous eyes stared at me. Warming to the task I spoke without thinking, "Yeah, we could make a play and show it to the kids at the school where you'll be going next year." They laughed, hearty belly laughs, as if my suggestion was too preposterous to be taken seriously. "What's so funny?" I asked. They laughed even harder. Suddenly I understood. "You're laughing because you think I'm making a joke but I'm serious. We can make our own play. We can do anything we want. That's why I'm here." Silence. Heads shaking their disbelief. They showed no spark of hope.

Once again I realized my words had no meaning. Years of being treated terribly could not be erased in moments. No matter how well-intentioned my enthusiasm, I was a stranger to them. "Okay," I said, wondering how to begin. "Let's imagine that I'm Cinderella and you're all her fairy godmothers. What would you do or say to make me feel better?" Entering into role, I bent my head down and began to sweep using an imaginary broom. I used my hands to fend off imaginary blows. The girls sat quietly. I sighed. I wished I could cry as Cinderella but my acting ability was not good enough. Still, I kept at my task for what seemed ages.

At first the voice was too low to hear so I kept sweeping. Then it grew stronger, "You a good girl Cinderella. You a good girl." I nodded my head in agreement but said nothing, sweeping, waiting, hoping. Nothing more was said and I was getting tired so I slumped against a desk, closing my eyes, as if to get some rest. I felt a hand awkwardly comforting me as the voice said, "You gonna be awright. I'm gonna help you. Just you wait. I'm gonna help you." The voice and hand disappeared. I waited a few minutes, opened my eyes, and joined the girls, sitting quietly, no sign of interest in their eyes, no evidence of who had spoken and acted.

"What do you think?" I asked. No answer. Asking questions proved futile. I pointed to one girl, "I'd like you to be Cinderella and I'll be the mean stepmother." She refused. "Okay, I'll be Cinderella and you be the mean stepmother." No response. Desperate, I suggested, "How about we both be Cinderella talking about our mean stepmother." A spark of interest.

Inspired, I said, "How about we all be Cinderella talking about our mean stepmother. Let's close our eyes and imagine that we've been sweeping the floor, washing the dishes, milking the cow, and picking the weeds out of the garden. All this before she'll let us eat our breakfast of dried crusts." I started, "I hate stepmother. I hate her guts."

An angry voice echoed my words, "I hate her guts." Soon we were joined by complaints of mistreatment and misunderstandings, almost like a spoken poem, with leader and chorus. When their words grew in intensity I stopped mine, listening intently to theirs. As the girls' words died down one voice grew in power, "I've had enough!" The others joined her, "We've had enough."

I entered the conversation with a different voice, "Oh my dears,

I'm your fairy godmother and I've come to help you. What would you like?"

"Rest."

"Food."

"To be treated good."

"Nice clothes."

"I want to go to the ball."

The last sentence was shouted quickly, then echoed by the others, "We want to go to the ball. We want to go to the ball."

Relieved to have broken the ice, I said, "Terrific. Great beginning." The girls opened their eyes and stared disbelievingly. I looked at my watch—our forty-five-minute session was finished. Where had the time gone? Still, we made progress, they had participated. I smiled, feeling hopeful, "I'm so pleased with what you've done. We're going to make a great play." They left as if I were some poor demented person, totally out of touch with reality.

It's extremely difficult to provide enough positive, healthy experience to counterbalance years of deprivation and discrimination so that children can feel confident enough to participate in creative activity. And, the larger the group, the more difficult the task. Every step has to be carefully thought through to ensure success; each time a child ventures to react, the response carries with it the seed of catastrophe.

Inadvertently, I found that laughing at my own mistakes in full view of the group was powerful medicine. During the second week I brought in clay, thinking the children would sculpt images of Cinderella at various times in her life. As I went to greet the children I tripped over the pile of clay which was standing in full view. Not only did I fall, but one of my shoes went careening into the air, landing at a rakish angle in the crack of a broken chair. I was mad at myself for being so clumsy but when I saw the shoe sticking up from the crack I laughed at my klutziness. The children, who had been cowering, afraid I would blame them, began to laugh. I put on a pout and grumped, "Aren't any of you Cinderellas going to help me up?" They stopped laughing but didn't know what to do. I continued, "I work my fingers to the bone for you and this is the thanks I get."

Thoroughly confused, one of the girls timidly asked, "Who are you?"

I rose to the occasion. "Who *am* I? I've been your stepmother for all these years and you ask who I am?"

The girls tittered but one of them said timidly, "Oh dear stepmother is it you? My eyes were full of dust from sweeping. Take my hand I'll help you up."

Continuing in role I glared, "Why haven't you finished sweeping? Where is supper? Your sisters and I are hungry. Being fitted for ball dresses is hard work. But what would you know? All you do is sit around and complain."

Another girl turned my book to serve as a tray and said, "Here's the food. Eat it while it's hot."

"Where are your sisters?" I complained.

Two more girls volunteered, "Here we are."

One girl pretended to trip. "That dumb Cinderella left her broom right in my way."

"What a stupid girl she is. Give her a good beating."

Encouraging interaction between the stepsisters and Cinderella until we reached a stopping place, I gathered them in a circle and told them that this was how we would make our play. Immediately one of the girls demanded, "Who's gonna be the ugly sisters and the step-mother?" No one was willing to play those roles. I couldn't blame them. Given their lives, why would anyone offer. I reminded them, "Without the ugly sisters and stepmother we have no play." They were adamant. If they couldn't be Cinderella, the fairy godmother, or the prince, they wouldn't be anyone.

I suggested compensation—maybe the sisters could have lovely dresses or bigger roles. Nothing moved them. We were just about out of time when one of the girls who'd never spoken said, "Maybe the ugly sisters and the stepmother are ugly because no one loves them. Maybe when Cinderella becomes a princess she loves them and then they not ugly." A chorus of "yeahs" greeted her suggestion. I was amazed and pleased but I could feel myself getting angry. These kids had been denied opportunities to learn for years, labeled with all the names that keep children isolated and ignored. Yet here they were, dealing with a difficult problem that I, with all my experience and education, couldn't solve.

Remembering my experience with the seven boys, I vowed to do better by this group and help them find a place within the system. I called the principal of the school the girls were going to attend the next year and asked if they could perform their play at an assembly. She was receptive, providing I obtained permission from the girls' school administrator. I carefully approached the school administrator who assured me this was beyond the girls' abilities. This time, instead of getting angry, I focused on the girls' participation and suggested she sit in on one of our sessions. The administrator didn't say no so I assured her she would be welcome any time.

Before the third session I went to a fabric store and asked the owner if I could borrow material for costumes for our play. He said I could have as much felt as I wanted with one stipulation—I could not cut the fabric. I took a bunch of brightly colored material, wondering how I'd make costumes with no cutting. Being a terrible seamstress, I bought a staple gun hoping to use it to drape the material so the girls wouldn't trip over the unused yardage—at least we could play with the fabric.

The girls decided to choose parts by lots and painstakingly wrote the names of all the characters on separate pieces of paper. Those who picked the roles of ugly sisters and stepmother were consoled and given first chance to pick fabric, for as soon as they saw the material they wanted to use it. I don't know what stories the girls told when they went home, but the next session, two mothers took time off from work to see what their daughters were doing. Grateful to have help with the stapling, we draped the girls, figuring out how to use the yards of extra material. The children, their mothers, and I laughed as we twisted the fabric into costumes and joked about our largess. The mothers shook their heads when they saw me clown around but they were totally entranced when we rehearsed. Our method was to play the play, letting the interaction evolve. Although I did not ask the girls to memorize their parts, each of them began to choose her words and actions.

Engrossed in our playing, with the mothers as our audience, when the school administrator entered the room no one saw her initially. Then, when she was spotted, the girls froze. The mothers stiffened. I forced a smile, invited her in, giving her a seat next to the mothers, and spoke in my most authoritative voice, "We appreciate your coming to see our work. We're working on the scene where Cinderella is first visited by her fairy godmother." I introduced each girl and the character she was playing, and then turned to the girls, "Let's begin with Cinderella weeping. Her stepmother has just beaten her for no reason." Although frightened, the girls overcame their terror and began to work. I kept to our normal routine, asking questions, setting tasks, easing them into the drama. Soon, they forgot about everything except making the play and we continued to work until it was time to stop.

I wasn't quite sure what to say to the administrator but while I was thinking one of the mothers told her, "We certainly appreciate this lady coming to work with our girls. We'll be here next week to help." The administrator nodded, then abruptly departed. Our spirits fell, but I pretended to ignore her action and complimented the girls on their fine work. It took two more visits to the administrator but I finally persuaded her to make arrangements for the girls to do their play at the school they would attend the following year.

The next week, eight mothers appeared. I was flabbergasted because

I knew all the mothers worked and everyone told me not to expect any help from parents. Their daughters beamed with delight as introductions were made. The mothers and I were initially rather shy with each other, but figuring out how to use yards of fabric without cutting it or totally covering up the girls created an instant rapport. The scene was a sight to behold. There were yards of material everywhere, each piece attached to a person, needing to be wound, draped, folded, or gathered in such a way that the child could move, act, and finally, get out of the costume without undoing all of the staples. There was so much excitement I thought we'd never get to work on the play but the children and their mothers insisted on rehearsing even though we were out of time. When the janitor came to throw us out, we invited him in. Having costumes and an audience had an amazing effect on the girls; they entered into their roles with newfound confidence. Weeks of talking and exploring bore fruit as the girls focused on deepening their character involvement.

The day of the performance I picked up the girls and found them excited, yet amazingly poised. Performance time came but my hands were shaking so much I was unable to put the needle on the record. One of the girls who hadn't yet put on her costume came out, smiled at everyone, put the needle on the record, and serenely disappeared backstage. So much for my help! Their performance was wonderful and entrancingly captured on the evening television news. The reporters said that although the whole piece would be filmed, they could only air a few seconds. In fact, they used over a minute of the performance and then interviewed several of the girls and one of the mothers.

Our last session began with excited and triumphant anecdotes, but I had more pressing business. "Would you like to have your play written down so that other children can use it?"

"Yes," they shouted.

"Who should do it?"

"You."

I looked straight at them. "But how will you know if I write down the words correctly?" They looked astonished. "Suppose I don't do it right?" Disbelief! "It's a pity you aren't willing to do it yourselves."

"You know we can't read."

"How we s'pposed to write?"

"If you can make a play, you can write it down."

"No we can't."

"You can if you want to. I'll help." Sullen silence. I put the names of the characters on the board and began to read them out loud. Eventually, I got every girl to find the name of her character. I wrote their names on the front cover of little books I had made for each girl and spent the rest of the session helping them to write their names, the name of their character, and simple sentences recounting the story.

These girls had no learning disabilities or other physiological impairment. What they suffered from was school administrators who condemned them to inadequate education. Once I was able to break through the girls' fears and "can'ts," they made rapid progress. I was allowed to extend the number of sessions so that by the end of the term, every girl was reading and writing well enough to be able to write down the play. We made their script into a book which the principal of the new school willingly put into the school library, a lovely reminder of their great success, and a welcoming connection to their new school.

Resonance

I have recounted some key personal experiences which shaped a way of working with children that encourages dialogue, exploration, forgiveness, mutual respect, and a profound excitement about learning. These experiences continue to reinforce my understanding that no real change or learning can take place unless there is mutual trust and caring. I also know that to be a good teacher I must continue to be an involved learner, and that no solution is right for every child or group. Knowing that I have made mistakes in the past and will do so in the future makes me unable to say to students or readers, "This is the *only* way." I am aware that no idea, no matter how brilliant, works all of the time, that teachers are rightly suspect of those who claim to have *the* answer. Often, adherence to one method is based on the rejection of all others, and such single-minded advocacy makes growth impossible.

When people are taught a system, information and experience are perceived through the filter of the system. Questions not satisfied by the structure can be labeled as unimportant or irrelevant. This book is not a cookbook for teaching and learning. Rather, it explores a variety of ways to make connections between who we are, what we are asked to learn, and the world in which we live. The stories in this book speak for themselves.

Groundwork

CHAPTER THREE

Teacher Preparation

Ideally, teacher preparation would include extensive experience in the use of imagination, creativity, and expression so that when teachers finish their professional education with confidence in their ability to plan activities that include divergent and convergent approaches to learning. In fact, because many teachers feel personally unimaginative and uncreative, they have difficulty designing and planning multifaceted approaches to learning. However, in courses and workshops I have led, I have seen many teachers who were absolutely positive they were not imaginative or creative regain access to inner resources and now use this newly descovered knowledge to significantly redirect their classroom practice. This chapter, written with the experience of these teachers in mind, is designed to help readers explore and develop their own creativity, imagination, and expression so that they too may design new approaches to learning.

The following story from Korea reminds me about the importance of becoming aware of how who we are affects what we see and the decisions we make. As I explore habitual response within myself, and consider altering my automatic behavior, I think about this story and find comfort in it.

Seeing is Believing

A long time ago in Korea there lived a young couple, very much in love. One day, as the husband was about to go on a long journey, he asked his wife, "What present shall I bring you?"

At first she replied, "Husband, all I wish is your safe homecoming." But the husband insisted; he so wanted to bring her a gift. The young woman finally consented, "I have heard of a marvelous invention. When you look into it you see amazing sights. If you are determined to bring me a gift, I would like to have such a thing."

The husband, pleased that his wife knew of such a wonder, promised to do his best to bring it back for her. When he arrived at his destination and finished his business, he set out to find the gift his wife desired. Although he did not know the name of the object he was searching for, his description soon enabled him to find what he was seeking. Pleased with his accomplishment, he put the thing they called a mirror into his bag and left for home.

Proudly, he handed the mirror to his wife, but when she looked into the mirror, and saw a beautiful woman she gasped, "I thought you loved me. Why have you brought home a new wife?"

"What nonsense is this?" He took the mirror and looked at it. Seeing a handsome young man he cried out, "Why have you brought a strange man into our house?" They began to quarrel bitterly.

The husband's mother heard them shouting and asked, "What is the trouble?" Her son gave her the mirror and told her to look at the strange man his wife had brought into the house. The old woman peered into the mirror and said, "Do not be so foolish. It is only an old widow come to borrow rice. She left to find the strange man who had caused the husband and wife to rage and weep and quarrel.

Soon the young man's father came in to ask why they were making so much noise. His daughter-in-law gave him the mirror to show him the beautiful young woman his son had brought home but when the old man looked into it he became angry, "Go away you stingy old man. I owe you nothing."

A neighbor, hearing the yelling, came in, gazed into the mirror and saw still another person. Another neighbor saw someone else yet again. The old man cried out, "Send for the magistrate. There are too many strangers. We must have peace."

The magistrate looked into the mirror, saw a stranger and took offense, "Pack my bags, a new magistrate has come to take my place." But his secretary, intrigued by the strange object, had glanced at the mirror over his master's shoulder and saw his master's face.

"Look master, it is yourself you are seeing." And the magistrate stared over his secretary's shoulder, saw his secretary and knew his servant spoke the truth.

Observing Patterns

One simple way to begin to explore our inner resourcefulness is to observe how we approach problems—considering as well as choosing solutions. Is our first thought that there is no resolution, that something can't be resolved or has no answer? Or do we brainstorm ideas either by ourselves or with others? Do we feel reasonably confident we can solve life's complex problems, or are we convinced that answers can only be given to us by experts other than ourselves? Is our first response to a difficult situation "I can't" or "I don't know how"? Or do we assume we can figure out a good enough solution?

Give yourself a week to notice your responses, and if possible, keep a journal or record so you can reflect on your initial tendencies. Don't make any judgments about your responses, just observe. If you've chosen a particularly stressful week, do it for a second or third week. Take as much time as you need to be able to identify your initial response patterns and to feel reasonably confident that you can observe your behavior without automatically making a judgment about the behavior.

You may want to give your students the same task, both in and out of the classroom. If so, encourage children to share their findings with each other. Set the task of observing as if you were approaching a research project. The first responsibility of a researcher is to study a particular area, issue, or problem in order to discover an important question or idea worth studying in greater depth and detail. Make an analogy between research to explore self and research to explore a question or issue.

Describing Patterns

When you are confident that you have some idea of your habitual response to a challenge, describe your patterns without being judg-mental. First responses might be, "I'm not good enough." "It's all my fault." "I'll ask someone who knows more than I do." "I usually figure out how to solve the problem." The best way to be clear about what you say to yourself as a first response is to observe your reactions to problems over time.

There are many ways to explore new approaches to problem-solving and all of them include breaking habitual patterns. Some people struc-ture their day to include a walk. Others sit with a cup of tea or coffee and stare at a wall. Many of the teachers with whom I have worked have found great success using fingerpaints and clay to develop access to knowledge for which they have no words. They paint images of "me as a problem solver," and list words or phrases that come to mind. You might sculpt an image of "me in relationship to my problem" and write down whatever ideas come to mind as the result of sculpting. Observe the colors you choose, the patterns you make, the feelings evoked by the way you put the paint on paper. When sculpting, pay attention to the way you manipulate the clay. Do you create one complex structure? A simple shape? Two or more shapes which are isolated from each other or related? Observe how you feel as you sculpt and note images, memories, or ideas which come to mind. You might write the words "Once upon a time" and let a story emerge. If you are really stuck try writing, "There was once a person who had no answers." Create an image, then see the person—what she or he looks like, where she or he is, neighbors, if any, what the problem might be. The story may turn out to be a metaphor for what you are experiencing.

Regardless of the medium, the goal is always to describe thought patterns more clearly, gathering information and describing what you want and/or need to learn. You might ask your students to explore their approaches to solving problems in similar ways. Using the analogy of research, we are gathering data about the issue we have chosen to study.

Designing a Study

Now it is time to explore possibilities, to design approaches to making whatever changes we choose to make, one change at a time. For example, suppose we decide our first reaction to difficulty is "I can't." What we want to do is to change our knee-jerk "I can't" into "What are some ways I can deal with the situation?" Notice, we don't demand that we immediately find the one and best solution. What we are asking of ourselves is to come up with ideas, to brainstorm. It may be that none of these ideas will work, but this is not our focus right now. What we want to do is to empower ourselves, to shift from "I can't" to "What can I do?" Keep a journal or record to help you recognize the enormity of the challenge and your gradually improving responses to difficult situations.

Similarly, when working with your students, encourage them to record or note their responses. Even young children can meet in small groups to discuss what is happening, whether in regard to work in school or to situations outside school. Encourage students to imagine many ideas rather than immediately to choose one. Help them to examine the part habit plays in discovery. Get them to look at their ability to be flexible and resourceful when initial ideas don't work as expected. Explore how humor helps us achieve perspective by laughing at ourselves, at our situation, at our responses, or at our anxieties.

Discovering Possibilities

Think of an issue or idea you want to explore, either theoretical or real. Paint or sculpt yourself in relationship to the issue or idea, writing down what comes to mind. Brainstorm by putting your thoughts down on paper listing the thoughts with the most potency toward the center and those with less vitality toward the periphery. If a thought that initially seems unimportant begins to feel consequential, put it down as many times and in as many places as necessary. Brainstorm with a friend or in a small group, but choose your partner(s) carefully. Remember, you are changing habitual responses and sometimes even people who love us don't want us to change. Encourage your students to participate at their own level.

I once worked with a group of first graders who were afraid to pass by an empty lot close to their school. They had convinced themselves, despite lectures from their teacher and the principal, that a witch lived there and would eat anyone who got close enough for her to grab. To encourage them to find new ways to respond to passing by the empty lot I told them to work in groups of three and to draw pictures of the witch. Afterward, I asked them to talk to the witch to find out why she was so hungry. The groups then shared their information with the whole class before returning to their small groups to invent a possible solution. The various solutions reported to the whole class ranged from starting up a witch patrol, to leaving a bit of food each day, to singing "The witch is dead" from *The Wizard of Oz*.

As a class we ranked the solutions discussing feasibility, practicality, effectiveness, and desirability. During the discussion, one child ventured, "Suppose there is no witch? Suppose we're pretending to be scared?" The answer came back clear and strong, "Well if there is a witch we certainly know what to do about it." Strangely enough, in a very short time the children stopped talking about the witch and walked past the empty lot as if they had never been afraid. Their teacher was able to build on the class's experience of finding ways to deal with feeling stuck when they encountered subsequent obstacles in learning.

Similarly, as you discover and develop potential solutions to particular problems, record your ideas in your journal. Noting feasibility, desirability, etc., without judgment, will develop resourcefulness. Very often we judge prematurely, which cuts off rather than encourages possibilities. Notice how you feel when you encounter a challenge and a host of possible ideas comes to mind. Note the solutions or ideas you are tempted to discard or which ones you immediately censor. Observe how easy or difficult it is for you to consider possibilities without deciding their immediate value.

Look at how you discover possibilities. What factors do you take into account as you make suggestions? How do you respond to unexpected inner feelings about what you are or are not doing? How do you decide parameters of feasibility? Are you able to play with ideas?

Choosing a Solution

When you have a number of possibilities, it is time to make a choice. Often, it is useful to imagine solutions and their potential consequences before making a decision. Some people find it useful to paint or sculpt their choice, writing down what comes to mind and noticing their reaction. I generally rank solutions if there is more than one that seems useful. Although I cannot always verbalize why I choose as I do, my sense of order usually feels right. When working with students who sometimes want to know which solution is best, the ensuing class discussion enables participants to look at elements of solutions and separate what makes something workable from something that is not. The collaborative process also helps reinforce the importance of being open to possibility and to new information.

Reflecting on Choice and Process

Usually, we have to decide whether our choice works and how well, or if not, why not. When reflecting, be kind to yourself. Don't automatically assume that if your choice proved less than wonderful you are fully to blame or that you are a failure. Separate out your reasons for the choice, look at consequences, examine what was and was not in your power to control. Similarly, when you work with your class, encourage your students to learn from their experience so that next time they will work with more resilience. No matter what size the catastrophe, we can always learn from it. When we do this, we honor our attempt, our courage to take a risk. Mistakes are often labeled failures but if we have learned from them is this not a kind of success? If we are more able to work effectively the next time have we not used our experience wisely?

The sequence I have described—observing patterns, describing patterns, designing a study, discovering possibilities, choosing a solution, and reflecting on the process—is always part of every research project. The more mindful we are of our thought processes, the less subject we are to acting automatically on past assumptions and practice. I believe this is an extremely useful way to introduce the place and importance of research to our students, to help them make connections between the knowledge learned in school and its relationship to lifelong challenges and choices.

Regaining Access to Imagination

I think of imagination as a muscle which becomes stronger and more flexible with use. Therefore, the following suggestions are a kind of image workout, a way to improve access to our imagination.

Think of a word which conjures up *place*, such as forest, desert, park, mountain, etc. Put your word at the top of a large piece of paper. Write down as many questions as you can think of which relate to the word. For example, I choose castle and my list includes the following questions:

What is the castle built of?　How is it defended?
Where is it situated?　Why was it built?
Who built it?　Who lives in it?
What is its history?　What is its current use?
How is the castle supplied?　What is the castle's mystery?
What lies near it?　What is the weather like?

Thinking about my list of questions I might paint or sculpt an image of my castle and then focus on what initially intrigues me about my castle. I find myself wondering about the young daughter of the woman who is in charge of weaving the cloth for those who live in the castle. Now I make a list of questions regarding this young woman.

How old is she?　What is her relationship to her
Where is her father?　　mother?
What is her full name?　What is the secret of her birth?
What does she look like?　What is her place in the castle?
What are her skills?　What does the mark on her
What does she want?　　forehead mean?
What does she yearn for?　What is her affinity to her life?
What draws me to her?　Why do others regard her as
What is the relationship, if　　special?
　any, between her mother　What is most significant about
　and father?　　her?
　　What helps or hinders her wishes
　　and dreams?

I feel myself becoming more interested in this young woman. Images form in my mind and the faint idea of a story begins to take shape even though I wrote questions as they occurred to me and I do not reorder them. At any point I can make another list of questions as

I pay attention to what is personally significant. Even if I don't continue my exploration and imaging, my imagination is engaged, my brain is stimulated. In quiet moments, when I'm washing the dishes or ironing, I find myself wondering about this young woman. I enjoy thinking about her, making up episodes in her life, considering her situation and what makes her who she is.

I have discovered that the more we allow ourselves to imagine, the easier it becomes, which is why I use the metaphor of imagination as muscle. Try it. Play with images and discard what fails to serve your pleasure and your purpose.

Regaining Access to Creativity

I think of creativity as a kind of faith in ourselves, that we have the inner resources to solve most of our problems in our own way. For instance, although initially I used a recipe when baking bread, I once found myself wanting to bake bread in a place where I had no books or mixer. My first impulse was, "I can't," but even as I thought this, another voice said, "Why not?" "Right," I told myself and bought yeast, flour, honey, and salt. I had no idea about proper proportion so I just fiddled around until the dough looked pretty good. I let it rise, punched it down, put it in oiled pans, let it rise again, and then baked it. I was astounded when it turned out well and, as an unexpected result, never again felt tied to a recipe. Reflecting on the experience, I recognized that because I really wanted the bread to be edible, I had to pay close attention to what I was doing. I couldn't take anything for granted and had to make a lot of decisions which required that I think about process and possibility, about what I remembered and what made sense.

I think paying attention is the secret wellspring, the source of our creativity. Taking chances, exploring, and discovering—are all part of creating, of making something that matters to us. Although we need a certain amount of knowledge and tools in order to create, what enables us to bring our ideas and dreams to fruition is our certainty that what we make or design for ourselves comes from a felt need inside us which cannot be answered by someone else's solution. Being creative is a way of life and comes from being our own authority on achieving our wishes, hopes, and dreams. It means looking first to ourselves for answers, solutions, and ideas before turning to so-called experts, authorities, and professionals. It isn't that we can't or don't ask for help when we get stuck; rather, we do as much as we can from our own resourcefulness before we ask others for the information we now know we lack. As we learn to look to ourselves, the process develops into a habit; relying on our own ingenuity and creativity becomes easier, more automatic, and a source of pleasure and comfort.

Suggestions

- Listen to your words and pay attention to your feelings when you are faced with either a small challenge or one that seems to be more than you can manage. Observe without judging your responses.
- Describe your automatic responses to yourself or to a friend. Notice how you respond to your own description.
- Design an approach to rethinking habitual responses which enables you to react and respond with renewed resourcefulness and ingenuity.
- Discover possibilities by playing with ideas, brainstorming notions by yourself and/or with a friend.
- Design new ways to deal with old issues. Take pleasure in the process.
- Choose some new possibilities and play them out in your imagination before actually trying any.
- Reflect nonjudgmentally on your experience. Articulate clearly what you have learned from your action.
- Discover what it takes for you to transform your internal "I can't" to "I can."
- Explore the development of creativity with your students as a research project. Encourage them to share without becoming judgmental in order to strengthen their internal resourcefulness. Teach them when judgment is appropriate and necessary, always focusing on what can be learned from the experience.

Ideas for Exploring Imagination and Creativity

Imagine a dream vacation. As you imagine, notice how or if you obstruct or censor your ideas. Allow yourself to be outrageous in your wishes and wants. In your mind's eye, play out several scenarios, each more pleasurable than the one preceding it. Create the space and time you most wish to enjoy.

Fingerpaint or sculpt an image of "myself at this moment." Write down any words or phrases that come to mind. If you don't have finger-paints you can use crayons, watercolors, or magic markers, but these are much less forgiving than fingerpaints or clay. Repeat this activity a few times a week for several weeks, always working without judgment—this is not about making art, it's about knowing yourself. Keep all your images, dated and labeled, in a three-holed notebook for future reference. Notice how you feel when you think about and/or do this activity. How can you relax and enjoy yourself? Notice whether you make jokes about your work at your own expense. If so, why? Think about the times you tried to explore your feelings—in art classes, singing, dancing, playing an instrument. What stops or encourages playing, the pleasure of expressing yourself?

Read or tell yourself an old story (folktale, myth, legend) that pleases you. Using a package of nonhardening clay, sculpt a moment from the story that piques your interest. If the scene includes one or more characters, sculpt them in relationship to each other or to their environment. Think about why the moment is so telling for you. Change your sculpture as you acquire new information.

After doing this by yourself, try it with a friend. Age or experience matters very little. What counts is the interest and willingness to try something new. Share sculptures and talk about what's going on in the moment for each of you. Explore how this moment relates to your own experience. Consider what the moment evokes, both in relationship to the story and in connection to your life. Have fun!

By yourself or with friends, think of a word that conjures up adventure, intrigue, or mystery such as *forest, apartment building, castle*, etc. Write down as many questions as you can think of to ask yourself. Share your list of questions and add to each other's list. Pick one aspect or question that interests you and focus in on it. Perhaps you chose the word *beach house* and you want to explore the person renting it for the week. You might paint an image of the beach house, the person in relationship to the house, and/or the environment. Now ask yourself questions about this person, writing them down any way you choose. Perhaps the ones that interest you most will go toward the top and those that seem perfunctory will be listed down near the bottom.

Choose a question or an issue that intrigues you, and as you think about it, paint or sculpt a few images. Write down what comes to mind. If you can't think of a beginning start with "Once upon a time . . ." or "In days long ago and a place far away . . ." Let yourself write without stopping to censor or rewrite. Leave space between the lines so you can add information as you choose. Stop when you feel tired or your story is finished. If you're tired and not finished, and you have no *ending* place, be sure to create a *resting* place (like a drink of water on a hike) or a *stopping* place (like staying overnight on a long trip) so that you can stop writing yet still feel okay about stopping. If you find it difficult to get back into the writing mode, ask yourself who, what, where, when, and why questions, or paint some images that come to mind as you imagine what might happen as the story unfolds. When I write I never know what will happen ahead of time—I tell the story to myself as I write it. Just make sure that when you think you are finished, you feel finished.

Occasionally I have worked with students who started what they thought was a short story only to discover their ideas could not be explored as a short story but needed to be a long story, a novella, or, in one case, a novel. Share your writing with a friend, asking for questions, wonders, or reactions that will allow you to deepen your work. Explore responses to your work or the work of a friend by sharing what the story evokes in you, what it makes you feel, what interests you about it, what questions the story elicits, or what the story reminds you of. Be easy on yourself and others. Consider what it takes for you to enjoy your work for its own sake without it having to be judged "good" by someone.

CHAPTER FOUR

Tools for Teaching Language Arts

I use the word tools to describe imagemaking, storymaking, movement, drama, soundmaking, and music because they are the means by which I teach reading, writing, and speaking. Although paints and clay are key materials, they are used to enhance knowing, not to make art. It is extremely important that teachers not allow themselves or their students to judge imagery because criticism is totally irrelevant and, if permitted, can cause great damage to students' ability to learn. Even very young children, often assumed to be "naturally" creative, may have experienced painful moments when teachers or students laughed at or denigrated their work, thus losing confidence in their ability to rely on inner resources. Teachers who want students to be open and imaginative have to be extremely conscious of what is said, stopping all comments which focus on artistry rather than on knowing.

If a class is suspicious of the use of imagery, teachers may want to paint or sculpt with their students as part of the initial exploration of a particular idea. For example, when studying the terrain of a country, a teacher might ask students to paint images of what the country looks like in a particular area. Follow-up use of imagery might center on exploring ideas about how people live in the places evoked by the imagery. Because the initial treatment of imagery affects subsequent use, teachers need to take special care to prevent inappropriate commentary during discussions.

Generally, I do not participate when students paint, sculpt, make stories, etc., because I sometimes become so interested in or affected by what I make that I have difficulty focusing on my students. However, if challenged to take part by students with whom I am just beginning to work, I generally do so, at least once, to demonstrate that I too use paints and clay to learn about my knowing. What matters is that they understand we are using imagery only as a way to discover and articulate ideas and feelings.

49

Imagemaking

The words teachers use to describe tasks are as important as the tasks themselves. For example, asking students to paint an image of *the* hero evokes a different response than asking them to paint an image of *a* hero, even though the task, painting an image, is the same. Telling children to paint a picture seems to be more threatening than asking them to paint an image, probably because picture connotes paintings hanging in a museum while image evokes something we see, either in our mind's eye or in the outer world. I introduce fingerpaints and clay by explaining that these materials are important tools which help us discover and learn what we know, especially when we have no words. Imagemaking, working with paint, clay, words, music, sounds, movement, or drama, enables students to make a spontaneous response, to discover the germ or seed of the idea being explored. Because students often take their behavioral cues from their teacher's attitude, it is crucial that teachers explain how imagemaking is central to learning.

I give children very little time to make the image, always less than one minute, and allow them no time to plan ahead. What I want them to do is to respond without self-censorship and that means time is of the essence. Although initially many students complain about not having enough time, as they become more familiar with the process most accept the time constraint and some are grateful for it. If teachers prepare their class properly, students generally work with good intention, especially after they see the rest of the class begin. Should some students refuse to paint or sculpt I give them time and space to change their mind without making a fuss, and most begin to work when they understand they are safe from criticism, that whatever their response might be, it will be taken seriously. If a student behaves inappropriately by throwing clay, using too much paint, or mocking others, I remove the student from the group by isolating the child physically, making sure he or she knows the door is always open and the only requirement for reentry is respect.

Imagemaking is most useful when teachers want to explore the essence of an idea, a piece of literature, or a problem, especially when students have trouble engaging with the material, or when the complexity of the inquiry leaves them no place in which to enter the material easily. For example, suppose the class is studying westward migration. Perhaps the teacher has read or told the class about a particular area in terms of climate, topography, economics, and history. The teacher might then ask the class to make an image of a factor which influences people's decisions about moving westward. If the teacher tells the class to use fingerpaint, students will use color, shape, and placement to uncover information. I always tell students to write the date and the title of the image on their paper so that when they reflect on their work they will know what it was they were doing. If the teacher asks the class to use clay, students will explore the relationships of people to the place in which they settle and the neighbors they have, using space, texture, form, and dimension. If drama is used, children will probably explore more personal interaction, giving them a sense of who and what is involved in leaving one's home to move westward toward the unknown. Whatever the medium, teachers can use images to explore issues and the connection between learners and the material being studied.

When given a task children often ask, "Do you mean . . . ?" or "Do you want . . . ?" My answer to these and similar questions is to repeat the task. If the questions persist I remind students that their questions are really about wanting to know what will please me but that I want them to please themselves. This is why it is important to delineate the task explicitly, so everyone knows without having to ask the teacher when the task has been accomplished.

Even if young children cannot write, their images still provide valuable opportunities for learning about their thoughts and feelings. I once worked in a shelter for battered families where I had a session with a mother and her three children, aged four, three, and two. After telling them an African folktale I asked them to make an image of a helper in a time of trouble. The four-year-old quickly painted a swirling image and when asked to talk about it said, "It's a wind. It blows away all the bad people." His sister, a year younger, had smeared gobs of orange paint all over the page. He looked at it intently and then said to her, "That looks like a fire."

She agreed, "Uh-huh. Burns up all the bad people."

To underscore the importance of images, students keep their images in a looseleaf notebook, arranged chronologically, according to a theme or idea, so that all images made in response to a particular text or subject are grouped together in one section. Then, when students need material for reflection, storymaking, or writing book reports or papers, the images serve as an excellent resource for evoking and stimulating ideas.

Imagemaking provides an opportunity for even the shyest child to speak by explaining, describing, or exploring the image the student has made. Even if the child simply says, "This is my image," the ice has been broken and in time, most children find more to say about their images, especially if the teacher has taught the class how to ask questions which help the image maker define or describe ideas more concretely.

An unexpected benefit occurs when children who think they are very different from everyone find they have made an image similar to someone else's. This unexpected response can provide the opportunity for isolated students to make important connections. For example, when teaching a seminar for teachers of deaf children I was informed by the principal that there was considerable tension between teachers who could hear and those who could not. After telling a Chinese folktale about a young girl who defeats a huge serpent, I asked the teachers to paint an image of something evoked by the story that was extremely important to them. Imagine their surprise when almost all the participants, deaf and hearing, painted a hand (which to them symbolized communication of ideas).

In the discussion that followed, many hearing teachers talked about feeling unwanted and pushed out by the deaf teachers, who in turn complained the hearing teachers did not understand the culture of deaf people. The conversation got so heated that the interpreter could not keep up. To give her some rest, I asked people to form groups of three (without regard to hearing capabilities) and to create a one-minute drama arising from their discussion of the images. After sharing their dramas, I asked them to freeze in the position of the most important moment of their drama, wanting to give participants time and space to consider what was going on without the need to react immediately. When each group of three had shared their drama I asked half of the groups to restage their highlighted moment so that it could be contemplated by the other half. There was silence as each half looked at the other, and more silence as they returned to their seats. No one could avoid noticing the similarity of the highlighted moments. The group's subsequent discussions continually made reference to their astonishment at the similarity of their moments and helped them begin to heal their hurts and reflect on their misperceptions.

Storymaking

After the image comes the development, the deepening, the story—the process whereby participants make a whole from the parts. Whether the storymaking is oral or written, the process is complete only when the story is shared. It is through this sharing that the teller fully senses the empowering effect of creating a story. As one young child said after telling her story, "I like it when everyone is listening to me." Teachers with whom I have worked, who make time for children to share their stories by designating periods for children to gather in an "Author's Corner," notice that many children, regardless of ability, soon want to participate and to be known as an author and a storyteller.

The amazing thing about storymaking is that often, perhaps usually, we have no idea we have a story to tell until we begin to speak or write and the story emerges. Where does it come from? Where is the story before we give breath to our thoughts and shape them into words?

I don't differentiate between stories children make from stories they already know and stories they make up themselves, either about their lives or from their fantasies, because in the telling, children add something of their own. Even the process of selection, which is often unconscious, allows children to put their unique stamp of being on the story.

What I find particularly fascinating is the emphasis each child brings to the story. For example, I asked fourth-grade children to write their version of "Little Red Ridinghood." Before writing, I asked, "When is a story a variation and when is it a new story?" As a class the children decided each version had to contain the following elements: a little girl given a basket filled with food by her mother; a mother telling her daughter to take the basket to her ill grandmother who lives in the woods; a wolf that the girl encounters on her way.

Then they were asked to explore how to decide the time and setting of the story, and to what degree this mattered as far as the "truth" of the story was concerned. To the teacher's surprise, there was an animated and vigorous discussion. One child said, "It doesn't have to be set in a real forest. It could be set in a bad neighborhood. That's as bad as being in a forest."

Another child said, "The wolf could be a gangster because gangsters are scary." Others argued that a forest was a forest and not a bad neighborhood, that a wolf and a gangster were not alike. The discussion enabled the teacher to talk about metaphor and the possibility that the traditional story could fuel a retelling that used modern equivalents for traditional experience. She asked how many children had ever been in a big forest. Only two of twenty-five raised their hands.

One child quickly defended the traditional story, "So what if I've never been in a real forest, I can use my imagination."

Another child countered, "Yeah, but when they made up that story people lived in forests, that's why the story takes place in a forest. We should make our stories be where we live."

Still another child asked, "Why does there have to be only one way? Why do we have to decide a forest is right and a bad neighborhood is wrong? Why can't we retell it how we feel? Like how the story lives inside us."

This was unacceptable to some children, who argued, "This is a very old story. If you take out the wolf and put in the gangster you're changing the story. Years from now children who hear the new version won't ever know that in the original story there was a scary wolf and not a bad person."

After much discussion and argument, the class decided as a group to write their "official" version of "Little Red Ridinghood" and to use the class's version as the basis on which to write their own versions. They labeled their collection, *Stories Inspired by Little Red Ridinghood.* This experience not only enabled each child to explore metaphor, choosing individually how much to depart from the original story, but provided a frame of reference from which to begin. Although some of the stories departed very little from the "official version," what mattered to the children was their freedom to tell the story in a way that was personally satisfying. Toward the end of the year, about four months after the original experience, on a whim, the teacher asked the children to repeat the activity, making their version of "Little Red Ridinghood." Without needing to hear the story retold, the children created new stories, all of them significantly more developed and with greater attention to detail, characterization, and plot than the first interpretations. After the stories were shared, the teacher asked the children to account for the richness of the new stories. One child answered nonchalantly, "Well, we're more experienced now than we were back then."

Children can make stories from any source. One interesting way for children to examine the contours of history is to ask them to write a diary as if each student in the class was a child living in a particular time, during a specific period. For example, if the class is studying the American Revolution, each child could pick one of the original thirteen states and select an incident around which to frame the diary entries. In order to write the diary, each child would have to research the incident and decide how to use fiction in the service of historical accuracy. Children might also use the information they uncover to write short stories about the life of one character imagined by the writer.

Teachers can encourage children to work in teams to use storymaking to make up math and science problems. Teams can then exchange problems, solve them, and discuss the issues and ideas involved in each problem. Storymaking connects the imagination with the capacity to make order out of chaos. In my experience, it is virtually impossible for children to make stories out of material which does not interest them. If they have to make up a story, they generally find ways to make the material of sufficient interest to allow them to create the story. By broadly framing material to be explored, teachers enable their students to use storymaking as an effective and challenging learning technique.

Movement

Movement and dance exist on a continuum, with dance at one end and movement at the other. While dance is based on formal use of pattern, rhythm, design, and style, movement embodies the informal expression of ideas and feelings based on ordinary human motion. Everyone moves. Everyone can use their ideas and feelings as the basis for their own movement. Teachers who use movement in the classroom as part of the traditional curriculum provide students with a nonverbal approach to discovery. Although we know that children learn in different ways and that some children learn best through a kinesthetic approach, few are enabled to learn this way. Teachers may not know how to structure appropriate movement activity or they may equate movement with dance and feel unequipped to incorporate movement activity into classroom education.

However, the benefits outweigh the possible disadvantages when teachers understand how to use movement to promote learning. First, teachers must decide what they want children to learn and how movement can be used to enhance the learning. Second, teachers must structure the movement activity to stimulate imagination in a clearly framed way that relates to what students are studying. Third, the movement activity must not only have a clear beginning but also a well-defined ending point. This enables participants to exercise discipline regarding their inquiry. I always limit the amount of time and space so that students know they don't have to keep going "forever."

Children studying what it is like to survive in a desert climate might do well to get out of their seats, clear a space, close their eyes, and imagine who they are, where they are going, and why they are in the desert. In groups of three or four they might move in ways that suggest heat, sand, arid landscapes, endless sun, uncertain water supplies. Not only does the imaginative activity spur questions and stimulate thinking, it provides an antidote for restlessness and purposeful activity after too much sitting. Encouraging children to share their exploration with another group or with the whole class deepens their thinking about the topic and encourages discussion based on personal discovery. If teachers ask their students to respond to the movement done by classmates I suggest they not ask them to guess what is going on. Guessing presupposes one right answer and inhibits spontaneous response. Much more helpful is the phrase, "What do you think (or feel) is going on?"

Teachers can use movement to introduce concepts in science as one first-grade teacher did when he asked the children to think of something that could be solid or fluid, held in the hand or breathed in through the nostrils, and affected by heat and by cold. When the children couldn't think of the answer he asked them to divide into small groups and to move both as individuals and as a group, exploring what the magical substance might be. Each group shared their movement exploration and as they were watching each other's work, several children shouted out, "Water! Water is solid when it's frozen and fluid when it's above freezing. When it boils it becomes steam." What a wonderful way to introduce a science unit.

Young children can explore arithmetic concepts of addition, subtraction, multiplication, and division through movement by manipulating small groups within the class to explore particular functions. As a group, children can explore what happens when you add, divide, multiply, or subtract by two or three or four, depending on class size. With the whole group moving as smaller units within it, abstract notions are more easily concretized.

When children read books teachers generally devise ways to ascertain children's comprehension through testing, book reports, or oral reports. Why not suggest that children, who tend to be great mimics, do a report using movement? For example, suppose they are reading "Snow White." Each child picks a character and a part of the story which is personally meaningful. Each "moves the story." One child might choose to be Snow White moving in the forest after being released by the woodcutter who was supposed to kill her. Another child might choose to be the dwarf who first sees Snow White. Before children do their movement report they describe the setting and the intention of the character. Children have to make decisions about their character's behavior at a time of crisis. What happens to a normally assertive Snow White who has to plead for her life and then manage to find her way out of a dark forest at night? What might it be like for a dwarf to share a meal with Snow White for the first time? Each decision the student makes depends upon her or his understanding of the book in general and of the character's actions in particular. Even when students choose the same passage to explore, each child's interpretation is unique, making for an interesting discussion and a diversity of thought and action based on a text.

Movement can also serve as an entry into drama and verbal communication when students explore the physical basis for characterization,

setting, emotional environment, and relationships among characters. Using "Hansel and Gretel" as an example, I once worked with a second-grade group whose teacher wanted to help some of her children who were less verbal than others to become more active participants.

We asked the children to pair up with someone who was either larger or smaller than themselves. We asked them to imagine what it was like for each of them to walk in the forest as it was growing dark, not knowing where they were going. In order to keep the children from generalizing we asked them to create an incident as Hansel and Gretel (with a definite beginning and end), but they couldn't make noise because they didn't know who might hear them. We did this to keep the focus on movement and feeling.

When we asked for volunteers no one offered. This is not an uncommon reaction and one way to encourage participation is to make the space more cozy. We asked the class to form a circle, to close their eyes, and to make sounds they thought the children might hear. When we once again asked for volunteers several pairs raised their hands. Even when children created similar incidents such as tripping over a log, being frightened of a sound, or losing each other temporarily, we helped the group to notice what made each pair's work unique. When we asked the children to tell us how they felt and what they were thinking, even the least articulate children had something to say and their words flowed easily.

If teachers are anxious about movement in the classroom, children will pick up their anxiety. One way to lessen this worry is to have volunteers work inside a circle made by the class while they offer helpful suggestions. Using the example of Hansel and Gretel, the group might suggest questions such as: How do the children feel at any particular point? How do their feelings affect their being in the forest? Their connection with each other? Do feelings affect action and behavior? If so, how? Always?

If children don't have ideas, they need to be encouraged to ask each other for helpful suggestions so there is no onus to being stuck, admitting it, or asking for help. If children are taught to explore ideas as a group, even when only a few members are actively exploring, the whole class will benefit in every future learning situation.

It is useful to outline an area of exploration and then to ask the children to devise their own ways to delineate and identify approaches to examining the issue through movement. This challenges them to use their imagination and creativity as problem-solving techniques. For example, when looking at the effect of weather on human beings, teachers might ask students to examine how temperature, wind, and humidity affect human behavior such as walking through a desert, running down a steep hill, etc. Exploring ideas about a subject or a text through movement encourages those whose primary mode of communication is kinesthetic and gives all children another way to think through questions and to approach learning.

Drama

"Let's pretend . . . I'll be the princess and you be the witch."

"I don't want to be the witch. You be the witch."

"Okay, we'll take turns. I'll be the witch first, then you be the witch."

Young children make drama as easily as they breathe. Yet, somewhere around first or second grade, self-consciousness sets in, and what was once natural becomes strained and uncomfortable. I think this change occurs when teachers and/or parents begin to comment on the dramatic play, letting children know in a variety of ways that there is something wrong with "pretending" or that it's "cute." However, drama is such an incredibly rich and useful method for exploring, developing, and extending oral and written language that it needs to be part of every teacher's methodology for teaching language arts.

Through the centuries, theatrical activity has often been looked on with disfavor. There is something about a person playing a role—taking on the behavior of a created persona, wearing a mask, assuming a new personality and disguise—that makes some people uncomfortable. It's as if we can't tell who or what is real when the person in front of us transforms into a character. Teachers often tell me that when students work in role something happens to the classroom environment, as if the classroom and the students are transformed. I call this transformation magic because we who are in the class feel a shift in the environment, as if we are invited into the world of the text or subject being explored. It's an important and healthy learning experience and usually means students are purposefully involved, actively taking on a role, entering into the life of an invented character, and making decisions about who this person is, what she or he wants, why, how, where, and so on. The more absorbing the character and situation are, the more potential there is for student learning. When this intense and focused concentration occurs, the whole class becomes involved in the learning process.

I think about a group of third graders with whom I worked as part of their interdisciplinary study of the history of the United States from its beginnings to the 1800s. The teacher was leading a discussion about the lives of the early settlers and I learned from the children's talk that "the settlers saved the Indians and taught them how to survive by hunting, fishing, and planting corn." I tried not to react but when I was asked to participate, I suggested we divide into two groups, settlers and Native Americans, and to examine how the two groups might have interacted in their first meetings. The teacher volunteered to work with those who chose to be settlers and I offered to join those who wanted to be Native Americans. We asked the class, "Who wants to be a settler?" Every hand went up.

A bit daunted, I spoke up, "I'm going to be a Native American and I welcome anyone who'd like to work with me. I'll be starting our exploration by telling stories from Native American cultures."

"There aren't any. They didn't speak English," sneered one of the children. I had to bite back a quip and keep my voice calm.

"Well, as a matter of fact, there were Native American peoples all over what is now the United States. Every tribe had stories and language and customs. They were living here long before the first settlers arrived. Come with me, we'll discover all sorts of interesting things they knew." Five children eventually, reluctantly put up their hands.

"Okay, here's what we'll do. Let's agree that our drama will be about the first meeting between the Native Americans living here and the settlers who have just arrived on these shores from another country." The teacher and her group decided where the settlers came from, where they landed, and what group of Native Americans they would most likely have met. "We'll need to do research about who we are, what our lives are like, what we want from each other, and how we relate among ourselves. The settlers will also have to decide why they've come to this land and what they hope to gain after having survived such a long and difficult ocean voyage."

For the rest of the afternoon we looked at library books; I told some stories from Native American peoples living in the area where the settlers landed; and we talked about who we wanted to be. Because there were only six of us we decided we would have a chief, his wife, and their four children. The students wanted me to be the chief but I suggested they would learn more if one of them took on the role. One of the boys finally agreed but stipulated he would not kiss his wife which we all agreed was reasonable. I offered to be one of the children but they didn't like this idea. "I have to be someone, why can't I be one of the children?" They fidgeted, unable to agree about my identity. Time was running out—I suggested we role-play, hoping we could discover the role they wanted me to play. Since we were only six, we decided that we had been chosen by our tribe to represent them, and then explored our ways of hunting and gathering food, clothing ourselves, and relating to each other. Slowly, the five children became quite involved, forgetting their initial reluctance. By the time we were to meet the settlers the children had a sense of pride about their heritage.

Just before the drama began one of the girls said, "I know who you are, you're our storyteller, sort of like our historian. You tell us stories when we need to know something." By unanimous consent, I had my role.

After arranging the room to represent the shore and the meeting place, we agreed that the drama would end after half an hour of playing, regardless of where we were in the action. We also agreed there would be no violence, that if people wanted to grab or push they would mime it. With the teacher and her group at the edge of the "shore," and my group at the edge of the "forest," we began.

The nineteen settlers strode off their ship and onto the shore, guns drawn, those playing the women and children huddled together in the rear. "Hello! Hello! Is anybody here?"

The chief walked slowly into the space, keeping his distance from the settlers. He spoke in our made-up language.

"Can't you speak English?" complained the head of the settlers. The chief looked puzzled and repeated his greetings. The settlers began to get restless, shouting, "Get out of our way." When the chief refused to move, some of the settlers yelled, "Kill him. He's in our way." The chief maintained his composure and repeated his greetings. Two of the settlers came over and "grabbed" him. The head settler did not stop them until the chief's wife and three children came over and quietly stood by him. I decided to stay out of the drama until I was needed. Nonplussed, the two settlers backed off. Now the two groups stood staring at each other. The settlers began to talk among themselves.

The class's teacher had also decided not to take a main role and kept silent while the children talked about what they would do. Although she and I had not discussed how we would participate in this particular drama, we had previously worked together in a workshop and shared a commitment to promote active participation by the class. However, in the workshop we had also talked about signals and signs that indicated a group might be in trouble and had examined possible ways to deal with difficult situations such as when groups or individuals are stuck, essentially saying or doing the same thing over and over again.

My group had determined before the drama began that we would maintain our dignity regardless of what the settlers did, but if given the chance, we would offer them some of our food—dried corn, deer meat, and sassafras tea.

While the settlers were talking among themselves, my group decided it was time to offer food and mimed bringing baskets of food and hot tea to them. The settlers were resistant at first but the teacher took the cue and said how hungry and thirsty she was. Others followed her lead and soon almost the whole group was eating and drinking. Two boys refused to join saying the Indians couldn't be trusted. They stood guard, guns drawn. Tension was high.

The chief, uneasy about the guns, decided it was time for a story and led me over to the group. With only gibberish at my command I had to use lots of gestures and expressive sounds to tell the story I selected. I focused on the two with the guns, hoping I could interest them to the point that they felt safe enough to put the rifles at their sides, if not down. They kept their watch, the guns remained pointed at us. The half hour ended.

Breaking role, I suggested everyone stand up, shake out their hands, talk to their classmates, and get out of role. The children refused, they wanted to keep going. The teacher pointed out that school was almost over for the day and that it was important to process our work before they left for the day. "Can't we talk in role?" asked one of the students. After a spirited discussion we agreed to talk in role for half the time and to speak as ourselves, out of role, for the second half.

"We have to speak in English," demanded the head of the settlers. The Native Americans fought hard to have the discussion in their "language" but the head settler concluded the matter by saying, "There are more of us than there are of you. Majority rules! We speak English."

Spirited dialogue among the Native Americans brought home a telling point for all of us when one said, "How come it's always us who has to give in? We were here first. We were doing just fine without you."

The group subsequently decided to exchange roles; settlers became Native Americans and Native Americans became settlers. Each group noticed how uncomfortable they felt in their new roles and they came to appreciate how difficult it is to be part of a disempowered minority.

Soundmaking and Music

Rhythm and sound have an immediate impact on our brains. Many of us have had the experience where we feel terrible, put on some music, and soon our mood is transformed. Our spirits lift and life seems possible once again. Because music can alter moods so effectively, there are teachers who use music to teach alternatives to violence. They help children learn how one can shake hands in friendship as well as punch, push, or shove by having students put new words to popular songs which reflect desired changes in behavior. Even young children respond to the challenge, learning to sing about how they feel and what they want. In some classrooms children engage in mock operatic debates where participants frame their complaints both in verse and melody. One fourth grader who was furious at a classmate faced him and sang, "I'd like to punch you in the face."

The teacher led the rest of the class in choral singing, "Punch. Punch."

His antagonist sang back, "I'd like to zap you to the moon."

The chorus sang, "Zap. Zap." Each time one of the combatants sang, the chorus echoed. After a few exchanges the chorus began to mix up the responses, "Zap, punch, blast, boom," faster and faster until some of the children began to laugh. The laughter spread until even the combatants were laughing. With the tension released, the class went back to work. The whole episode took less than five minutes.

In a class made up of "slow learners," as part of a reading program, the teacher and I helped the children make drums from a variety of materials—oatmeal boxes, coffee tins, industrial-size tin cans, etc. We explored the concept of African talking drums as a way to communicate in a world without telephones, newspapers, and radios. The children created a vocabulary of rhythmic patterns to indicate common experiences such as danger, welcome, and flood. Initially, the patterns were simple and easily remembered, but as the children wanted to increase their ability to communicate, the patterns became more complex. Finally, after one of the children kept forgetting a sequence he complained, "This is too hard to remember. Can't we write some things down?" The teacher used his complaint as the opening she'd been looking for, a way to make reading and writing necessary, relevant, and important to children who had previously not been interested in learning.

We divided the class into two groups, each "translating" rhythmic sequences into verbal equivalents. When each group had about ten phrases we divided them into smaller groups, each with a few phrases to teach another group. As the class's confidence grew, their ability to learn improved yet the drums continued to be an important method of communication. Children learned to share their feelings by drumming out what was going on inside them. Those listening responded by drumming rather than talking yet there was significant communication, satisfying to all participants.

Another way to use music in the classroom involves putting new words to old songs, which is not only an interesting technique to develop discipline in class, but also serves to improve and increase vocabulary. Using a familiar tune like "Here We Go Round the Mulberry Bush" with children in a Head Start program enabled them to make up lines about what they were doing which were then echoed by the rest of the class. If a child got stuck, he or she would sing, "I'm stuck," and classmates were encouraged to suggest ideas to get unstuck. The singing unified us as a group, made what we were doing more fun (such as cleaning up our mess), and allowed the children to practice commenting on what they were doing. One child, who hated to work with clay, sang, "This is the way I hate to play, hate to play, hate to play. Working with clay is terrible, so early in the morning." Somehow, having the rest of the class sing his song made it easier for him to join the class even though he never learned to like messing about with clay.

With older groups, creating songs and chants enables students to write poems without thinking of them as poetry. Although teaching the class to sing your group's song can be initially embarrassing because most of us have been told we can't sing or are tone deaf, it is a good opportunity for students to reclaim their rights to their own capacities. Teachers can use the occasion to talk about how we let the judgment of others ruin our faith in ourselves.

Although enabling older children to sing in front of their peers is sometimes difficult, it helps to divide them into groups of four and to have each group make up a chant, which they then teach to the whole class. The following Native American trickster story about coyote has provided students with powerful images and has served as the basis for many chants.

Coyote and His Name

Great Spirit called the people together to tell them that a new time was coming. Soon the animals would be all-together animals and there would be people who would be all-together people. Every animal was to come before Great Spirit the next morning to receive the name by which each would be called for eternity.

Coyote did not like his name. He wanted to have a powerful name like Grizzly, the strongest of all the animals who walk on land. Or Eagle, the most powerful creature who flies through the air. Or Salmon, the mightiest of swimmers who live in the water.

Coyote tried to keep himself awake all night so that he would be the first to greet Great Spirit at dawn. When he arrived and saw no one, he congratulated himself for being first. Great Spirit asked him what name he wanted. "Grizzly," he said in a loud voice. Great Spirit told him Grizzly had already come and gone. The name was taken. "Eagle!" said Coyote, willing to take his second choice. But this name had been taken by Eagle. "Oh, well," said Coyote, "in that case I will be called Salmon." Great Spirit quietly told Coyote that Salmon too had claimed his name. In fact, the only name not taken was Coyote the trickster.

Coyote felt sad and discouraged. He told Great Spirit, "I do not want to be Coyote the trickster. I do not like my name. I want a new name."

Great Spirit listened to Coyote's complaints. When Coyote grew quiet, Great Spirit said, "You must be Coyote the trickster, the shape changer, because I need you to help me. The people who are coming know nothing. You will have to show them how to hunt and to fish. You will have to help them to be sad, and happy, and brave, and cowardly, for this is what it means to be human. You will have to teach them. No one else can do this because no one else can change their shape."

So Coyote the trickster, the shape changer, accepted his name and prepared to teach the people who were coming what he knew.

One of the ways I begin an exploration of this story is to ask the class to suggest powerful and important qualities such as bravery, fear, joy, cowardice, or anger, which are written on the board. Each quality is then written on a piece of paper. The class is divided into four or five groups, depending on the size of the class. Each group selects a piece of paper with a quality written on it, and creates a short chant, no more than two lines, which Coyote chants to himself in a time of need or crisis or just because it feels good to chant. Each group teaches the class the chant they've made up. Often, we make a circle and chant, playing with rhythm and harmony, until we have learned all the chants and put them in an order which feels satisfying. Sometimes each student writes the chants down for the class to use in the future. Occasionally, when a class is having difficulty, someone will chant the appropriate chant or make reference to it, and somehow, with everyone chanting, the difficult moment is eased. The experience provides us with a good opportunity to talk about what it is that makes us human, what we need to make us feel better, or how we can celebrate a moment of triumph, while writing, reading, or expressing feelings.

Ideas for Exploring Imagemaking, Storymaking, Movement, and Drama

Carefully structure the activity so that students know what the task is, where the beginning and end points are, and how much time they have.

Design the activity so that there is no one "right" answer.

Encourage diversity. If an answer seems peculiar or strange, resist the urge to judge it. Instead, ask the person or group who devised the solution or response to share the thinking that led to it.

Teach the class how to respond to work without being judgmental. Encourage students to explore how the work shown connects to them, what it makes them think about, feel, remember, wonder. Help students to formulate questions which further the work and make possible new exploration.

Create an environment where students can easily say they are stuck and need help. Encourage the class to think of themselves as the resource for one another. Show them that part of learning is helping others to think through issues, problems, questions, and challenges.

NEVER allow a student to make fun of, denigrate, or casually dismiss the work of class members. Creative work is impossible when students suffer from being put down, threatened, or devalued.

Teachers participate when they help students to process their work, but occasionally the class benefits from a teacher joining in by painting or sculpting an image, creating movement, making drama, or sharing a story. The teacher's active participation in making an image, a story, a drama, or movement demonstrates that this work benefits all participants. I often bring in examples of how I've used imagemaking or storymaking to solve a problem just to show my students that these techniques also work for me in my professional life. In fact, I use them in my private life as well, and share these occasionally when it is appropriate.

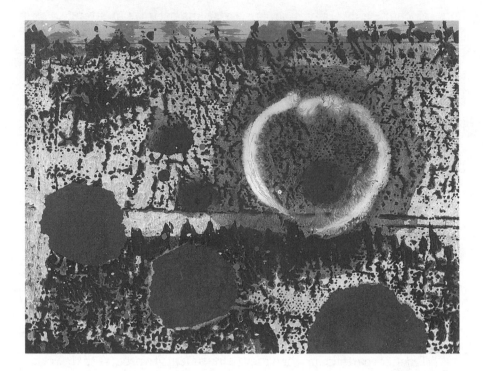

CHAPTER FIVE

Classroom Management

When I think of an issue, a story usually comes to mind. "The Poor Tailor" from eastern Europe reminds me that imagination, creativity, and expression are not only essential to education, but also to living a life that is full of hope and possibility.

The Poor Tailor

There was once a poor tailor who felt sad that he could never afford to buy material to make himself a coat. One day he realized that if he saved the scraps of material left over from all the clothes he made, he just might have enough cloth to make himself a coat. Happy to have a plan, the tailor kept all the left over pieces from all the clothes he cut and sewed, until the day came when he decided he had enough material to make his coat.

That night, working until dawn, he cut and sewed himself a fine coat which he wore with great pleasure. However, in time his coat wore out. He looked at the shabby garment and decided he had enough material to make himself a jacket which he wore happily until the jacket was in tatters.

From the scraps he made himself a vest which he wore until there was not enough material to patch the frayed garment. From the bits and pieces of the vest he sewed himself a cap, but in time this too raveled.

He cut the useable bits of material to make himself some buttons. And, when the buttons wore out, he used the material to make himself a story.

Children who are encouraged to think for themselves develop inner resources that help them respond to challenge with resiliency and ingenuity. Children who are discouraged from becoming active learners do not. If children are to acquire the skills necessary to become vigorous participants in their own learning, teachers need to develop educational activities designed to evoke interesting and creative responses rather than those which focus primarily on the one "right" response so often required. For this to happen two things must occur simultaneously: teachers' lesson plans must include activities that involve and encourage divergent and convergent thinking, how we learn as well as what we learn, invention and memorization. And, teachers need to feel comfortable in the role of facilitator, the "one who creates dialogue and partnership" as well as the "one who knows and tells." The teacher who welcomes exploration believes that what is taught in the classroom must result in the competency we need all our lives as well as the ability to do well on a test.

How we teach reflects our notion of the world and our place in it. We are affected not only by our sense of the present, but also by our past experience and our view of the future. As human beings, we create and assign meaning based on our understanding of the importance of particular symbols in our lives. Symbolization is the beginning of all human intellectual activity. The degree to which we are aware of this personal symbolic meaning is the extent to which we can be cognizant of how we make sense of our world. For example, an apron can be a symbol of tyranny for a child who is forced to cook. The very same apron can be a symbol of love to a child who enjoys cooking with a nurturing adult. Fortunately, we can also explore symbolic meaning through using our imagination. We can ask ourselves how we would feel about an apron we are forced to wear to cook food we are not allowed to eat. What might this apron symbolize? In constrast, we might imagine wearing the apron to cook food for people we love, knowing we will all sit down together to eat it. How might this scenario affect what the apron symbolizes? Because our understanding of what symbols mean to us personally is greatly enhanced by our capacity to visualize and express our inner vision, encouraging the use of imagination in the classroom improves abstract thinking.

Invoking the imagination is the beginning of knowing and is the first step in creative learning. Given that children currently watch a great deal of television, which eliminates the viewers' need to make images and to visualize, it is not surprising that some children come to school with poor access to their imagemaking capacity. Thus deprived, it is difficult for them to read and to imagine what characters look like, where they live, how they interact, or how they are affected by situations and issues.

The capacity to see and differentiate among images plays a critical role in reading and writing. When I was teaching young children in a Head Start program, the director wanted me to teach the alphabet to children who could not differentiate among circles, squares, and triangles. I could see no way to teach a child letters if this child could not recognize and name shapes. When we give children tasks for which they have no preparation, we condemn them to a failure from which they cannot easily emerge. We certainly make it harder for them to learn in the future. Yet when these same Head Start children learned to recognize shapes and to differentiate among various colors, they quickly began to recognize their names, which I wrote in a variety of ways: with icing on the top of a cupcake, with pancake batter cooked in the shape of their name, and on pieces of paper I placed around the room.

In the beginning, after I told a story to these children, none of them could imagine what scenes in the story looked like. Yet later, after practicing and exploring the possibilities, all the children were able to describe what they saw in their mind's eye, adding and inventing details as they gained experience. Children's lack of ability to visualize fundamentally affects all aspects of their ability to learn and must be addressed before we can hope to teach more complex subjects such as reading, writing, science, and mathematics.

When children recover their imagemaking capacity and discover what makes them unique in their reactions and responses, they are more able to make connections between their inner and outer worlds. Teachers inhibit or facilitate this freedom to learn by the way they structure exercises for their students. I cannot overemphasize the importance of paying attention to classroom activity that focuses on process as well as content. We need to foster the sharing and use of imagery which freely express ideas, feelings, and attitudes directly related to the question or task at hand. It is the teacher's function to set the agenda, create a framework, and enable students to focus on specific tasks.

Teachers sometimes fear that the use of imagemaking and creative approaches to learning will inevitably unleash emotional and psychological chaos. In more than forty years of teaching and consulting, I have never experienced a group of students reacting poorly to the opportunity to engage in dialogue or explore powerful issues. I believe that a teacher's fear of losing control in the classroom comes from insufficient education in teacher preparation and a lack of positive personal experience. As a professional working with children, a teacher is accountable to administrators and parents. The fear of losing control can be so strong that teachers focus on that fear, rather than on ways to diminish their anxiety. Tightly structuring lessons, making very small changes at any one time, differentiating what they fear from what they want to achieve with their students, and sharing ideas and questions with other professionals all help to alleviate fear and anxiety.

I addressed these issues in a school where the principal had terrified teachers by stressing the importance of order and silence in the classroom to the exclusion of all other classroom possibilities. The teachers with whom I worked could not tolerate the slightest bit of sound, which created great problems for normally noisy youngsters. I proposed we do some drama using "wind sounds," all breath and no voice. One teacher agreed, more out of frustration than belief, but when she saw the difference in her students after we had worked for thirty minutes, how much calmer and more focused they were, she agreed to continue exploring. I discussed with the children the importance of moderating their voices and they agreed to try. The work in drama made such a difference in the children's receptivity during regular classroom study that we decided to share our experience with the principal. Eventually he visited the classroom to see for himself that children talking in the classroom is not necessarily bad nor is silence and order synonymous with learning.

The incorporation of the arts is a central part of education because the skills required to make drama, poetry, images, movement, songs, and stories encourage divergent approaches to solving problems even as arts education improves cognitive functioning. Children have to think about the task at hand in order to create particular and individual solutions, rather than respond with pat or automatic responses. Not only do students improve their ability to learn, they approach learning with confidence and high self-esteem.

Structuring activity that encourages individual learning styles and develops the roles and responsibilities of active learners transforms the classroom from a place where memorization is the primary skill taught to one where inquiry, choice, and change are the norm. I believe that children who are actively engaged in learning tend to do better on standardized tests than children who are taught by teachers who teach "to the test," because active learners are more confident of their skills and have more resources to solve problems than do passive learners.

Many of my ideas about learning come from examining my imagemaking experiences, both in school and at home. As a young child I liked to read and to pretend I was a character in the book I was reading. I spent hours imagining plays in my head, needing nothing more than an empty space to entertain my fantasy. As I grew older, around age eight, I integrated my feelings and ideas into more concrete play. Because I always wanted to be a teacher I created an imaginary classroom of children with whom I became very involved. I made up and gave tests which I graded, sent report cards home, and commented on students' behavior, all of which was predicated on my creation of interesting lessons which I then imagined teaching. Although my dramatic play took place in private, the enquiry which fueled my actions is common to all children involved in dramatic play.

The first question children engaged in dramatic play ask is, Who am I? This generates other questions. Where am I? What am I doing? What do I want? Why do I want it? What stands in my way? What will I do to get what I want? What are the possible consequences of my action? Who or what hinders and helps me? How does the story/conflict/situation end? Although we may not consciously ask ourselves questions as we play out our fantasies, our actions are informed by them. Skills acquired in developing dramatic play can be applied to traditional academic study when children use their ability to formulate and incorporate questions in drama to explore, examine, and discover other aspects of learning such as math or science.

While teaching math to a group of twenty-two slow learners, I asked twelve students to move into the center of our circle. The children tediously counted from one to twelve until they were satisfied there were twelve children in the middle. Then I asked them to divide the group of twelve into two equal halves. Blank stares. "Okay," I said, "how about putting one-half of the children on one side of this chalk line and one-half on the other side?" Laboriously, the ten children on the outside moved the children in the middle until they had six children on each side of the chalk line. They were pleased when I congratulated them, yet puzzled and intrigued as I helped them figure out what they had done to divide twelve by two. In the course of the session we added, subtracted, multiplied, and divided, processing what we had done immediately after each activity. The children were helped to ask questions and to consider applications for each activity. When I brought the children, brimming with excitement, back to their teacher, he built on their new energy to enhance their self-esteem and willingness to help each other learn.

Participants in arts-centered activities find they have to ask questions that are interesting enough to keep them exploring and discovering. Although people can suggest possibilities, only we, the ones who are creating, can finally discover our authentic response and solve the problem or question we have set for ourselves in a way that is personally satisfying. Thus we learn to be active explorers, aware of what we want and what we need to do to please ourselves. Even when we fail to accomplish what we intend, we learn, for now we know what we need to learn, and what might have been lacking in our previous attempts. We are empowered because we emerge from the experience more resourceful and knowledgeable. We understand the importance of making decisions, not as a one-time right or wrong experience, but as the means by which we continue to expand our knowledge.

Engagement

We tend to learn most effectively when we find pleasure in a process which encourages deeper and more focused participation. While selecting children to participate in the Stories Project, I met a boy who told me he hated to read and write. "I'm not gonna do it," he said emphatically. I explained that I certainly wouldn't force him to do what he didn't enjoy doing. Suspicious, he asked, "How come you want me?"

"I'd like to see you participate. Let's make a deal. You come with the others and do only what you want to do." After his reluctant agreement, his university tutor and I devised strategies to help the boy want to read and write.

When he came for his first session, his tutor told him a folktale from Africa and then brought out fingerpaints. He asked, "What do I have to do?"

"Nothing," she said. "I just like to make images of the story." She painted while he watched. Casually she said, "You can paint with me if you feel like it." The boy continued to watch. When the session was over he asked her, "What you gonna do with them pictures?"

"After they dry I put them into a book." He looked somewhat interested so she asked, "Would you like to see my book of pictures?" He nodded and she promised to bring them to their next session. Later she called me, worried about his lack of participation. I told her to keep sharing interesting stories, using the fingerpaints to record her thoughts and feelings. Under no circumstances was she to force, cajole, or use pressure to get him to do anything. Part of her worrying stemmed from her inability to join the other university students when they shared their children's stories in class; she had none to recount. I reminded her this was not a competition to see who was most successful as tutor, but a powerful struggle to help a child recover his sense of curiosity and pleasure in reading, writing, and talking.

When the tutor next picked the boy up from his classroom he immediately asked to see the book of images. When he looked at the third painting he asked her what it was about. She said, "I painted it after hearing a story I liked a lot."

"What's the story?" he asked.

"The picture isn't about the story I heard, it's about the story I made up from the story I heard." The boy looked confused. She asked him, "Which story would you like to hear? The story I heard or the story I made up?"

"Both!" So she told him the original story, a myth from Polynesia, and then shared the story she had written. By this time, although the session was almost over, the university student asked if he would like to paint. The boy said no, yet watched intently as she painted her impression of the session. When she finished he wanted to know about her painting.

"I feel good about sharing the stories but I'm a little sad that you don't want to paint." Before he could say anything she reminded him their time was up. Silently, he helped her pack up the paints.

The tutor began their third session by sharing a Korean folktale. The boy informed her that his father had been a soldier in Korea and had written him letters describing the country and what it was like being there. "Would you like to paint an image of Korea from descriptions you remember from your father's letters?"

"No."

"Do you mind if I make an image of Korea?"

"No." Watching her paint he said, "You got too many trees in your picture. My daddy said there were no trees 'cause people cut them down to burn for cooking."

The tutor said, "This is my picture, not yours. You want to make an image, be my guest." The boy painted a treeless landscape. Gently she suggested, "How 'bout I show you my image and then you show me yours."

"Okay," said the boy, "but you got to remember, I know what it's really like. You only know about the story."

The university student replied testily, "You know what it's like from your experience—your father's letters. I know what it's like from my experience—the story. Yours isn't better than mine, it's different."

"You're wrong! My father was there. He knows."

"Well, the story was told by a Korean. Doesn't a Korean storyteller know about Korea?"

After some silence, the boy took her painting and studied it. Then he looked at his own. "Look," he said, "we both got mountains in our pictures."

"Yes, and we both painted them purple," said the tutor, surprised. The boy looked at the pictures while the university student waited.

"That's funny, us both painting the mountains purple. My dad didn't say the mountains was purple."

"Neither did the storyteller," said the tutor.

"So how come we both painted the mountains purple?" asked the boy.

"I don't know."

The boy began to laugh, mimicking the tutor's tone of voice. "I think we been using our 'magination."

"How about telling me the story of your purple mountain."

"I ain't got no story."

"I think you do. What you don't know is how to find it."

"Where is it?" he asked.

She laughed, "In your imagination."

"Well, if it is, how come I can't find it?"

"Because you're looking outside and you need to look inside. Want me to help you find it?" He nodded. "Close your eyes and imagine your purple mountain. Can you see it?" He nodded. "Okay, now look and see who lives there."

"A purple rabbit."

"Does the rabbit live alone or does it live with other rabbits?"

"He's the only purple rabbit. The others are white and brown."

"So how does this purple rabbit feel?"

"Lonely."

"What would the purple rabbit like?"

"A purple rabbit friend."

"What does he do to find one?"

"He looks everywhere. Up and down the mountain. He gets very tired. He sits down and cries."

"Then what happens?"

"A red rabbit finds him."

"A red rabbit?"

"Yeah."

"Is the red rabbit happy to see the purple rabbit?"

"Yeah."

"Why?"

"'Cause the red rabbit is lonely. The brown and white rabbits won't play with him."

"Do the two rabbits become friends?"

"Yeah. And then they're not lonely any more."

"Thank you for telling me such a wonderful story."

He opened his eyes. "I didn't tell you a story. I just told about a rabbit who lived in the purple mountain."

"But that's a story. It's your story."

"How can it be a story, it doesn't even have a title."

"So give it a title."

"I can't.

"Sure you can."

"I can't."

"Okay, I'll give it a title. The Brown and White Rabbits."

"But it's not about brown and white rabbits, it's about the purple rabbit being lonely."

"Oh, so your title is The Loneliness of the Purple Rabbit?"

"Yeah."

"I told you you could title your story."

"Did you play a trick on me?" he asked.

"No. The words are yours." She could see the boy thinking so she waited a bit before asking, "Would you like me to help you write down your story so you can read it?"

"You know I can't read."

"Just like you can't tell a story?" He smiled sheepishly. "Reading is easier than telling a story, you only have to learn some letters." She wrote his title, "The Loneliness of the Purple Rabbit," on a sheet of paper. "This is the title of your story. Now tell me the first sentence and I'll write it down for you."

He hesitated, sighed, and then said, "Once upon a time there was a purple rabbit who lived on a purple mountain. He was very lonely. All the . . ."

"Wait, I can't write so fast," protested the tutor. She slowly printed his words saying each word out loud. He repeated her words. They continued until she had written down his story. He picked up the paper and stared at it.

"This is my story?"

"Uh-huh. Word for word. Just what you told me."

"If I give it to my mother can she read it?"

"Try. See what happens."

He did. She could. Utter joy.

Many aspects of our capacity to learn are called into play when we are allowed to absorb knowledge and process information using all of our being. We know that people learn differently, primarily processing information visually, kinesthetically, aurally, or in some combination. When the mode of learning involves the entire sensory system this greatly increases a learner's chance to succeed. The little boy in the above episode was given the opportunity to participate and learn in his own time, in his own way. Once he experienced the joy of making up a story and reading his own creation he came to look forward to working with the university student, and eventually asked if they could work together after the sessions were officially over.

Although it may be easier to work one-on-one than it is to work with an entire class, the essential process of involving students in their own learning remains basically the same. When teachers make it possible for children to have a personal stake in their own learning and the opportunity to have some control regarding their education, children usually respond positively even though this may take a while. We all need different amounts of healthy experience before we can trust our teacher and our new skills.

Making, telling, and/or writing stories as a central and essential mode of learning is one excellent way to engage children. When we make up a story, whether we are retelling a familiar tale, sharing something that happened to us, or inventing a new story, we collect disparate bits of information in order to create a new whole. Gathering the fragments requires that we make choices; we add this bit but not that bit. We sequence the information in this way, not that way. We shape our story to this purpose and not that purpose. Our choices, many of which are unconscious, help us become more aware of what we know, who we are, how we feel, and what matters to us.

Every child with whom I have worked, who has written, illustrated, and learned to read her or his story, feels a sense of accomplishment, and, at least for the moment, an enthusiasm for reading and writing stories. When we tell our stories to others, we positively reinforce our self-image; we are people with unique ideas worth sharing. We establish the purposefulness of expressing what we know and how we feel.

Discipline

Discipline promotes active learning and growing. Not the passive "sit-at-your-desk-and-fold-your-hands" type, but the active experience of making choices, honing possibilities, seeking responses, reworking ideas, and exploring alternatives—all in the service of making what is inner and private, outer and public. The kind of inner discipline students develop as active learners evolves slowly, as children recognize that the vision and impulse they seek to make articulate is theirs alone. No one can give this to anyone, it must come from inside. The struggle to make what is inchoate articulate and/or visible is a metaphoric struggle for life, for all learning. Others can help, but only after we make the initial decisions about who, what, where, when, why, and how. Even then, *we must hold to our vision* as we explore, consider criticism, and make changes. This is not an easy task—it takes time to establish trust—but each time children ask for and receive nurturing help, their opportunities for learning are expanded and enriched.

I developed an appreciation of the importance of inner discipline from a group of four- and-five-year-olds who weren't supposed to know much about discipline. We had just gathered on our "storytelling rug" when a program assistant dumped twenty milk cartons on the floor and shouted, "We're making trucks today. Visitors are coming to see the children's work." After piling the cartons on the tables we had pushed together so that all twenty of us could sit around as a community, everyone looked at me, waiting for directions.

Unaccountably, I felt angry and did not trust myself to speak. The children began to squirm. My aide spoke worriedly, "What do you want us to do?"

"Nothing." She recoiled, as if I had struck her. The children's fidgets increased. Why was I so mad?

My aide asked, "What's the matter?"

I blurted out, "The matter is I don't know how to make a truck from milk cartons."

"You're the teacher. If you don't know who does?"

I asked the children, "Who knows how to make a truck from a milk carton?" Silence. More fidgeting. "What does it take to make a truck?"

They looked uncomfortable and confused but one of them said, "Wheels?"

"How many?" No answer. "Well, where do the wheels go?" No answer. I tried again, "What do wheels do?" Silence. I began to understand what to do. Smiling, I asked, "What would happen if a truck had no wheels?" The children laughed.

"It couldn't go."

"Why not?"

"Cause wheels go 'round and the truck is on the wheels. When the wheels go, the truck go," said a five-year-old whose father was a mechanic.

"Yeah, and if a wheel is flat the truck moves funny," said his sister, who proceeded to give us a demonstration of a truck out of control. Great roars of laughter as the children got up and moved and made sounds as if they were trucks with flat tires.

One child acted out his words, "If the wheels is flat the truck be st . . . u . . .ck." Immediately the class echoed his words and moved to the rhythm.

The aide told the children to return to the table and behave.

Reassuring her that their reactions were purposeful, I asked, "Do all trucks have the same number of wheels?" I heard yeahs and nahs. "If we're going to make trucks how will we know how many wheels we need?" The children waited for me to give them the answer.

One child ran to the window, "Look, there's a truck with lots of wheels." We piled up against the window to watch a huge truck back up to a loading dock.

Another child shouted, "Look over there. I see a little truck." We all looked. We had explored numbers up to ten but few of the children could count accurately.

"Let's count the wheels on the big truck." I began to count and my aide joined in. Quietly the children joined us, mostly copying our sounds, "One, two, three, four, five, six, seven, eight."

"There's not so many on the little truck," piped up a shy little boy.

"I'm gonna make me a big truck, with eight wheels," said the boy whose father was a mechanic.

"What will your truck be used for?" I asked.

His sister answered for him, "Toys. Lots of toys."

"Yeah," her brother agreed, "toys."

"I want a little truck," said a small girl.

"What will your truck carry?" I asked.

"Ice cream. Cones and pops. Lots."

"So why doncha make a big truck?" asked one of the boys.

"'Cause it gonna come to my house. My street be too little for a big truck." The children stared out the window watching the trucks and cars zooming down the busy road visible in the distance.

My aide was worried, "Don't you think we should get started? Lunch is in half an hour." I didn't see how we could get the trucks made in half an hour and I didn't feel like rushing, especially when I overheard two children talking as seriously as if they were actually buying a truck.

"I need a truck with lots of wheels so mah milk won't spill."

"Well I have to have a skinny truck 'cause I drive in the city. You know them cars is parked everywhere."

One of the children started to draw a picture of her truck. Another child saw her and ran to get his own paper. Soon, the children were drawing the trucks they wanted to make. Their drawings gave me an idea.

"Let's go back to our drawing boards." The children looked puzzled. I explained what the term meant and they look pleased, even proud. Another "big word." "Let's pretend we're a company that makes trucks.

Each truck is specially designed according to what the customer wants. Design the truck for your customer and then take one of the milk cartons and make your truck."

"What do we do for wheels?"

"What do you think we should use?" I asked them. My aide looked at her watch. The children walked around the room, examining paper, rooting through the button box, the bottle cap collection, even the blocks. One by one they returned with their choices, focused on what they wanted to make.

"I'm stuck," shouted one of the children. "How'm I gonna 'tach the wheels to the body?" Several children made suggestions which he rejected out of hand.

"You too choosy," complained a classmate. "We tell you what to do and all you do is shake your head. Why you ask?"

"It don't fit mah customer's needs."

"What your customer want?"

"He want a big truck with big wheels. They got to go through mud."

Several children who had been absorbed in making their trucks looked up. One girl offered, "You can do like me. They goin' to different customers so it don't make no difference if you copy me."

"You sure?"

"Yeah." He went over to her, watched for a bit, went back to his truck and attached the wheels in his own way.

We were busy working when the director came in with two visitors. She was visibly displeased at our lack of progress. "Your group is the only one not finished."

My rage rose then transformed into pure joy when a child said, "We ain't finished 'cause we got to design trucks for our customers. Some of them is plain fussy." I stifled my impulse to laugh as children explained what the trucks they were building were supposed to do. We'd done a lot of dramatic play and as the children spoke, they took on the role of designers trying to please difficult clients, describing their various tales of woe.

One of the visitors entered into the dramatic play, "I own a large company that makes trucks. I'd like to see your finished trucks. When do you think they'll be ready?"

The children talked among themselves and then one suggested, "What about a little after lunch?"

The visitor said, "I have to leave soon after lunch. Suppose I come back just before I leave. Can you be ready then?" The children nodded. Lunch was served, eaten, and cleared away in record time.

As they returned to making their trucks my aide and I took on the role of shop supervisor. "We've got a big order and you'll probably need help so just ask." Each child worked intently and purposefully, as if this were a real job. Their excitement grew as we carefully arranged a display of the trucks, each one different from the others. What had been scheduled as a half hour "copy-the-teacher's-model art project" became a day-long learning experience that began with looking at trucks on the road, followed by thinking about how the function of a truck affected its design, making up stories about the truck drivers' lives on the road, and finally, talking about how we came to make the trucks we did.

These four- and-five-year-olds were not specially selected—just normal kids whose lives were marked more often by chaos than calm. They learned to focus their minds and discipline their thoughts as they worked together sharing questions and ideas, as a natural, everyday experience. When children's ideas are respected and personal and collective exploration is valued, students also learn the function and significance of discipline, a vital skill rather than a punishment.

Imagination, Creativity, and Expression

My experience in the classroom suggests that the most important and fundamental benefit of arts activities is that they help children to regain access to their inner resources. Those who study creative development in children notice that five-year-olds are generally more enthusiastic and curious about learning than are nine-year-olds. Educators with whom I have spoken tend to assume that this is a developmental phenomenon, that except for the small number of talented children who become artists, the creativity a child is endowed with at birth lasts for only a few years. I believe that children lose access to their imagination, creativity, and expression only when these traits are deemed undesirable by administrators, teachers, and parents who value rote learning more than individual engagement with the learning process. Ironically, not only do children retain very little when memorization is the primary learning tool, but often, bright children drop out, normal children think learning is drudgery, and children with learning disabilities give up.

In every classroom where teachers use arts activities as a fundamental learning tool, I find children who are engaged, excited, and eager to share their work, performing at or close to their potential. I believe this happens because children start their project with an idea or a question. If they get stuck or discover they lack skills or knowledge, most want to learn what they don't know so they can finish what they started. At the same time, even when the whole class is working on the same assignment, each child's work reflects the child's singularity in an important way. The more learning is linked to the use of imagination, creativity, and expression, the more likely it is that children will be active learners.

One second-grade teacher with whom I worked on a storymaking project decided to have each of the children in her lowest reading group write a story based on a story told to them. While discussing the project she asked what constituted a story. I laughed and said, "A sentence."

"One sentence?"

"Actually," I said when I thought about it, "in the beginning, one word can be a story." We talked about using stories to spark children's interest in reading, writing, and sharing stories, and we agreed that each child needed to feel good about the experience. The next time I visited her class, I told the children in the lowest group a story from the Canadian Indians about a spirit that couldn't make up its mind. I had the children fold their paper in half and asked them to paint an image of how the spirit might be feeling about being unable to make up its mind on the left side of the paper. On the right side of the paper I asked them to write down some words which came to mind, either about the spirit, or a time when they couldn't make up their mind, or about what it might be like to be of two minds. Many children knew words they wanted to use but didn't know how to spell them so I wrote all the words they asked about on the blackboard, assuring them that words belong to everyone, that they could use any word on the board which suited them.

As we shared the images and words we talked about what it might be like to be responsible for taking care of people and not be able to make a decision. I then asked the children to look at their images, to think about the story I had shared with them, and to make up a "very, very short story" to share with the group.

"How short?" asked one dark-eyed boy named Tiko.

"As short as you choose," I answered.

"Okay," he said, "stupid. That's my story." Without a word I helped him write—Stupid. He looked slightly uncomfortable, as if waiting for me to make fun of him.

I asked the children, "Does anyone want to know anything more about Tiko's story?"

"Yeah," said a pigtailed girl named Annie, "I want to know who's stupid."

Tiko looked worried. I reassured him, "If you don't want to answer you don't have to. Your story is your story." He squirmed a bit.

"Well, there's this old man who thinks he's really smart so he tells people what to do. But he don't remember what he says."

Amazed, I asked him, "If you would like to include this in your story I'd be glad to help you write it." He nodded, looking surprised yet pleased.

After reading what he had told me to the group I asked, "Is there anything else you want to know?"

"What happens to the man? I mean after he says one thing one day and somethin' diff'rent the next?" asked a tiny little girl named LaTonya.

Tiko countered, "What do you mean what happens?"

"Well," she said, "just because he can't remember don't make him stupid. My grampa has trouble remembering and he ain't stupid."

"I didn't say he's stupid," grumped Tiko.

"Yes you did," insisted LaTonya.

"The old man ain't stupid. The people who get mad at him for not remembering. They're the ones who stupid."

I intervened, "Tell us some more about the old man."

Tiko's words tumbled out of his mouth. "There's a kid on the block who's doin' bad in school. He comes home from school. He's crying. The old man sees him crying. He asks him, 'What's wrong?' The little kid tells him, 'I forgot how to spell a word. The kids in my class was laughing at me. Sayin' I'm stupid.' The old man says, 'I forget lots of things. Am I stupid?' The little boy says, 'You're a grownup. How can you be stupid?' The old man says, 'Happens.' The little kid says, 'The people who make you feel bad are stupid.' The little kid and the old man take a walk."

It took a while for me to write his story the way he wanted it to be but the group members were surprisingly patient. When I read the completed story to the group, everyone complimented him, saying what a great story he had written. I had to promise to help each child make a story before I was able to leave. The teacher typed Tiko's story on the large-print typewriter around the images he had painted; for the first time he asked if he could take schoolwork home to show his mother. The next day, the boy offered to read his story during "Author's Corner," a time when children shared their stories with the class. Even though he was in the lowest reading group, he read his story perfectly.

Legitimizing the idea that one word can be a story allows children to relax about writing "a good story" and often enables them, through questions from the group or teacher, to go deeper, to find the underlying story, without stress or feelings of inadequacy. One-word stories are a bit like the tale of "Stone Soup" where the soldier makes delicious soup after asking for a stone to put in the boiling water. Casually he asks the woman of the house, "Might I have a bit of carrot? A tiny onion? A little potato?" Soon he has a pot full of goodies yet the woman keeps talking about how the soldier made soup from a stone. Similarly, children who have low self-esteem and/or poorly developed writing, reading, or speaking skills often do surprisingly well with the one-word storymaking approach because it is something they can easily do. Afterward, when they have responded to questions and deepened their story, many still seem amazed "you could get such a good story out of one word."

Time and time again people ask me where stories come from. How can one word contain a story without the story being known to the storymaker? I don't know the answer. I think storymaking is a function of being human; it is the way we make sense of our life and the world. We all have stories to tell—the question is how to help the teller tell the tale. Using small steps to ensure success, children experience themselves as storymakers. Their self-confidence often rises, as does their ability to attempt what previously seemed impossible. The boy who wrote "Stupid" felt stupid and one experience with storymaking did not automatically transform him into a great reader. The teacher had to help him each time he wrote a story and at first, although he "read" the story, he was actually reciting it from memory. But his teacher persisted and, periodically he told her he had a story inside him that needed to come out. No one is quite sure when he actually began to read rather than recite his story from memory, but once he knew he could read, his skills developed rapidly. He worked to improve his writing so he could write his stories by himself. Near the end of the year, the teacher wrote a note home, sharing the boy's success with his mother and stepfather. The mother called the school to castigate the teacher, "You know my boy is stupid. Stop telling lies about him." To protect the boy, the teacher copied all of the boy's stories before he took them home, collected them in a portfolio, and at the end of the year, sent the portfolio to his next teacher with a note describing her experiences with the boy, suggesting ways to continue helping him to flourish.

As educators, we know that none of us works to our full potential. It often takes a crisis, catastrophe, or difficult situation to make us use unused or unknown inner resources. In the classroom, teachers can use arts activities to enable children to connect and reconnect with themselves and their classmates, to develop basic and complex skills which heretofore seemed unattainable. Instead of deciding what children can or cannot do, teachers need to plan lessons which are explicitly designed to enable children to discover their abilities. As with the women in the mental hospital, supposedly incapable of active participation, who one day, after weeks of no response, returned the ball I threw to them, no one knows what children can do. No label is absolutely accurate for all time and under all circumstances. We are all capable of growth given the right teacher, time, and place. What makes teaching so exciting is the opportunity to help children discover and develop hitherto unknown resources, skills, and abilities.

Creating Community

Not only is learning affected by the relationship between students and teacher, it is also directly influenced by the relationships among individuals within the group. When the group is healthy and can act as a source of information and support for every individual within the group, students more easily admit they are stuck or want information. But when the group is unhealthy, individuals have difficulty working together, and often there are bouts of fighting, yelling, and other disruptive behaviors. Group well-being depends upon healthy teacher/student interaction and on a teacher who knows how to process difficult experiences so that individuals can learn and grow from the bad times. This is always the teacher's responsibility.

Structuring activities which help children to imagine, create, share, and explore are important experiences that teachers can use to facilitate healthy interaction. Yet, the less healthy the group, the more necessary it is to work as a whole rather than to divide the group into smaller units. Activities to create community have to be carefully planned and be the primary objective if group health, fundamental to effective individual learning and all classroom practice, is to be achieved.

This became apparent when I was working as a consultant in a small elementary school, helping teachers use the arts to teach traditional school subjects. The teachers' attitudes toward me ranged from welcoming to hostile; they had not been asked whether they wanted me to observe their teaching; they were simply told I would work with them in their classrooms. Not an auspicious way to begin. My initial classroom experience involved working in a first-grade classroom with a teacher who was absolutely wonderful—open, interested, eager to learn, and devoted to her students. The children, with their teacher's blessings, responded to every activity with good concentration and enthusiastic participation.

Not only did the children write and share stories, they also improved their oral expression by making drama from their favorite stories. Normally, first-grade children do best when everyone in the class plays the same role at the same time, as one group. Young children generally do not have the ability to create differentiated characters where each child plays a singular role, a skill usually developed in second or third grade. But these first graders were able to work in small groups with every student playing a chosen character.

What helped to make their responses possible was their teacher's practice of regularly telling a story to the class as a continuing part of her language arts program. The class's "job" was to listen and then to ask questions or talk about what each child thought or felt after hearing the story. The children were taught how to listen and how to share their responses without being judgmental. The teacher did this by helping them to consider how a story made each of them feel, what it made them think about, and what they might want to know about the story that wasn't told. For example, when she told them "Jack and the Beanstalk" one of the children asked, "How come the mother's so poor? Where's Jack's father?" The teacher explained that this was not in the original story and wondered what the children thought. She encouraged them to devise many ideas without deciding which idea was best. When one of the children demanded to know, "Which is right?" the teacher talked about how stories could be used to make new stories. She divided the children into small groups and asked each group to create "The Story of Jack's Mother and Father." The students also learned to talk about what a story made them think about, and what events, if any, in the story reminded them of their own lives and selves.

After working with this first-grade class, the principal assigned me to a poorly functioning fourth grade. I planned my work with the older children based on what I had been able to do with the first grade. Big mistake. One should never assume automatic development just because a group is older or more experienced. I walked into the fourth-grade room and was greeted by total chaos. The teacher was shouting at the children, who paid no attention; they were too busy fighting, screaming, and throwing objects. "Oh boy," I said to no one in particular, wanting to run back to the warmth and peace of the first-grade room. I introduced myself to the teacher who muttered something, grabbed her purse, and ran out the door.

Knowing better than to try to outshout screaming children I stood quietly in front of the room mouthing words. Eventually, some of the children became curious, stopped what they were doing, and stared at me. When the class was temporarily quiet I introduced myself, purposefully speaking too softly for them to hear easily. Finally, one child raised her hand and timidly asked, "Please miss, could you speak a little louder?"

I barely said two words when a few boys started punching each other. Without thinking I yelled, "No!" They stopped, shocked. Taking advantage of the momentary lull I told the class to sit in a circle in a small area free of desks, hoping there would be enough room for all of them. It was as if my request was so extraordinary they could do nothing but comply. Once they were seated I explained why I had come, what I wanted them to do, and how I wanted us to work together. I didn't dare ask individuals to do anything so we huddled together while I told them "The Ant and the Elephant," a story from India.

The Ant and the Elephant

Once upon a time, Elephant, huge and forceful, ruled as king of a very large jungle. Every animal, whether they were big like Giraffe, powerful like Tiger, or small like Hummingbird, obeyed King Elephant. Very soon, all this power went to King Elephant's head. He began to order animals to do whatever he felt like having them do, even if it meant they had no time to find food for their children.

The animals began to grumble quietly among themselves. Some of the braver ones began to suggest, politely and gently, that perhaps King Elephant did not realize the effect his commands were having on their lives. They tried to tell King Elephant about the difficulties he was causing but he was not interested. The animals spoke up, a little louder, a bit more often. King Elephant ignored them and made even more demands.

Fear and terror reigned in the jungle. No one was safe from King Elephant's charges. Children were starving for lack of food.

The animals decided to hold a meeting to discuss the situation. Perhaps someone could think of a way to end their misery. Most of the animals were too frightened to consider possible solutions. Some were too angry to think. Everyone felt wretched.

Tiny Ant spoke up and said she knew how to put an end to their troubles. The animals had a good laugh. How could such a puny creature like Ant do anything to stop a huge and powerful animal like King Elephant? Ant persisted, "Please listen to me. I can make King Elephant stop his bad behavior. I will even force King Elephant to apologize!" The animals insisted this was impossible but Ant refused to give up. "None of you have any ideas. Give me a chance. Let me help." Finally, muttering how foolish Ant was for falsely raising their hopes, the animals reluctantly agreed.

Ant carefully observed King Elephant, waiting for the right moment to put her plan into action. She noticed that every afternoon, after eating a large lunch of sugarcane, he took a very long nap. She also noticed that nothing, not even the buzzing of bumblebees, disturbed his sleep.

When Ant was satisfied that King Elephant was sleeping deeply, she crawled up his trunk, into his brain, and danced.

Ant's dancing put pressure on the delicate tissue in his brain and caused King Elephant to have a terrible headache. The faster Ant danced, the worse Elephant King's head ached.

Many animals hid in terror as King Elephant tore down trees and smashed rocks, trying to stop the agony in his head. A few animals were so frightened they confessed to King Elephant that his pain was caused by Ant who was dancing in his brain.

King Elephant roared, "Get out Ant. Leave now or I shall kill you." Ant laughed as she continued to dance.

King Elephant yelled and screamed but Ant quietly said, "I will not come out until..."

"Until what?" yelped Elephant King. His head hurt so much he could hardly see.

Ant spoke firmly and gently, "I will come out when you agree to change your ways. You must promise you will not order us about any more. You must give us your word that you will treat us kindly." The pain in King Elephant's head was so excruciating he felt he would die if the agony did not stop.

"Very well Ant," he said grudgingly. "I agree. . . Anything to stop your dancing."

"Anything?" asked Ant, who began to dance slowly.

"Anything," shouted King Elephant.

"Good," encouraged Ant. "I think you should apologize to the animals. I think it would be a very good idea if you tell them you are very sorry you treated them so poorly." Ant danced a little faster.

"I will! Just to stop your dancing. GO. Leave me in peace." Slowly, Ant crawled out of King Elephant's brain, down his trunk, and onto the earth.

King Elephant breathed an enormous sigh of relief. The pain in his head was gone. Ant said nothing. She stared at King Elephant. When he did not move, Ant said, "I'm waiting."

King Elephant called all the animals together. Ant watched him very closely as he said, "I am sorry I treated you so poorly."

Ant smiled. When the animals had gone, she said to King Elephant, "Remember your promise. I have many relatives and we all love to dance."

I was just finishing the story when their teacher strode into the classroom, saw us sitting on the floor, and screamed, "Get up! Go to your seats immediately. How dare you sit on the floor! Get up! Get up!"

The children scurried to their desks. "Sit up and fold your hands." Frozen, the children sat, hands clasped. Then she turned to me, "Get out of my classroom. I won't have your nonsense in my room." Face burning, a thousand unspoken words rushing to my head, and with my hand ready to open the door, I calmly turned and said to the children, "Thank you for your cooperation, I'm pleased you liked the story."

I left before the teacher could respond, wishing I could run to the principal and demand he fire the teacher. Instead, I asked him about the class. He told me the children were doing poorly, parents were complaining about the teacher, and he had asked me to work with the class hoping I could change the unhealthy dynamics. I knew the teacher, not the children, was the source of the problem; I wondered what I could do to help her want to teach differently.

Fate intervened. Two days later the teacher was hospitalized with pneumonia. The principal asked me to teach the class until an experienced substitute could be hired. My first tasks were to tell the class what I expected and how I intended to restore order. I knew this would take more than a few days, but I hoped that by concentrating on creating community, I might help them function better. Since the children had listened well enough to the story I'd told them the first time we met, I decided to begin to change the class dynamic by telling stories. Every story I shared had the same theme, that of a small and "insignificant" person, animal, or creature who figured out how to overcome great odds to complete an important task successfully.

After each story I asked the children to draw whatever came to mind as they thought about the story. When they showed signs of restlessness I gave them movement exercises to do and encouraged them to "shout" using wind sounds (voiceless sounds such as whispering). Although they were persuaded by me to talk about their pictures while sitting close together, I had to reassure them repeatedly that sitting on the floor was acceptable classroom practice.

We were sharing images when the principal and the substitute teacher entered the room. Immediately the children fled in terror to their seats, folded their hands, and looked down at their desks. I gulped and said, "Would you like to join us in our circle—we're sharing images and we haven't quite finished." Only after the two sat down did the children slowly return to the circle, warily checking the principal to make sure sitting on the floor was really permissible.

The substitute teacher and I worked out long-range plans and then developed ways in which she could comfortably continue the story work, using the stories to teach reading and writing. We also worked out some math and science problems using characters and situations from the stories. I recommended that she do a lot of work in the circle on the floor because this seemed to reinforce healthy interaction and certainly reduced behavior problems. It took her two weeks of remedial interaction before she could begin more traditional fourth-grade work, yet she continued to use stories as her way of reinforcing the community structure we had begun to build.

Although I was pleased with the class's progress I knew only too well how quickly things could change when their regular teacher returned. I decided to send daily reports to the regular classroom teacher telling her what the children were doing, the stories they were being told, and ways in which the stories were being used to teach subjects. I had to leave before she was scheduled to return but the substitute teacher agreed to continue the practice of using stories as the basis for all her teaching. As the children calmed down, parents were so relieved and pleased that many called the principal to demand that the substitute teacher be hired full time. The principal promised he would work with the regular teacher but parents were adamant—they did not want her back. In the end, he effected a compromise. The substitute teacher would stay for two weeks after the teacher returned, helping her to learn the new methods. Frequent intervention by the principal reinforced the necessity for her to incorporate the new curriculum into her daily lesson plans. She was not a mean or bad person who purposefully created terror and chaos. Rather, she was without knowledge about how to make things better. Although she was never as relaxed and comfortable as the substitute teacher, the children continued to respond and make progress.

After the teacher's return I wrote her a letter suggesting that when chaos threatened she might find it useful to tell a story. She wrote back a cordial note and said she had and it had worked. To my surprise, she requested that I share with her the story I initially told the children. We continued our correspondence for a few months, discussing ways to use stories to encourage children to imagine, think, explore, and express.

One of the first issues we examined was whether to tell the moral of the story or to make one up if it did not come with one. I have learned that when you tell children what the moral or the meaning of a story is you deprive them of the opportunity to decide for themselves what a story means, how they connect to it, and whether or not they like it. Very often, before there is any discussion of the story, I ask children to sculpt, draw, or paint a telling moment, a point which resonates inside each child, the highlight of the story for them. Sharing images enables even the shyest of children to say something, even if it is only, "This is my picture." With practice, children become used to exploring their images as a way to share ideas about the story. When twenty-five children come up with twenty or so different telling moments they understand that as long as an idea can be supported by the text, all answers have validity. As students listen to ideas which are both similar to and different from their own, they can better appreciate both commonality and diversity

Often, after children have discussed their ideas about the story they spontaneously share stories of their lives. With a bit of encouragement, these life stories lead to "made-up" stories, all of which can be collected and put into a book of the child's own stories. Sharing stories always creates a sense of community among those who listen.

Often, a class has a favorite story which they repeatedly ask for, until one day, for no apparent reason, they suddenly request another story. I heard Bruno Bettelheim theorize that a particular story may have a healing effect on the listener, and that when the healing occurs, the story is no longer so meaningful. In my own life I know that certain stories are very significant to me, serving as a source of comfort, information, encouragement, or humor, but after a time some of these stories cease to be the ones that come to mind; other, newly found stories have taken their place.

The class's sense of community can be strengthened by giving a copy of a favorite story to students who then draw or paint images of or from the story, illustrate a cover page to personalize their copy, and then bind the pages to make a book which becomes part of their personal library. This often leads to discussions about the relationship of a book cover to the book, the nature of illustration and imagery, and what it is that attracts readers' attention when they look at books. When all the books are finished we display them, allowing everyone to see the range of ideas and expression evoked by the same story. This reinforces community and personal accomplishment, without sacrificing diversity or individual imagination.

Subsequently, when differences of opinion arise, children can be helped to use their experiences with books to work out difficulties without immediately resorting to violence. Teachers can use characters and events in texts to enable children to role-play or talk about resolution. Children need to learn that there are essentially two responses to conflict—talk or violence—and that violence never settles an issue, often leading to more and increased violence. In the end, talking is the only way to resolve conflict.

Even after community in the classroom is established, it cannot be taken for granted. Like a plant, it needs constant nourishment and attention. Short daily meetings to discuss issues or raise questions can be a useful way to accent the importance of sharing and connecting. I usually begin my classes by asking, "Questions? Complaints? Comments? Happenings of note? Anything we need to know for the good of the company?" A few seconds of silence give students time to decide whether they want to speak; most often they do not. Sometimes it helps to begin with a few minutes of silence, perhaps with the class and teacher sitting in a circle on the floor. Whatever technique is chosen, the "ritual" reinforces community—what affects one, affects all.

Collaborative Learning

Probably nothing is more basic to effective learning than the environment in which it occurs; time spent developing collaborative learning strategies is always time well spent. Yet we are formed by our culture, and many of us experienced the classroom as a place of competition rather than cooperation. Some teachers fear that if the competitive edge is blunted children will not perform as well. I think the opposite is true. Students who learn to think and comprehend when they are interested and relaxed retain much more for longer periods of time than do tense students whose primary classroom function is memorization. Students who are taught to ask for help have more opportunities to learn than do students who are afraid to admit their lack of knowledge. Although stories about the importance of asking for help and the necessity of cooperation can be found in cultures throughout the world, the following Sufi story is one of my favorites.

The Journey of the Stream

There was once a stream which came to life in the highest of the high mountains, moving through dense forests, wide plains, and deep valleys until it came to a huge desert. No matter how hard the stream tried to pass through the desert, its waters always evaporated beneath the hot sands.

The stream was afraid it would disappear if it did not find a way to cross the desert yet was soon exhausted by its futile efforts. While the stream was resting, a voice whispered, "The wind crosses the desert and so can you."

"How?" asked the stream. "I am not like the wind. I cannot fly. I make my way along and under the ground."

"This is true," said the voice. "But the wind can help you cross if you are willing."

"How? I am water, not wind," protested the stream.

"Let the wind carry you over the desert. Allow yourself to be absorbed by the wind. If you continue as you have, you will disappear forever," answered the voice.

The stream did not like this idea. It had always been its own master. It did not want to change into something else, not even for a short time. How could the stream be sure it would find itself again, once it had traversed the desert, carried by the wind?

The stream did not believe the voice. It kept trying to cross the desert and continued to disappear. The voice whispered again, "Do not be afraid. You will once again become a stream if you let the wind carry you across the desert."

Too tired to keep fighting the sand, the stream, which was now just a trickle, sadly agreed to be absorbed by the wind. Gently, the wind cradled the stream across the desert, onto the top of a very high mountain where, as raindrops, it fell softly onto the welcoming ground and transformed once again into a stream.

A teacher has to want to create a collaborative environment in her or his classroom, for it does not happen by itself or by the teacher simply asking for cooperation. Even the conscious determination to make cooperation, rather than competition, the operative classroom mode has to be a decision. For most of us, both as teachers and learners, past conditioning and experience comes into play when we enter a classroom. Often, the classroom has been the place where we learned that we must rely only on ourselves. Asking for help is difficult, if not impossible, and admitting we don't know is usually painful.

Given that creating a collaborative learning environment takes time from instruction, is often difficult to establish, and is not an issue on standardized tests, why should we bother? There is no comparison between the quality of learning in a collaborative environment and that which takes place in a traditionally competitive classroom. When I tell principals that little real learning can occur if a class is out of control, or if students are extremely tense, I seldom get an argument. Yet when I suggest that the remedy lies in classroom management, eyebrows often lift and I'm given a polite smile, as if I can't be ushered out of the office soon enough. But in every case where I've been given a chance to work with a class, whether it's because the teacher is desperate enough to take whatever help is given, or because the teacher wants a better teaching/learning environment but doesn't know how to achieve it, the change in atmosphere immediately and directly affects the quality of learning. Regardless of the situation, teachers and children interact most effectively when they teach and learn in an atmosphere of support and mutual respect.

The following example is one of many where the teacher had a lot of experience, liked her job, wanted to help her students, and was doing the best she knew to do, yet her classroom was a place of misery. As a consultant in a project using movement and drama to teach reading, I entered a third-grade classroom where there was so much tension I felt like walking out just so I could breathe more easily. I had come to tell a story which would become the stimulus for further exploration. The teacher introduced me and then spoke to the twenty-seven children: "Clear your desks. Fold your hands, face front, and pay attention."

For myself as much as for them, I told the class: "I want each of you to take a deep breath. Now shake out your hands and feet. Allow your hands and feet to find a comfortable resting place." When the teacher seemed ready to intervene I added, "It's difficult to hear a story unless you feel comfortable. So without bothering your neighbor, relax and listen." I began to tell them one of my favorite stories, "The Queen Who Couldn't Bake Gingerbread," an old German folktale retold by Dorothy Van Woerkom (1975), about a king who is looking for a beautiful, wise wife who can bake gingerbread. After I was about one-third into the story I drew a total and complete blank—I could not remember the rest of the story. The children stared at me. Feeling helpless, I could only tell the truth: "I can't remember what happens next." They were incredulous and I was embarrassed.

One of the children quickly looked at the teacher and then said to me, "But how can you forget such a good story?"

Another child asked, "Are you sure you can't remember?" The teacher, somewhat nonplussed, tried to help but nothing worked; my mind was a blank.

I had counted on the storytelling to take half of the time allotted to me but now I had to come up with another plan. The first thing I thought of was to ask the children, "What would you write if you were the author of the story?" No hands went up. No one spoke.

The teacher admonished them, "Surely one of you can tell our guest what she wants to know." I cringed. When no one spoke she berated them, "Is this how I've taught you to behave? You know better. Our guest has asked you a question. Answer her!" There was no doubt, we were in a lose/lose situation which was disintegrating, fast.

When I'm stuck, the best way out for me is to talk about being stuck, so I said to the children and their teacher, "Let's look at what is happening. I was invited to come here, tell you a story, and help you explore the joys of reading. Instead, what we have is a mess. I forgot the story and you're having difficulty thinking of ideas to make a new story. What do you suppose would make all of us feel better?"

The teacher, upset and embarrassed, answered first, "For the children to behave as I've taught them." What to do? Take a deep breath.

I said to the class, "I'm sure every one of you is trying to figure out something good to say, yet to me, we feel like a group of people who are stuck in a big hole. Try as we may, we don't know how to get out. Let's take a deep breath." They did. "Now I want to ask a favor. Get a pencil and take out a piece of paper." I asked the teacher to join us.

"The last bit of story I remember is the part where the king is going to take a trip to look at the eligible princesses. I'd like you to write down one, thing the king decides is important to the success of his journey. Don't worry about spelling, just write down the first word that comes to mind." With encouragement the children nervously began to write.

"Your teacher and I are interested in your ideas so you tell me your choices and I'll write them on the board." No response.

"Okay, before you share your choice with me, share it with a neighbor and talk about what makes it so important." No response.

Frustrated and worried I took a huge chance, and asked their teacher to tell us her choice. She looked as uncomfortable as her students, but with all their eyes focused on her, she later told me, she felt she had no choice but to say something.

"Gingerbread."

"Tell us why you decided this was so important."

Embarrassed, she said, "Well, if it's so important to me that my wife can bake gingerbread I want to be sure she bakes the kind I like."

"That makes sense," I responded. I noticed a child looking at her paper and then at the teacher, and asked her, "What did you bring?"

Almost whispering she said, "I brought the recipe for the gingerbread I like because I don't know how long it's gonna take me to find my princess. If I bring gingerbread I'll prob'ly eat it all up before I find my princess."

"Clever thinking," I said. "I'm impressed.

After a short silence another hand went up, "I brought along the baker to teach the princess how to make the gingerbread I like."

One of his classmates asked, "Well, if the king has a baker why does he want his princess to bake him gingerbread?" The boy shrugged his shoulders.

The teacher came to his aid. "Perhaps the baker is getting old and tired. Maybe he's only waiting for the prince to find his princess so he can retire." The boy looked grateful and a bit surprised.

"But what's so special about gingerbread? Why can't the king bake it himself if he wants it so badly?" asked another child.

The teacher looked at her watch and said that it was time for math. There was kind of a collective sigh, almost a palpable sense of disappointment, as if none of us were ready to move on. I asked the teacher if we could explore the math lesson using the story. She looked puzzled so I asked the class, "Let's pretend we're all math teachers. What problems can we construct using the story we've been exploring?"

One child asked, "You mean like how much gingerbread would the king need to take with him if he wanted it to last the whole trip?" I nodded and wrote the question down on the board.

Another child suggested, "How many times would he have to bake his recipe in order to have enough to last the whole trip?"

A classmate interjected, "Stupid! A king doesn't bake his own gingerbread."

The teacher did not respond so I quietly spoke, "Let's think about what was just said." The class looked uncomfortable; the teacher was surprised. "How does it help us to learn when someone calls us stupid?" No answer.

The teacher spoke up, "He has a point. A king doesn't bake his own gingerbread. We have to learn to take criticism."

Not wanting to take on the teacher, I looked at the child who'd been called stupid and said, "Well, I like your question; it's kind of tricky. Suppose the king has eaten the last of the gingerbread. The baker is sick. No one else in the palace knows how to bake gingerbread. The king is so desperate he decides to bake gingerbread even though he doesn't know how. He might have to bake an enormous amount of gingerbread before he baked any that tasted good enough to eat."

"Yeah, that's what I was thinking," he said gratefully. Silence.

"Okay, we have two problems, anybody think of another?"

"We could make up the recipe and then figure out how much stuff we need in order to bake the amount we want."

One child volunteered, "My mom makes gingerbread. I could ask her to write down her recipe."

I quipped, "Maybe she better send along some gingerbread with the recipe so we can see how good it tastes." Everyone laughed.

A serious-looking child asked, "How long does gingerbread last? Maybe we have to figure out how long it will take before it spoils 'cause the king doesn't know how long he's going to be on the road. He might have to stop someplace and pay a baker to bake more. My mom baked some cookies for my sister when she was at camp and by the time the cookies got there they were all moldy and my sister had to throw them away."

"Yeah," chimed in a classmate, "My father bought some donuts and the next day they tasted awful; all dried up and hard as rocks."

"How much is all this going to cost?" asked another.

I looked at the teacher and decided to admit my growing discomfort. "I think I'm out of my league with the math stuff. You take over. You're the expert on math problems." She blushed. To my great relief, she walked to the blackboard, looked at the list, and said: "Let's suppose that we eat one piece of gingerbread a day. Our trip will last . . ." The transformation had begun.

Most teachers want to teach. They don't want to spend their time yelling or punishing, yet this often happens in classrooms where teachers lose control of themselves, their class, and/or the situation. Collaborative learning techniques cannot promise that a teacher will never have a problem class or situation, but they do guarantee that when teachers and students work together, change is possible, even in the worst of situations. Looking back and reflecting on my teaching experience, I believe collaborative learning is what always saved me from the "full catastrophe." Important components have been convincing students to give me a chance to make things better; helping students become active participants in their own learning; encouraging students to let me know what's going on inside them; and engaging students in a cooperative effort to help transform the classroom into a place where it's safe to say, "I don't know."

Teachers are responsible for the atmosphere they create in their classroom. Although we have all had classes so difficult to reach we feel lucky just to survive, there can still be one or two students who respond positively. It is for their sake that we must continue the effort to make learning a cooperative, mutually engaging experience. We who teach collaboratively know the benefits far outlast the time spent in the classroom.

Components of Learning

Whenever you enter a classroom and see children busy, by themselves or in small groups, studying, reading, consulting, or examining, you know the teacher has helped students become active learners. I have found it useful to identify and discuss aspects of the learning process with my students so they can use this information as part of their educational development. Students who understand and appreciate the components of learning are forever empowered because all learning, whether in the arts, sciences, or humanities, employs similar processes of inquiry, discovery, examination, reflection, and revision. Teachers who understand that effective self-directed learning and creative expression are dependent upon disciplined approaches to learning will foster this way of working as part of their day-to-day teaching. The components of learning can be described as follows:

> *Initial activity:* Reading a text, doing a task, or fulfilling requirements for an assignment, either individually or as a member of a group.
>
> *Deepening the initial activity*
> 1. Observation:
>   What is going on? What do I notice? What do I think? What do I feel? What creates the strongest impression? What influences my perception and response? What obscures or enhances my observation?
> 2. Description:
>   Define, describe, delineate what is happening. Do oral and written expression differ in terms of information? If so, how? What defines and differentiates subjective and objective reporting? How do I differentiate between description and judgment?
> 3. Reflection:
>   Considering what has happened, and what I have observed and described, how do I think and feel about my experience? What do I remember most clearly? What ideas, attitudes, feelings, memories, or stories come to mind? What connections do I make between the initial activity, what I have observed and described, and what comes to mind?
>
> *Action:* Assignment relating to initial activity. Perhaps students will do a research project, either alone or in small groups. Students might write a story, make a book, do a report, explore a special homework assignment, write a book report using their imagination and creativity. Record experiences in their journal. Select material for a portfolio of work in progress.
>
> *Revision:* What questions or ideas come to mind about my work? How do these questions or ideas affect my work? What changes, additions, deletions, rethinking are evoked by my questions? There can be many revisions but each needs to be preceded by reflection and, if possible, feedback from trusted sources.
>
> *Evaluation:* What have I learned? Were I to continue this work, what questions might I ask myself? What questions have

others asked? What changes might I make in my learning process? What are current areas of strength? What skills might benefit from further honing?

Recording: Students keep a record of what has been learned by creating a learning journal, an experience log, a diary, or a portfolio of work. Teachers record students' progress by notating selected pieces of student work and by selecting particular papers or tests which demonstrate specific difficulties in learning or exemplary work.

Process-Centered Learning

Students who cause trouble in the classroom often feel they have nothing to lose because no one cares about them, and they don't care about what they are supposed to be learning. When students feel they have nothing to lose they can cause great devastation, both to themselves and to those around them. One way to begin to help troubled students is to have a discussion where the class is encouraged to give voice to what is going on, to name what is happening so that students and teachers can explore effective solutions.

In a second-grade class where I was working with drama as part of the language arts program, there were two boys who were repeating second grade. Angry, taller, and heavier than their classmates, they caused havoc wherever they went. Many of their classmates were fearful of them; even their teacher seemed reluctant to "take them on." As I was thinking of ways to help them and the class work together more peacefully, I remembered when I was in a ninth-grade science class. Our teacher continually made sarcastic comments about six boys who were repeating the class, treating them as if they were scum. They responded by mocking, cursing, disrupting her lessons, and threatening to beat up anyone who didn't let them copy answers on a test. I often had stomachaches as I forced myself to go to class. One day, we were greeted by a young man who told us he'd been hired as a long-term substitute while our regular teacher recovered from surgery. The boys cheered. I felt ill. If our regular, experienced teacher couldn't control those boys, how was a brand-new college graduate going to manage?

What he did was talk to them in front of the whole class. He asked for their help in doing our next project, weather experiments. They were so taken aback they didn't respond. He took their "response" as consent and divided the class into six groups, one boy in each group, all of us responsible for a specific section of the United States. Our job was to observe weather patterns in our particular region, and to look at the elements forecasters used to predict weather. Before he told us how to complete our assignment, he engaged the class by having us ponder the ramifications of accurate forecasting. When he asked, "Why is it important to know about the weather?" the boys howled.

Playing to his friends, one answered, "So if you're planning to rob a bank you don't pick a day when there's going to be an ice storm which could cause problems getting away." They laughed uproariously, exceedingly pleased with themselves. My stomachache worsened. But the teacher took the answer very seriously.

"Right. If you're going to rob a bank you certainly want to be able to drive away as fast as possible. Any other reasons to know about the weather?"

"Well, if you were sailing in a small boat, you'd want to know if a storm was coming up," ventured a class member timidly. The teacher nodded and asked for more possibilities. By the end of our first class with him the dynamics of the class had changed significantly. In an amazingly short time, we were working together. The teacher praised the ingenuity and humor of the six boys.

No longer dreading science class, I looked forward to it until the last week of the school semester, when our regular teacher returned. Within minutes, her sarcasm and disrespect once again poisoned the atmosphere, permanently evaporating our class cooperation and interest. Indelibly imprinted on my mind was the idea that there might be ways to remedy even the worst situation if I were willing to address perceived injustices and ills. I could not label students and think I had no further responsibilities toward helping them and the class reconnect.

With the memory of the substitute teacher's skills in mind, I asked the children in the second-grade class if they had a favorite folktale. Because "Jack and the Beanstalk" was mentioned by a few, I asked if they would like to use it as the basis for our drama. The two boys, Joseph and Alfilio, who were repeating second grade, grimaced; children around them looked worried. The teacher stared at the boys. I asked them the first question that popped into my mind, "How strong do you think the giant is?"

"Strong as me," laughed Joseph.

"How strong is that?" I asked.

"Stronger than anyone in this class," he boasted.

"Do you think you'd like to play the giant?" I asked.

"No," he said.

"Why not?" I asked.

"'Cause the giant's dumb." The class snickered.

I was taken aback, "Why is the giant dumb?"

"'Cause he lets Jack take everything. That's dumb."

"How would you play the giant if you could make him into any kind of giant you wanted him to be?"

"The first time Jack came up the beanstalk I would eat him. He wouldn't get away from me."

"But if you did that, there'd be no more story."

Alfilio spoke, "So what? It's a dumb story."

"What makes it dumb?"

"Jack does everything right. The giant does everything wrong. That's dumb." The class looked interested so I decided to open up the conversation.

"What do the rest of you think?"

"I like the story. Even though Jack is little he tries to help his mother."

"He's smarter than the giant."

"He gets the hen that lays the golden eggs and then he takes the golden harp." Others chimed in, everyone talking at once. The teacher, alarmed by all the noise, moved to take control.

Quickly quieting everyone down I suggested, "Let's divide into groups. Each group will tell the story from the point of view of any character they choose. You can tell the story from the point of view of the mother, or Jack, or the beanstalk, or the giant, or even a neighbor."

"But, does the giant always have to lose?" asked Joseph.

"That's a good question. Why don't you make your story and see what happens."

"Yeah, but if we do and you don't like it we'll be in big trouble," said Alfilio.

"What makes you say that?" I asked.

"'Cause that's what always happens," said Joseph. I could feel the class's tension rise and remembered my stomachaches in science class.

"Well, when you make a story from a particular character's point of view, let's say you choose the giant, as long as you really consider how the giant thinks and feels, and what he might say and do, you'll be fine."

"But that's changing the story," objected one of the children.

"We're using the story to make drama. We're not making a drama out of the story, although you can do this." The teacher and the children looked thoroughly confused.

One of the class members asked, "What's the difference?"

"If we were making a drama out of "Jack and the Beanstalk" we would choose the elements of the story we wanted to dramatize. We would follow the story line exactly. But if we're making drama and using the story as our point of departure, we can play with it. What I'm suggesting is that we tell the story from a variety of viewpoints and that means there will be some elements of the story which remain the same, such as Jack selling the cow, Jack exchanging the cow for the beans, the beanstalk growing so tall, and Jack meeting the giant. But the giant tells a very different story than Jack. Jack's mother's story won't be the same as the story told by the giant's wife."

The children still looked puzzled. I tried again. "How many of you have brothers and sisters?" Many children raised their hands. "How many of you have had the experience where you and your brother or sister or a friend were fighting, and someone got hurt or something got broken?" Lots of children raised their hands. "Suppose your parents or your friend's parents or a babysitter wanted to know what happened and who was responsible. Do you think each of you would tell the same story?"

One child raised her hand, "Me and my brother was fighting and he knocked down a jar with flowers in it and water went all over the place. The babysitter blamed me 'cause I'm older, but he did it."

"So each of you told a different version of what happened."

"Yeah but he was lying."

"Did he say you were lying?"

"Yeah but he's the one who lied. He bumped into the jar. He's always doing stuff like that and blaming me, and my stepfather believes him, just 'cause I'm older. It's not fair."

"Sounds like you might like to tell the story from the giant's point of view."

As a class, we chose to tell the story from three points of view: Jack, the beans and beanstalk, and the giant. After they divided into three groups I asked them to sit on the floor in their group, and think about what Jack, the beans and beanstalk, and the giant knew. They looked baffled so I asked, "What do you think the giant knows about where Jack lives or how poor Jack and his mother are?"

Alfilio raised his hand and said, "This giant is really smart. He knows everything." I asked what the others in his group thought.

The little girl with brother troubles spoke up, "The giant doesn't care about Jack. He just wants to eat. He's so big it's hard for him to find enough food. Most of the time he feels bad because he's hungry."

"Good. Each of you is thinking about the giant you see in your mind. Take a few minutes and talk among yourselves about your story."

From the initial activity, we moved to observation and description, making sure that the children understood which events they wanted to include in their drama. After the teacher and I worked with each group, helping the children write the sequence of events on which they could all agree, we set the task for the next session—to reflect on their ideas and to begin making the drama. Alfilio and Joseph remained absorbed for the whole session and were fully integrated into the group. The teacher noticed that the children were talking to each other more than they had previously; the topic of conversation was their character's point of view.

In subsequent sessions, the teacher and I were able to maintain the two boys' interest in the drama so they continued to be involved. They definitely wanted to make sure that in their drama, the giant was smart and sympathetic. There were also unexpected discussions such as the one I overheard where the two boys were telling the little girl with brother problems how she could get even with her brother without getting herself into trouble.

The teacher and I kept the children focused on the task at hand. When a group shared their work with the class we prefaced discussion by asking the group what they'd been working on, what they felt good about, where they thought they might need help, and how they were feeling as a group. The children learned to ask for help, even if they were in the middle of the drama.

At the end of the last session, I asked the class what they thought of the process; what they had learned; what they might do differently next time; what they thought they needed to learn; and what questions they had.

Alfilio shot up his hand and grinned, "What story we working on next?"

Children shouted out their suggestions with great enthusiasm.

The teacher, who had trouble with noise, calmed them down and said, "One at a time, tell me your story suggestion, and I'll write it on the board. Then we'll think about what we want to do." Immediately the children quieted down and patiently waited for everyone to make a suggestion. Then the teacher said, "Let's sit in a circle and think about how we might want to do the next drama." Alfilio and Joseph sat with their classmates in the circle, no longer outsiders. The teacher subsequently capitalized on the boys' attitudes regarding their work in drama and found ways to help them feel successful in other areas of learning.

It's not always possible to help troubled children reintegrate into the group, nor does it happen automatically, just because a teacher offers them a new way of being. If students get stuck in a role and have no idea or way to get out, an observant, caring teacher can sometimes devise ways to help students make more productive choices which may then lead to behavioral changes that make a significant difference in their classroom functioning.

Suggestions

- Design tasks so that children create unique responses using a variety of media, and know when they have completed their task without having to ask an authority.
- Set out a topic, issue, or skill to be learned, and ask children to suggest ways in which they can accomplish their learning.
- Encourage children to admit when they are stuck so that others can help them become unstuck in a variety of ways.
- Design activities to foster curiosity, focused observation, independent investigation, and wondering.
- Enable children, as a group, to explore approaches to learning as well as to discover answers or solutions. Facilitate cooperation and collaboration rather than competition.
- With your class, preferably two or three times a week, make a point of sharing stories from around the world, especially those focused on children solving problems and meeting life situations with resourcefulness. Tell the story rather than read it even if you think you can't tell stories. Start by choosing a short, simple story which catches your attention, and as you speak, focus on your students. Let the telling come from your heart rather than your mouth. Consider the story a means of developing inner resources and establishing community.
- Instead of asking children what the story means, ask them to contemplate a particular aspect such as: What is a memorable point in the story for you? What makes it memorable? What does the story make you think about? Feel? Remember? What would you do if you were a particular character in a specific situation? Ask students to paint, sculpt, or explore ideas using drama or movement, with a partner or in small groups.
- Encourage many answers, rather than the "best or right solution," as diverse as possible, using the text as the basis for choice. Appreciate and nourish diversity by noting the richness of different ideas, approaches, and possibilities.

- Use problems such as pollution, traffic, drought, crime, violence, drugs, or homelessness as a way to incorporate real-life experiences into reading, writing, and discussion skills. Design language arts programs to increase interest in the development of students' problem-solving skills.
- Incorporate the use of visual media, videotape, drama, movement, music, poetry, storymaking, or journalism in all aspects of learning as a way of discovering information, ideas, and attitudes.
- Design approaches to learning which include divergent and convergent exploration to enhance imagination and cognition.

Response-Tasks

Children who are active listeners retain more than when they are passive, yet too much activity can obscure or hinder listening. To facilitate engagement give children small tasks, called response-tasks, which help keep the listener and the speaker connected. For example, when children are listening to a story you might ask them to paint images evoked by the story. After hearing the story students might use their images as the basis for discussion, a report, or to make a new story.

As a way of helping listeners enter into the story of "Cinderella," students might paint a gift of encouragement for Cinderella. After hearing the story students might talk about what they painted and how they think their gift will help Cinderella feel better.

When a child tells a story and is sad or angry or frustrated, classmates might paint an image of a helper to make life more manageable, giving the images to the storyteller. Sometimes the given images become the basis for a new story.

To design a response-task, teachers need to consider the connections between the task, the person, and the event which is being responded to. The tasks need to be contained, easily finished, and purposeful. It helps to give students paper, precut to the desired size, before the story begins. The instructions have to include what students are to do, when they are to do it, and how their response-tasks will be processed afterward.

Sharing response-tasks serves to reinforce community as classmates respond to a character in need, a story, or a classmate. The response-task enhances listening skills and can also augment good group dynamics by helping children to think about each other. In a tension-filled class I ended a session by telling students to paint an image of a blessing, and to write a few encouraging words. I collected and folded the images and put them into a large hat. Each child picked a blessing and then we went around the room, sharing the images and words. By the time we were finished, children were smiling and there was considerably less tension in the room.

Sourcework

CHAPTER SIX

Framework for Designing Classroom Activity

I title this section Sourcework because the ideas contained in these chapters provide source materials, specific stories, and techniques to help teachers and administrators design and explore imagemaking and storymaking activities in the classroom.

Components of Program Design

The success of an activity is often determined by the degree to which the teacher prepares the class physically, mentally, psychologically, and emotionally. Therefore, it is important to note that the following concepts underlie each activity in this book and are crucial elements in all program design:

- Promote or regain access to imagination
- Stimulate individual and group ingenuity
- Facilitate critical thinking
- Foster self-esteem
- Respect and value diversity
- Welcome unique responses—make productive choices rather than look for the one right answer
- Nourish creativity
- Improve and develop oral, written, and symbolic language
- Enhance creative expression
- Nurture self-confidence

Organization of Activities

It is extremely difficult, if not impossible, to develop an activity that works equally well, with no exception, for every group of children in a particular grade. To help teachers choose appropriate tasks for their students, I "explode" one activity in movement and drama to open it up and show how a basic activity can be deepened and made more complex to meet the needs of older or more experienced class members. Teachers can use the suggested explorations as a guide, to design activities commensurate with the experience and needs of their students. If you are unsure about the level of activity appropriate for your class, start with the first task in each section. Even a simple task such as painting an image of a telling moment, creating a short monologue as if you are a character in the story, or telling how you are feeling at a particular moment can stimulate interesting sharing and reflection.

The description of each activity, whether we are exploring movement, drama, imagemaking, or storymaking, begins with the *focus*, the point of concentration within each experience. If the exploration is text-referenced, the *text* is stated. Directions for *activities*, such as "paint" or "sculpt," are always the instructions teachers give to students. Most explorations include *sharing*, either with the whole class or with smaller groups within the larger group, and all include *reflection*, providing the opportunity for teacher and students to consider what has been done, to express responses to the experience, and to share thoughts about possible ways to go further or deeper. Often, there are *questions* to further stimulate teachers and/or students but they are not meant to be answered methodically, as a part of each lesson. Rather, they are examples of questions participants can ask themselves—their function is to help participants make up their own. Evolving questions based on personal and group experience and on students' understanding of the work helps them to develop critical thinking skills. *Exploring Connections* will be found at the end of many exercises. These are not so much particular recommendations, but ways of thinking that connect the arts to other areas of study such as math, physics, and geography, and to real-life situations.

Participation

Self-consciousness

Self-consciousness is probably the biggest difficulty teachers and students face when working in new ways. It arises from feelings of disconnection, when students don't know what they're doing, what they're supposed to accomplish, or what the assignment has to do with them. When students feel self-conscious they usually don't know how to approach the task given to them. When teachers are self-conscious they usually feel insecure about the material and uncertain of their approach. The best way to deal with self-consciousness is to help people connect through inner imagery and a clear understanding of the task at hand. For example, when students, especially those approaching puberty, are initially asked to create a character, they often feel unsure and uncomfortable because they don't exactly know what is required or how to "act," and they are already self-conscious about their changing bodies.

One way to lessen self-consciousness is to state the task and then ask students to close their eyes and imagine themselves solving the problem, addressing an issue, or devising a solution. I first ask students to consider what they perceive to be stumbling blocks or stuck places, and then have them write down what they discover. As a group we explore techniques to address the difficulties noted. If students are working in role I ask them to imagine what their characters look like; where they are; what they want; why they are in the situation they are in; and why they are doing what they are doing. Often, I ask them to share this information with a partner so the partner can respond by asking questions and commenting on ideas to develop a particular character. As one way to explore a text I ask students to share ideas, feelings, and questions about aspects of the text in role as their character. This helps students to understand more clearly how working in role permits the reader to enter into the text and to explore it from the inside out.

If I hear inappropriate laughter, a common sign of self-consciousness, I ask the class what is happening, what further information they need, and why they feel uncomfortable. The more discomfort a group feels, the more necessary it is for the teacher to define each task very carefully and clearly, and to structure the activity so that only one new, small step is required at any point in the learning process. For example, if I am doing drama with an inexperienced group I might begin our work by asking the students to paint an image of their character in his or her familiar environment. I might then ask students to give their characters names and have students share the images of their character as a way of introducing their characters to others in the class.

However I structure the activity, my objective is always the same: I want students to be successful, to feel good about what they're doing, and to feel comfortable about the challenges involved in the educational process and environment. For learning to occur, we have to recognize the boundaries of our knowledge and be willing to leave the known to enter into the unknown. Too much comfort suggests we probably aren't learning much, yet too much discomfort creates so much tension that learning becomes difficult, if not impossible.

Disruption

When students refuse to participate, mock the process, disrupt the activity, or challenge those working, the teacher must take immediate action, for the situation can only get worse. The teacher must establish control, make the participants feel safe, and isolate the troublemakers so they cannot continue to do damage. Although there are many ways to remedy difficulties, it is most important that the teacher appear calm and confident. Solutions depend on the situation, the number of troublemakers, and the degree to which the teacher knows the class.

If one person refuses to paint or sculpt and is otherwise not disruptive, I generally allow that student "to pass" this time. Sometimes children just don't feel like participating and if no fuss is made, they will often join the group when they feel better.

If those refusing are making jokes and actively disrupting the process, the teacher has to stop them. Telling a trickster story where the trickster gets his comeuppance may help to relieve tension and give the offenders a chance to save face and rejoin the group. If the school has a "time out" room, the offenders can be sent there. If the classroom is large enough and the teacher has sufficient power, the offenders can be isolated in a section of the room.

However, if the offenders are a continuing problem the situation may require both private talks with the individuals and a class discussion of the crisis. When the teacher discusses the disruption, care must be taken to avoid blame and judgment. Instead, the teacher needs to talk about what she or he envisions the class learning and why the chosen techniques have been selected. Inviting the class to offer suggestions as to how to make the environment more conducive to learning often brings about surprisingly helpful ideas. What is most necessary is that the class experiences the importance of their active participation.

Suggestions for Planning Tasks

- Design activities so they have clear beginnings and endings. Always know how you will create closure. Be prepared with an alternative ending in case a task takes longer than planned.
- Be careful how you describe what you want the class to do. There is a big difference between painting an image of *an* apple and painting an image of *the* apple. One connotes any apple, the other a specific apple.
- Differentiate between questions which come from lack of understanding about the required task, and those which

come from students trying to figure out what will please the teacher.

- Always include time for sharing and reflection because these activities promote growth and group cooperation. Require the students to use "I" rather than "you" when talking about their ideas and feelings.
- Consider your own experience and feelings when designing tasks. Keep your discomfort level manageable. If you are trying new ideas it often helps to let students know this and to ask for their perceptions of the activity.
- Decide how you want to approach the idea of commentary before you ask students to give their opinions about shared work. One way to help students understand elements of judgment and perception is to ask them to phrase all responses in question form. If students want to say they liked something suggest they talk only about what it is they like and why. Encourage students to associate what they see with how they feel or any memories that come to mind so they talk about their personal reactions and responses to the work that has been shown, rather than simply saying "I like," or "I don't like."
- Consider the nature of an activity so that students are supported as they explore. For example, if you want students to sing a song, you need to help them prepare their voices and practice making sounds before they actually sing. If students are going to participate in vigorous activity, they need to do warm-up exercises to avoid strain.
- Consider the place of the task in the total school day to design ways in which you connect the preceding activity with the task which follows.
- Develop fail-safe methods of calming and controlling the group. For example, if students are louder or wilder than I think is appropriate I often ask them to sit in a circle on the floor. This helps them calm down, is comforting, reinforces the concept of community, and allows me to discuss what is going on.
- Develop a nonverbal sign that everyone in the group understands is the signal to stop immediately, regardless of noise level. I find it useful to raise my arm as my signal and for students to stop and raise their arms as soon as they see me. This eventually creates enough stillness and quiet that the rest of the group will stop, allowing me to give further directions or necessary information without being harsh or autocratic.

Warming Up

Children easily tire of sitting. Although they need more activity than adults, it is often the teacher who moves and the children who sit. Warm-up activities prepare the body for vigorous and concentrated activity, allow children to let off steam safely, and also provide transitions from one activity to another. They improve communication, relieve fatigue, and reduce tensions in individuals and within a group as people work together in easy and relaxed activity. Warming up as a group improves concentration and focus, providing a passage from one class session to the next.

By moving all or part of the body, everyone can swing, stretch, bob, vibrate, move smoothly, move percussively, and relax. These movements are good preparation for academic tests as well as for drama, sports, and performance. When warming up, avoid muscle strain, forceful exertion, and quick jerky movement. When working on hard, cold floors, warm up the feet by doing small, easy jumps, hops, and leaps in place and in space keeping the knees bent.

Warm-up Suggestions:

Types of movement:

- *Stretching*: Smooth, sustained extension of part or all of the body as far as possible without strain or pushing. Move alone, with a partner, or as a group. Explore various levels using all parts of the body.
- *Swinging*: Loose, relaxed movement that starts with energy, continues with momentum, and ends with energy. The free-flowing ease of the swing corresponds to the breathing cycle of inhalation (energy), exhalation (momentum). Explore ways to swing all parts of the body (torso, head, legs, arms, hands) separately and together.
- *Bobbing*: Gentle, easy, up-and-down movement of the body in any position. To use the feet properly, land first on the toes, then on the ball of the foot, then on the heel with the knees bent. Keeping the knee bent is particularly important, especially when jumping or bobbing on cold or concrete floors.
- *Striking*: Short, clearly defined movement done with as little tension as possible such as when the fingers curled in a fist are thrust open or a leg is kicked in karate style. The more relaxed you are, the easier and more effective is this activity.

Striking helps use excess energy, often a problem for young children. Use various parts of the body to explore striking from a sitting or lying position, always starting from a relaxed position.

- *Vibrating*: Shaking movement that resembles shivering. It is hard to do and harder to sustain and is extremely effective in ridding the body of strain and tension. Use various parts of the body or the total body, standing, sitting, and lying.
- *Collapsing*: Total release of the body, like a balloon stuck with a pin which slowly deflates. Collapse can be partial or total and must be practiced on soft surfaces. It is important to remember when falling that the body needs to be rounded and soft. Fall only on padded parts of the body and avoid landing on knees, elbows, shoulders, or wrists. For safety reasons, start exploring collapses on the floor with only part of the body raised.

Parts of the body

- *Head:* Circle the head around slowly, keeping the shoulders still, first to one side, then the other. If neck muscles are sore or tense, bend the body slightly forward at the waist keeping the knees slightly bent.
- *Shoulders:* Circle one shoulder, then the other, going around both forward and backward. Work both shoulders together at the same time and/or sequentially. Keep fingers and wrist relaxed, torso lifted, knees slightly bent.
- *Wrists and arms:* Extend arms out to the sides, flex wrists, extend and wiggle fingers. Move arms around in a circle, stretching or swinging, forward and backward. Shake out fingers and hands to release stress and strain from writing. Play an imaginary piano in various positions.
- *Torso:* With arms relaxed at sides, and head in line with body, circle the torso first to one side, then to the other, with knees slightly bent. Extending the arms over the head increases the difficulty of the movement. Be careful when circling to the back by moving gently to avoid strain. Explore ways to move the spine in figure-eight shapes. Move both forward and back and from side to side.
- *Legs and feet:* Keeping the body as still and relaxed as possible, do small bobs, hops, and jumps in place, keeping the knees

slightly bent. Swing the legs in standing, sitting, and lying positions. Shake the feet in sitting and lying positions to release tension.

These activities can be done with and without sound, with and without partners, using all or part of the body. Variety can be achieved by moving quickly, slowly, up, down, circularly, and with and without accent. I encourage teachers to do these activities regularly, especially during periods of great tension such as at exam-time, when it seems to be a bad day, or when children have trouble focusing.

In general, the younger the children, the greater their need for frequent, vigorous activity. A few minutes of warm-up activity every hour helps to avoid pent-up energy which may result in loss of concentration, fatigue, dullness, and restlessness. Warming up can be silent, but activity is enhanced if children make wind sounds (breath sounds with no vocal involvement such as whisper sounds, whooshing, mouth sounds, and playing with the breath as the mouth moves in various positions) or body sounds such as clapping, beating the thighs with palms, or tapping with fingers or toes. Encourage children to create their own warm-up activity, by themselves, with others, or in a group.

Relaxation

Teachers and their students benefit when relaxation activities are a regular part of classroom routine and can be used as part of any warm-up activity. Like the warm-up activities previously described, they defuse tension, provide a transition from a difficult situation to the next activity, and enable the class to "breathe" during periods of concentration.

- *Centering:* Standing, slowly and smoothly move your body any way you choose, as far as you can in any one direction, and without losing balance or control. On signal, stop, close your eyes, and imagine yourself being gently pulled toward your center. Move your body until you feel centered. Breathe deeply.
- *Quick release:* Sitting, inhale and tense your body. Release the tension and breathe deeply. Repeat three times. Shake out fingers, wrists, toes, and feet.
- *Imaging ease:* Lying down, close your eyes, inhale deeply, and tense your body. Slowly, starting with the feet, then the thighs, torso, arms, hands, and head, release the tension as you exhale. As you gently and deeply breathe from the abdomen, imagine warm air softly moving all excess tension

Framework for Designing Classroom Activity

.... 117

out of your body. Keeping your eyes closed, scan your body
for tension and imagine warm air gently dispersing it. Open
your eyes, gently shake out hands and feet, and breathe
deeply before slowly standing up.

- *Gibberish*: Children can release a lot of tension by working in
pairs, telling each other the most horrible, upsetting things
that have ever happened to them using gibberish—made-up
language. If noise is a problem, suggest that students use
wind sounds such as whispers, coughs, or mouth sounds as
well as body sounds like tapping, clapping, etc.

The warm-up and relaxation activities are valuable techniques that
teachers can use either separately or together to improve circulation
in the body, release bodily tension, reenergize, and defuse tension in
the class. Activity choice depends upon the amount of time, space, and
class dynamics—how well children function as a group or in small
groups working cooperatively.

CHAPTER SEVEN

Exploring Nonverbal Communication

We live in a verbal culture where much depends on how quickly we find the right word or the appropriate phrase. Although we know words are symbols and not the things themselves, most of us come to believe that if we have the right words, all will be well. When we run out of words, can't think of the right word, or don't know the word we want, we often feel stupid or helpless. The nonverbal activities in this chapter are designed to help students begin to find the words to express their thoughts, feelings, and attitudes as they look inside themselves and interact with others.

Nonverbal activity stimulates verbal acuity by helping us to see what it is we know. Einstein, when asked how he knew what he knew, told about making images, then scribbling words and equations that came to mind, making more images, and so on, until he finally discovered and understood what he was thinking. I believe the process of making images helps us to find words because we tend to think in images and then have to translate the images into words. I have helped many students who were unable to write papers for which they had done the research by having them paint and/or sculpt images of their ideas—in a sense, they "wrote" their research paper in images first and then used the images to find their words. After the imagemaking process was complete, they were always able to complete their assignment.

An important part of imagemaking occurs after the images have been made, and we share them with others. As we describe what we painted or sculpted, we discover ideas, feelings, attitudes, even memories. Only by knowing and expressing what is going on inside ourselves can we authentically communicate who we are and what we experience to those with whom we share a world.

Exploration of Imagemaking

Imagemaking is used to discover knowing; it is *never* about making art. It is an important tool used to develop access to imagination, creativity,

119

feelings, and ideas. How a teacher approaches imagemaking has a great effect on how students respond to the activity. Children who are used to working with clay and fingerpaints as part of their study of art need to reframe their view of imagemaking. They have to learn that making images with paints and clay is part of studying language arts, separate and different from making art.

When students paint or sculpt in an art class, the picture or piece they create is the object of importance. When students make images as part of a language arts activity, the imagemaking technique is used to uncover meaning in a text or to explore a telling moment in a story. The images are made quickly (in less than a minute) and are explicitly designed to help students learn about a particular idea, experience, or relationship, and to evoke and deepen verbal expression. Although my students keep all their images in a notebook, dated and referenced with a few words, the images themselves are not finished products. Students do not comment on the quality of each other's images, although they may ask questions about what an image means or how a symbol reflects the text. When working with clay, students use nonhardening clay, usually crushing their work after each use. Sculpting responses to stories allows students to change their images as their ideas and feelings about the text change. This process can be enlightening as children observe how new information affects currently held opinions and ideas.

I use fingerpaints rather than crayons, felt markers, or watercolors because fingerpaints are more forgiving, more easily blended, and not associated with making fine art. Usually, three or four students share a set of six to eight colors which I keep in little plastic pots about two inches wide and deep. The paint doesn't spill, is nontoxic, easily refilled, and lasts a surprisingly long time. Paper towels are used to wipe fingers so that paint colors are not mixed in the pots. Water is not used, either to mix paints or to clean fingers. Students paint on plain, ordinary, 8½-by-11-inch white paper. Children who make images to evoke stories may want to keep their images with the stories they have written. In this case, if possible, laminate the images before putting them into book form to keep the paint from flaking off.

Students paint images to discover feelings, ideas, and relationships through color, shape, form, and intensity of hue. Keeping all images in a notebook allows students to create an image diary which permits observation, reflection, and discussion of these images at a later date. Clay enables students to play with relationship connections in three dimension; sculptures can be put inside, on top, around, in front, or behind other images. Each choice affects and perhaps changes meaning.

The first time teachers use paints or clay for imagemaking sets the tone for future use, so it is extremely important that teachers take the time to create an appropriate experience which is seen by students as "serious" work, a vital part of their language arts study.

Teachers ask what happens if a child refuses to paint. The response depends on why the child is saying no. If the child doesn't want to get his hands dirty he can use a popsicle stick. If a child doesn't like to paint it may be that he feels he can't do it well enough. Teacher attitudes play a big part in the class's response to being asked to fingerpaint. If the teacher considers the activity important, necessary, and legitimate, so will most or all of the children. The most effective way to help children participate is to be calm and firm without making it a big issue. Children who refuse eventually participate when they feel reassured that the imagemaking is not about making art and that there is no best or most beautiful image.

In the beginning, students may not know what to say when asked to speak about their images. Ask them to talk about whatever comes to mind, whether it is the colors they used, the forms they made, what they think of when they look at their work, or how the image connects to an important moment in the story. Do not let students make comments about the quality of the image or denigrate images. Remind students that the importance of imagery lies in the way it evokes ideas, thoughts, feelings, or memories in relationship to the story. Have students date the image, and when possible, note ideas about the image so that they can reflect on the image at a later date. If students want to know about each other's images, teach them to respond without being judgmental. For example, "Can you tell me more about that patch of blue?" or "What were you thinking about when you painted your image?" or "Your image reminds me of a time when . . ."

As part of creating an effective working environment, allow silence to be productive and natural by using it as "thinking time." Prompt students to respond by asking questions of the whole class without expecting an immediate answer. Sometimes I write questions on the board to encourage students to suggest their own questions. At times I go around the room asking each student to comment on some aspect of the work we've done. Students also meet in groups to discuss their work, creating a group comment or question to share with the larger group. When questions are suggested or comments made, I connect them to the text or issue we are exploring. Even young children learn to ask questions or to suggest ideas when they know their responses are taken seriously.

Before any images are shared, teachers need to stress the importance of being faithful to one's vision. People approach stories in their own way; there is no one right answer or correct way to think about a text. Help students to talk about why their chosen moments are important to them by stressing the importance of personal vision and the connection between vision, experience, and the meaning we make and find in a text. Do not allow students to mock or disparage someone's ideas or feelings. This is crucial because initial experiences of sharing influence all later interaction and response.

During early discussions about work children must learn that it is all right to have their own ideas about what matters in a story, and to support their ideas by referring back to the text. It is not that *any* idea is valid, but rather that any idea that can be supported by the text is cogent. Some ideas eventually seem more powerful or productive than others, but this happens as the result of extended exploration where the work is deepened rather than from any initial judgment by the teacher.

Students may ask if they have to sculpt "everything" or if they should just sculpt one particular thing. This is an attempt to find out what will please you. What you want is for them to please themselves. I answer this question and others like it by repeating the task. If questions persist I remind students that what I want is for *them* to decide how to approach the task and how to decide if they have completed it. These first tasks involve helping children to become accustomed not only to working with new materials, but also to the importance of making decisions and taking responsibility for their choices and work.

Sometimes children have trouble choosing the one image to paint or sculpt because there are so many points of interest. Helping children to make a decision is an important part of learning; if you tell them to choose one point, make sure children choose only one point. They have to learn that we cannot go wide and deep at the same time. We can look at a whole tree but once we try to describe it we can choose only one thing to talk about at a time, the roots, the leaves, the trunk, etc.

Be careful when children with different approaches share their paintings or sculptures; some classmates may condemn what they see as different and therefore unacceptable. The important question for the class to focus on is, "Did . . . solve the problem?" If the answer is yes, students will soon learn that honoring one's own ideas is important, supporting one's ideas by referencing the text. If the answer is no, gently help the child to relate back to the text to find an idea which does connect to the story.

The first time children use a new material such as clay to explore text, they may have to be reminded again that they are not making art; they are exploring the nature of relationship (three dimensionally when they use clay). Discourage children's comments about "how real" a statue looks or "how good you sculpt." Instead, focus on the ideas which the sculptor used to make the sculpture, and the ideas and feelings evoked by the sculpture when others look at it. Invite children to consider changing their sculptures after working with the story. This enables students to understand more clearly that ideas and opinions do not have to be fixed and that new information enables us to make new choices.

The following sequence of activities ranges from simple to more complex and demonstrates how the initial activities can be deepened. When in doubt about where to start, it is always safe and productive to start with the initial activity. Student responses reflect the experiences they bring to each task and therefore the more accomplished they are, the deeper their work.

Initial Exploration

Focus:	Visualizing a character
Text:	"Jack and the Beanstalk"
Tell:	"Jack and the Beanstalk"
Paint:	An image of Jack at a particular point in the story. *(From the beginning, teach students to particularize rather than to generalize. This is the first step in learning to enter into a text, to explore the connection between self and text. Even the youngest children can do this, although they may need help deciding how to choose one point.)*
Share:	Images *(Talk about the point that has been chosen. Encourage students to think about why they chose this point and to express their ideas. Recommend that children ask for help if they have trouble finding words. The sharing can also become a vocabulary lesson if words describing Jack at different moments in the story are put on*

*the board. For example, in the beginning Jack
might be seen as shy, quiet, polite, good. When his
mother yells at him students might describe Jack
as unhappy, misunderstood, frightened, etc. Later
on, when he confronts the Giant's wife and the
Giant he might be described as wicked, brave,
worried, lucky, etc. Do not let children say,
"That's not right," in response to someone's answer.
Instead ask, "How did you come to decide as
you did?" Encourage children to explore their
thought processes and how they use information
to answer questions or explore tasks. It is important
that children learn to begin textual exploration
using the text to support an idea rather than merely
judging the worth of an idea.)*

Reflect: On the various points you have chosen, the reasons
you chose your points, and how you feel about
what is going on at the particular point in the story
you have chosen
*(Emphasize the importance of paying attention to
their own thoughts, experiences, and points of view
using the text as the frame of reference for all
information and support for ideas. Teach the
children to appreciate diversity.)*

Second Exploration

Focus: Visualizing a telling moment

Text: "Jack and the Beanstalk"

Tell: "Jack and the Beanstalk"

Select: A moment in the story that you remember most
easily

Paint: Image of moment

Share: Images
*(To begin, have each child hold up his/her painting
and say one thing about it, such as the moment
chosen, thoughts about the image, or feelings evoked
by the image.)*

Reflect: On what is special about the chosen moments
*(Consider the different moments selected and what
makes them singular for the imagemaker.
Discuss what might account for people choosing
various moments or assigning different meaning
to the same moment.)*

Third Exploration

Focus: Exploring a story through imagery

Text: "Jack and the Beanstalk"

Tell: "Jack and the Beanstalk"

Select: Three important moments in the story

Paint: Images of the chosen moments

Share: Images
*(Explore what makes the moments chosen
important. Discuss how the moments came to
be chosen.)*

Reflect: On the chosen moments
*(Look at variety and concept, reference to the text,
and personal response.)*

Fourth Exploration

Focus: Exploring character through sculpture

Text: "Jack and the Beanstalk"

Tell:	"Jack and the Beanstalk"
Sculpt:	An image of Jack at a particular moment in the story
Share:	Sculptures *(When students share their sculptures some may have sculpted Jack by himself, others may have sculpted him in his surroundings, while a few may have sculpted Jack in relationship to characters in the story.)*
Reflect:	On the variety of points chosen, on how we choose a point, on how we connect our ideas to the text

Fifth Exploration

Focus:	Exploring the effects of events on relationship
Text:	"Jack and the Beanstalk"
Tell:	"Jack and the Beanstalk"
Sculpt:	An image of Jack and his mother in relationship at the beginning of the story. Choose the point of view from which you will sculpt. Are you looking at them through Jack's eyes? Through his mother's eyes? Perhaps you see them from the point of view of an omniscient narrator?
Sculpt:	An image of Jack and his mother in relationship at the end of the story. Choose your point of view.
Share:	The sculptures. Talk about the point of view you chose and your reasons for choosing as you did. Talk about changes, if any, between the two sculptures. Did you sculpt both of them from the same point of view? If so, why? If not, why not? How does your choice affect your sculpture?
Reflect:	How do events in the story affect the way you sculpted the two sculptures? How does point of view affect

the way you sculpted the two sculptures? After listening to people's ideas, do you feel like making any changes to your sculptures? If so, make the changes. What changes, if any, do you make? Why?

Sixth Exploration

Focus: Exploring how feeling may affect perception

Text: "Jack and the Beanstalk"

Sculpt: An image of Jack in relationship to the Giant, focusing on size. How much bigger is the Giant than Jack? Now sculpt an image of Jack in relationship to the Giant, focusing on how Jack feels about the Giant.

Share: Sculptures. Talk about how Jack's feelings might affect the way he thinks about the Giant.

Reflect: On what enabled Jack to deal with the Giant the way he did. Think about strategies you might have tried had you been in Jack's place.

Exploring connections

Write a letter from Jack to someone in the story.
Create an adventure for Jack's mother.
Figure out how fast the beanstalk had to grow in
      order to reach its full height as quickly as it
      did.
Figure out what Jack did with the beans left on the
      beanstalk.
Do research to create recipes for beans.

Teachers might want to move from the story to the children's lives by asking them if they remember a time when their feelings affected their action. For example, they might sculpt themselves in relationship to a parent or an authority figure, then sculpt this same relationship when they are in trouble or when the authority figure is angry at them. Understanding how our feelings affect our perception is useful information and informs the process by which we come to conclusions and plan strategies. Perhaps a bully loomed too large to deal with until the time when the bully made the child so mad the child forgot to be afraid and stood up to the bully. If children do volunteer to tell personal stories, it is important for teachers to make the telling safe by accepting the story without digging for more details, judging, ridiculing, correcting, or otherwise commenting. Always relate the point of the story to the point in the text which is being discussed or to the issue being explored.

If disturbing information is revealed, do not allow children to see that you are upset. Remain calm and make a neutral transition from the troubling information to the next child's contribution or to the subject to be studied. Take time to check out the information privately. If the class is troubled by the information relate it back to the story. For example, if a child's story indicates child abuse, it may be difficult to comfort the class, especially if the children are young, but the teacher can say that the job of grownups is to make the world safe for children. If some grownups don't know how to do this, there are others who do and will when they find out what is going on. In any case, teachers are required to report suspected cases of child abuse to school authorities, who may also have skills and materials that the teacher can use with the class. Whether the difficult issues are about divorce, stepfamilies, or illness, the teacher might want to find stories from other cultures which explore these problems, letting children know that they are not alone, that children all over the world have to deal with unpleasant aspects of life.

One way to gauge younger children's feelings is to ask them to paint an image of themselves at this moment, or an image of themselves in relationship to the class, or an image of themselves in the class. Children can put their images in one place so the class can look at all of them at the same time, enabling the teacher to have some understanding of what is going on and how to deal with the issue and the feelings it evokes. When working with older children who can write by themselves, a teacher might ask the class to write a story using the phrase "Once upon a time," or "In a place far away and a time long ago." Sharing some or all of the stories is a good way to knit the feelings evoked by the original story into imaginative approaches to resolving the problem.

The activities suggested above can be finished in a few minutes or explored for much longer, depending upon how much time the teacher and students take in processing and sharing the images and ideas. In the beginning, it is best to keep the time for making and sharing rather short and completed within each session. New skills can be introduced such as learning to develop questions, learning to explore many answers to one question, or working in groups to develop complex responses. It is very difficult to say what works best for particular age groups because they differ depending on their collective health and background. I have used these activities with children as young as four years old, finding that with practice they were able to go deeper and work more intensively. Even with older, more experienced children, I start simply, using the group's response to gauge direction and depth. Each time we learn a new skill we feel successful. The more productive our learning, the more we feel we know what we're doing. We are empowered to continue exploring.

Exploration of Movement

Movement activity facilitates language, nurtures creativity, releases pent-up energy, nourishes the nervous system, and allows children to explore and express feelings without words. Children who routinely have nothing to say can use movement as their path to verbal expression by finding their ideas as they move, then talking about their experience afterward.

Teachers can help children capture the essence of a story or a character by having students move as if they were a particular character at a specific moment in the text. When children have no words to express their ideas about a text they are helped by the instruction, "Try to move as you think or feel, either as yourself or as the character." Movement can also be a wonderful introduction to drama, allowing students to explore environment, action, character, and relationships before they have words.

Teachers who routinely use movement in the classroom notice that afterward, children are better able to concentrate and sit quietly. I discovered this benefit of movement when my son was little. When he misbehaved I found that if I took him outside and made him run until he was too tired to continue running, he returned in better spirits, more pleasant to be around. Punishment would not have helped significantly—he simply had too much energy and needed a healthy way to calm down. Children often have too much energy to sit still in the classroom but teachers cannot let students run at will. One good substitute is to permit the child to relieve excess energy by doing some of the warm-up and relaxation activities on pages 114–117, as vigorously as possible. When children know their teacher wants to help them, they learn to ask for a movement break, realizing they will be able to concentrate better afterward.

Movement can help strengthen community through activities such as a "group bounce," where everyone bounces together in a small space until everyone is in sync, or a "group follow-the-leader," where one person starts a movement and, when everyone is moving as one, a new leader starts a new movement.

I am often asked to assign grade levels to each exercise, but this has proven to be impossible for me—no two groups respond the same way, differing even among themselves from day to day. Nevertheless, to show how one activity can be adapted to varying levels of ability, I have chosen a beginning exercise, balloons, to explore in a variety of ways for three levels of experience. It is always useful to start with a simple activity; children feel successful and this enhances the confidence with which they approach subsequent work. Suggestions are made to expand and deepen the elementary activity, thus making it complex and interesting enough to use with older or more knowledgeable students.

Level One: For young children or those with no experience

Initial Exploration

Focus: Exploring space using a common image

Move: Imagine you are a shriveled-up balloon slowly being blown up to full size. Now imagine someone sticks a pin in you and you slowly deflate.

Share: How you inflate and deflate your balloon

Reflect: On different ways people inflate and deflate

Questions: What does inflating and deflating make you think about? How does it feel to be a balloon? If you could go anywhere as a balloon, where would you go?

Second Exploration

Focus: Developing the kinesthetic sense

Move: Imagine you are going to be a balloon present for a child. Decide what kind of balloon you will be such as a bear, snake, dinosaur, etc. As you inflate yourself, create your special balloon. Experiment. Before you make a decision, inflate and deflate several times.

Share: Your choice of balloons. How do you remember in your body what you have created? Talk about how you created your balloon. How and why did you decide on your choice? Share the ideas you discarded and talk about why you decided not to use them.

Reflect: On the experience. Think about the ease or difficulty of inflating and deflating various body parts. Would you make the same choice again? If so, why? If not, why not? Do certain movements make you think about past experiences? If so, does this affect your feelings? How?

Questions: How can you use your body to create ideas? What do you think about as you use your body to explore ideas? What does it feel like to explore ideas using your body?

Third Exploration

Focus: Working with a partner to create an image

Move: With a partner to create a two-person balloon. Explore ways to inflate and deflate your balloon. Decide the pace and manner in which the two of you will inflate and deflate. Give your creation a name and purpose.

Share: Your two-person balloon. Talk about how you came to decide on the choices you have made.

Reflect: On what it's like to create with another person. How do you make decisions? How do you respond to each other's suggestions? How do you remember ideas that interest you which don't interest your partner?

Questions: If you were going to be given an extra special balloon, what would you like to have? Why? Have you ever been given a balloon as a present? If so, did you like it? Why or why not? How did you play with it? What happened to it?

Level Two: For children who have some experience

Initial Exploration

Focus: Exploring body movement using a common image

Imagine: You are a balloon being blown up into an extraordinary balloon for a specific purpose. Decide what you are and why.

Move: Create your balloon using your body and any props you might choose. Explore inflating and deflating so that this becomes part of your balloon.

Share: Your balloon with the class. Talk about how you came to be the kind of balloon you are. How you hope to be played with. By whom? What would you like to have happen to you?

Reflect: On the variety and purposes of the balloons. On any memories or feelings evoked by the exploration.

Questions: How does purpose affect choice of balloon shape? What ideas did you think about but decide not to use? Why? Have you ever had a special balloon?

If so, what was it like? Why did you get it? What happened to it?

Second Exploration

Focus: Exploring sound and movement

Move: As a balloon that makes a special kind of sound like a whisper, a whistle, a pop, etc. Give your balloon a name. Explore moving quickly and slowly. Alone or in the company of others. If you pass near another balloon, greet the balloon using your balloon sound.

Share: Your balloons moving in groups of three or four at the same time

Reflect: How sound affects movement and how movement affects sound

Questions: Does making sounds affect your feelings as you move? If so, how? Think about toys you have that are silent and those that make sounds. Do you play differently with toys that make sounds than you do with those that are silent? If so, how? Why?

Third Exploration

Focus: Exploring movement in small groups

Imagine: You are going to be a balloon in the Thanksgiving Day Parade in New York City.

Divide: Into groups of three or four

Decide: What kind of balloon you are going to be. Give your balloon a name and a brief biography (who you are, what you like, how you live).

Create: Your balloon, beginning with how it looks deflated and ending with how it looks fully inflated. Create

the parade announcer's introduction for your
balloon.

Share: Balloons. Tell the name and give a brief biography
of your balloon.

Reflect: On variety of balloons, biographies of balloon
characters. Think about how you worked as a
group. Who made the decisions? How? What
happened to ideas suggested but not used?

Questions: Have you ever seen huge balloon characters in a
parade? If so, which one (ones) do you remember
best? What made the balloon(s) memorable?

Level Three: For children with experience

Initial Exploration

Focus: Using movement to stimulate imagery

Move: As if you are the most wonderful balloon you can
imagine. Explore a variety of balloon possibilities.
Play with various ways to inflate and deflate. Imagine
and create the balloon you would like to see but
have never seen.

Share: Balloons with the class. Explore ways to enhance
your balloon.

Reflect: On the variety of balloons. Think about how you see
images in your mind and how, or if, you can
move the images from your mind to your body. What
makes a balloon wonderful for you?

Questions: What helps you to see images in your mind's eye?
What happens to these images when you move?
Does movement influence your feelings and
thinking? If so, how?

Second Exploration

Focus: Using movement to explore nonverbal
             communication

Create: A balloon that makes sound

Move: With a partner, exploring how the two balloons
            might interact when they greet and say goodbye
            to each other. Explore meeting, greeting, and saying
            goodbye, imagining a variety of circumstances
            and sounds.

Share: Balloon meeting and greeting with class

Reflect: On how sound and movement contribute to ways in
               which we communicate with others. How
               circumstances and situations affect movement and
               sound choice. How were choices explored? Who
               made the final decisions? What do you think and
               feel about the unused choices?

Questions: What information is transmitted through sound and
                 movement? How does this information influence
                 our thoughts about others? What experiences have
                 you had where you decided something about
                 someone based on what you saw and felt but had no
                 prior knowledge or information?

Third Exploration

Focus: Developing movement vocabulary

Imagine: You are a balloon flying to a place you'd like to go,
               where you have never been. Close your eyes and
               image what your balloon looks like. Using your
               mind's eye, imagine your trip to this wonderful
               new place. See yourself as a balloon arriving, being
               greeted, having a lovely time, departing, and
               arriving home.

Paint: An image of your balloon arriving and being greeted

Create: Your balloon and balloon trip using sound and movement. Decide how you will greet those who greet you using sound and movement.

Share: Your balloon trip with a partner. Create ways to greet each other and to interact using gibberish (sounds with no recognizable meaning). Explore what happens when you move slowly or quickly, when your movement is sharp or curved, small or large.

Reflect: On your experiences. Think about how you made your choices. What helps you to decide? How are your feelings affected by your sound and movement choices?

Questions: What is it like to communicate without words? How do you know if your interpretation is accurate? What would make you want to use words? Do words ever get in your way? If so, how? When?

Exploring connections

Write about an experience with a balloon.
Create a balloon adventure and write it as a story.
Measure air pressure needed to pump up a balloon.
Use balloons to track wind patterns.
Figure out how many balloons are needed for a party, allowing for accidents.
Do research on weather balloons.

The following movement explorations, like the balloon activities, also range from simple to complex. Teachers can always use beginning explorations to warm up their students as well as to discover a particular group's capabilities, and to design more complex activity specifically tailored to the class's needs. Factors which influence participation, such as weather, examination periods, etc., may make it desirable for teachers to deliberately begin with the basic activity in order to improve student focus and concentration.

As it is impossible to assign a particular grade level to a specific activity, it is also impossible to state how long an activity will or should last. I push students to work very quickly to enable them to explore their first, (mostly) uncensored thoughts. I respect teachers; they alone know their class and situation and can best determine how long and how complex an activity needs to be in order to provide benefit to students. However, always be sure to provide closure through reflection as a group before moving on to another area of study.

Working with a Partner

Focus: Exploring imaginative ways to be interdependent

Divide: Into pairs

Devise: An activity to do with a partner which you could not do by yourself

Share: Activities

Reflect: On activities selected. Share the kinds of activities pairs thought about but rejected. Explore how people negotiated what activity they would choose.

Questions: What happens when people of different height or weight work together? What if an accommodation is needed? What do you have to do to work safely? How do you think of ideas to try with a partner? How does it feel to have to work with a partner?

Exploring connections

Compare your experience with situations in literature where people need to depend on each other.

What factors hinder or foster interdependence?

Consider issues of dependency, interdependency, and
independence in a text you are reading.
What differentiates each issue from the other?
Look at ways in which culture fosters or makes
interdependency difficult.

Melting Snow, Quick Freeze

Focus: Creating and releasing tension

Move: As if you were snow swirling around. On a signal,
freeze into a snow statue. On signal, begin to
melt. On signal, freeze. Melt and freeze as many
times as desired. Even when statues are on the
floor, totally melted, the shapes can freeze, melt, and
refreeze.

Share: Some ways students created statues from swirling
snow, melting and freezing, melting and freezing

Reflect: On the experience and on the sensation of moving
from being tense to being relaxed. What feelings
or memories, if any, are evoked by freezing and
melting?

Questions: What would it be like if one or more statues melted
into each other and froze into a statue made of
two or more people? What memories do you have
of making snow statues? How does working in a
group statue differ from working by yourself? Do
you prefer making melting or freezing
movements? Why?

Exploring Connections

Explore effects of sudden frosts and thaws on nature
and created environments.
Write about an experience of freezing or thawing.
Research what happens to the body when
temperatures rise and fall quickly.

Following the Movement Leader

Focus: Exploring imaginative ways to move

Stand: In a circle

Move: One person begins a movement which everyone copies. As soon as everyone is doing the movement someone in the circle starts a new movement.

       Young children may need the teacher to select the next leader.

Consider: If two or more people introduce a new movement at the same time, explore ways for the group to decide nonverbally which person to follow. If both people give up their movement so there is no leader, the group might want to stop and start over by selecting one person to be the first leader. If the group continues to have difficulty, leaders can be selected before the activity begins.

Reflect: On experience. Consider how the group makes decisions about which person to follow and what influences choice of movement.

Questions: Do you generally start a movement or do you prefer to follow someone else? What would it take for you to change your pattern? What helps you to change movement? How do you achieve variety and avoid repetition when it is your turn to be the leader? What would help you to be more creative? What movement is difficult for you? What do you need to learn or know in order to do it more comfortably?

Exploring Connections

Consider how culture supports or discourages
    leaders and followers.

Explore the consequences of being a leader or a
    follower.

Write about a time of leading or following.
Consider the relationship between a system of
government and the ways in which the
society's children are educated.

Throwing and Catching

Focus: Working cooperatively from kinesthetic cues

Divide: Into pairs

Throw: An imaginary ball to partner. She/he catches it.
Continue throwing and catching, experimenting
with changing the size or weight of the ball. Explore
what happens when one partner throws the ball
with feelings such as anger, frustration, joy, or worry
and the other person decides how she or he will
catch it and then throw it back. Consider the cause
of the feeling.

Share: Some of the possibilities discovered by partners.
Explore ways to deepen and enhance ideas.

Reflect: On work shared. Consider when is a variation a
variation and when is it a new idea? Talk about
the cues and information we receive from nonverbal
interaction. When we have only nonverbal cues
to go by, how do we decide what we know? How
does the cause of the feeling affect its expression?

Exploring connections

Consider how we make decisions on the basis of what
we see and/or feel.
Research how culture affects or shapes nonverbal
communication.
Explore how we communicate nonverbally when we
are not paying attention to what we are doing.
Write a story based on an idea evoked by catching
and throwing.

Mirroring

Focus: To concentrate on precise external movement
direction and response

Divide: Into pairs. Face each other.

Move: One initiates the movement, the other mirrors it,
and then partners change place. Mirror imitates
partner's movement as closely as possible,
responding not only to shape but also to pace,
rhythm, and dynamics. The teacher will probably
have to give a signal when it is time to change
places. Usually forty-five seconds to one minute is
sufficient. Repeat the activity with a new partner.

Share: Mirroring with half the class watching and half the
class working, then change places.

Reflect: What makes movement hard or easy to follow? Does
being the mirror evoke any feelings or ideas? If
so, what? How do you feel when someone mirrors
your movement? Do you prefer to mirror or to
respond? Why? What might make you feel or think
differently?

Exploring Connections

Think of two characters in a story you have read.
Working with a partner, in character, explore
how the two characters might mirror each other.
What do you have to know about each
character to make your decisions?

Explore ways in which people might mirror each
other in social settings.

Consider how you decide what is correct behavior
in a new situation. What influences your
decisions? Your actions? Your feelings?

Write a story where one character mirrors another.

Using two different instruments, or body sounds,
mirror each other's sounds. Change roles so
that each gets a chance to make sound and to

be the sound mirror. Does mirroring sound
differ from mirroring movement? If so, how?

Creating Movement Images

Text: "Little Red Ridinghood"

Focus: Exploring imaginative movement and nonverbal
communication

Divide: Into groups of two

Share: Story with partner

Paint: Image of story that makes a great impression on you

Share: Image with partner

Move: Partner's image as if you are reading what you see.
Explore how the image makes you feel, what it
makes you think about. Use sounds if you choose to
do so. Share your painted images of your
partner's movement with him or her. Move freely.
Don't worry about whether you are working
"correctly." Each partner "reads" and shares images
before talking about the images.

Talk: With your partner about what was evoked by the
image. Partner shares what he/she felt and
thought when watching partner move image.

**Response-
task:**   Share some of the images and the movement evoked
by images with the whole class. As you watch people
move their images, paint an image of the most
powerful point in their movement.

Share: Response-task images with the person whose
movement evoked the image.

Reflect: On how moving images differs from talking about images. Listen to yourself talk. Describe what is going on rather than judging your responses.

Exploring Connections

Share a scene from a short story with a partner and move as if each of you are one of the characters in the story at the particular time you have chosen. Look at whether the characters move closer together or farther away from each other. Decide whether they are on the same level or if one has higher status than the other. If so, where do the differences come from? Explore ways to express the differences spatially as well as with eye contact.

Remember a powerful experience you have had. Paint an image (or series of images) of your experience. Share your experience with a partner by showing your images. Tell your story using movement.

Molding Statues

Text: "Little Red Ridinghood"

Focus: Creating character through movement

Tell: "Little Red Ridinghood"

Divide: Into pairs

Sculpt: Partner into one of the characters in "Little Red Ridinghood" by gently moving his or her body. Remember your position. Now partner sculpts you into a character. Each partner is a character but both can play the same role.

Move: In character, as if you are meeting each other for the first time. Feel free to use sounds but do not use words. Decide where you are, what you are doing, what you want, and what will end your improvisation. If both characters are the wolf or Little Red Ridinghood, partners explore their vision and version of the character, perhaps as if they are alter egos.

Share: Improvisations

Reflect: On what can be communicated nonverbally and what requires words. How do you decide this? What cues do you pick up on in order to respond when you have only movement to go by? What happens when you feel a person is communicating one emotion but the person denies this is so when you ask? How do you decide who is right? What do you do with your impressions when your partner denies your interpretation?

Exploring Connections:

Select a photograph from a newspaper and have people assume the position of the people in it. Those watching talk about what feelings are communicated. Explore whether you can communicate different feelings keeping the position the same but changing the levels of tension in people's bodies. For example, what happens when you talk and your whole body is very tense? If your left hand is tense? If your feet are curled up? If you are so tired you can hardly hold yourself upright?

Look at television, particularly the news from other countries. Explore how nonverbal communication, as shown on television, affects communication and understanding.

Create a two-person scene where people have simple directions such as first person enters the room, sits down; second person enters room, looks at person sitting and leaves. Those watching can suggest a situation to infuse the action with feelings such as first person is a father waiting for his teenage child to come home; first person is a teacher waiting for a student to come for a grade; first person is a person seeking a job, waiting for an interview. In the first case, perhaps the child is late and the father is worried, or the father has returned after being away for a long time and is anxious about how the child will react to him. In the second case, perhaps the teacher wants to tell the student she has received a huge scholarship or his paper is not acceptable. In the third case, perhaps this is the person's first job interview, or this interview will determine if the person can pay huge debts.

Set up each situation with clear nonverbal action (enter, sit, stand, run, turn away, etc.). Ask students to fill in the details which fuel the feelings and charge the scene between the two actors. When one aspect of the situation is changed, everything changes. Working with basic actions allows those working and those watching to explore the power and effect of nonverbal behavior and to understand the meaning of subtext—the ideas, feelings, and/ or motivation that inform the text.

Exploration of Soundmaking and Music

Music, often seen as the province of music specialists, can be used along with soundmaking to bridge the gap between oral and written stories. Soundmaking resembles music in that soundmakers use rhythm, volume, and tone, but musical instruments are not necessary. Soundmakers can use their voice, body, or objects to make sounds which can be very expressive while not being dependent on technique or experience. Although the following material depicts a particular experience, the methods described have been used by many teachers who know that the fastest way to help children stuck in the "I can't" mode is to assign seemingly unrelated tasks that the students enjoy doing and that help them learn what they had deemed impossible. The sequence of events described evolved from the class's prior responses and experiences and is included to suggest ways to use soundmaking and music in the classroom. Although teachers do not need to follow the structure we used, it is usually best to start with a simple activity and add complexity as the group becomes more experienced.

"I'm having a terrible time getting the boys in my class to write. Any suggestions? I'm at the end of my rope. I've tried everything," wrote a caring and experienced third-grade teacher who had explored many approaches. The boys in her class were willing to make up stories but refused to write them down. Since I had been working with West African folktales and noticed that messages were often communicated from village to village through drumming, using drums called talking drums, we devised our strategy beginning with the telling of the following West African story.

As we began to work in new ways, both the teacher and the boys seemed to forget about their previous frustrations, focusing instead on the fascination of exploring ideas through soundmaking. Reframing the learning experience, as we did in the following example, is a face-saving way for teachers and students to get out of the "corner or hole."

Ananse the Storyteller

Ananse the Spider wanted to be a storyteller so he went to Great One and asked, "What can I do to tell your stories?"

Great One said, "If you bring me a live leopard, a swarm of bees, and a live python, I will tell you the stories you wish to know."

Ananse the Spider went to his favorite place in the woods and sat and thought. For four days he sat and thought. On the fifth day he knew what to do. He found a calabash filled with honey and then found a huge swarm of bees. He sang to himself, "My jar is filled with honey. There is no room for those who make it."

The bees laughed and said, "Of course there is room for us." When they had all flown into the calabash Ananse immediately put on the lid.

He took the calabash filled with bees to Great One who said, "This is but the first of three presents to be given in exchange for my stories."

Ananse went back to the forest and made himself a sewing needle and thread. Sitting by the bank of the river, he sewed his eyelids shut. Pretty soon Leopard came by and saw Ananse. "Why are your eyelids sewn shut, Ananse?" asked Leopard.

"I sewed my eyelids together so I could see the wonderful visions no one can see if their eyes are open or closed."

"What kind of visions?" asked Leopard. Ananse told him about so many wonderful sights Leopard begged Ananse to sew his eyes together. Ananse pretended to think about it but in the end, he sewed Leopard's eyes until they were tightly shut.

Then he led Leopard to Great One who told Ananse, "Remember, this is but the second of three presents to be given in exchange for my stories."

Ananse went back to the forest, cut down a strong young sapling, and went to find Python who was sunning himself on a rock. Ananse whispered to Python, "The animals are saying that Green Mambo is longer than you are. Although I told them they are wrong, they continue to insist you are not as long as Green Mambo." Python was angry that anyone would doubt his size or strength. Ananse offered to help prove Python was longer. "Lay yourself against my stick and when you reach the end, I will tie you around it, just to make sure you keep your length." Python stretched himself out the length of the sapling and allowed Ananse to tie him to the stick.

He carried Python to Great One who smiled. "You have brought me my three gifts. From now on you may tell all my stories."

After receiving Great One's box of stories, Ananse went back down to the forest and opened the box. Out flew all of the stories.

Initial Exploration

Focus: Creating sound words

Create: A sound and rhythm name for yourself using your real name or a made-up name.
(The teacher had some rhythm instruments in the classroom but encouraged the children to use whatever they could find such as pencils tapped on desks, shoes clapped together, etc. As preparation she had brought in spoons, beans in plastic jars, and other homemade soundmaking equipment.)

Share: Sound name
(Some of the children chose to say their names as they played them; others just played their names on their instruments. After children heard the sound name they repeated it.)

Reflect: On the process of turning your name into a sound and rhythm.
(Some children liked having a sound and rhythm name instead of a word name; others thought it was

too complicated. I introduced the idea that they could use their sound and rhythm names as a way of keeping information secret, which caught their interest. Their teacher and I told them about how people in African communities used drums to tell friends and relatives living in other villages what was happening in times before telephones, fax machines, and television. This was hard for the children to imagine so we talked about how we might tell people who live more than a day's walk away from us what is going on without telephones, fax machines, or other modern conveniences.

Before the end of the session we asked them to make their own instruments, out of whatever they could find, and bring them to class the next day. Two children who had beautiful voices chose song as their instrument. One child said she would bring in her violin. We reinforced each child's choice and made it clear that anything that made sound that could be repeated was fine—no choice was better than another.)

Second Exploration

Focus: Sound stories

Text: "Ananse the Storyteller"

Tell: "Ananse the Storyteller"

Divide: Into groups of four

Select: One aspect of the story to work with such as Ananse and the bees, Ananse and Leopard, or Ananse and Python.
(To make sure each group had appropriate material we went around the room asking every group to tell which bit they had chosen. Immediately the children let us know they were worried about their choices. Had they chosen correctly? The

teacher and I helped them examine what goes
into making a choice, reassuring them that we
weren't thinking about right and wrong choices.
What tumbled out were some of the arguments they
had had among themselves about which bit to
choose. We spent almost all of the time dealing with
issues of right and wrong and good and bad,
leaving little time for actual work. We asked one
group to volunteer to work with us so the rest
of the class could understand the process better.)

Tell: The bit of the story you choose to work with using
only your instruments
(The children needed some help so we asked them
to first decide how they wanted to begin. Then
we asked them to make their story into one or two
sentences. We purposefully did not ask them to
write down their stories.)

Share: Story
(We helped the volunteer group to tell their story
by sharing their sentence. The class made suggestions
about ways of translating words into sounds and
rhythm.
*   The next session we picked up from where we*
had stopped. All the groups chose the bit to work
on and then each group decided for themselves what
sounds they would make. Each group played
their stories.)

Reflect: On the process of telling a story in sound
(The children wanted to talk about how "you know
you're right" rather than what the sound stories
evoked. The teacher and I were amazed at how much
the children had to say about their worries. When
we finally brought the conversation around to the
sound stories, the children had little to say except
that it was fun. Several commented it turned out
to be a lot easier than they thought, although
when we asked them why they thought this was,
they had no answer.)

Third Exploration

Focus: Creating a sound story vocabulary

Text: "Ananse the Storyteller"

Introduce: Yourself using your soundmaking names.
*(We asked the children to use their sound and
rhythm names instead of their given names to
introduce themselves. Several children used the
same rhythms and seemed unhappy that their
names were not unique. Their teacher and I decided
to use the situation to help them think about
empowerment. We asked the children how they felt
about sharing names and eventually got them
to admit they didn't like it. We asked what they
could do about it, and at first they had no idea
they could do anything. With a bit more questioning
one child decided to add to her name to make
it unique. When the others saw this was acceptable
they too changed their names. The teacher and
I may have made too much of this but we wanted
the children to understand they could speak up
and affect their learning.)*

Divide: Into groups of four. Think about the Ananse story
and choose three words which are important to
you. Create sound and rhythm patterns for these
words.
*(Before they began we asked the children for word
ideas so every group had something with which
to begin.)*

Share: Sound and rhythm patterns
*(Some of the children wanted to guess what the
words were. I hate guessing because the child who
guesses wrong often feels stupid. Instead, I suggested
they say what the words felt like or seemed to
be. The first phrase was "watch out" and many
children named it. After a few minutes there
were so many sound and rhythm patterns to listen*

*to we were all exhausted. One child complained
he had already forgotten the words and patterns his
group had chosen.*

*The teacher and I did not look at each other
but we both knew this was the moment we had
been waiting for. Casually, we asked the class what
remedy they could suggest. "We need to write
down our words. We need to figure out how to write
the sound patterns," shouted several children.
There was immediate agreement and the groups
huddled together, writing down their words. I
showed the class a simple way to notate the rhythm
using dots and dashes. Sharing resumed after
each group wrote down their words and
soundmaking patterns.)*

Reflect: On process of creating a sound story vocabulary
*(We talked about ways to connect the three words
each group had chosen so that each group's words
contained important messages such as Watch out
for Leopard or Python is coming. One of the
children asked, "What happens if the person who
has the words and pattern written down takes
it home and then is absent from school?"*

*The teacher said, "Maybe everyone in each
group should write down the group's words and
patterns, just in case."*

*By the end of the session every child had
written their group's words and notated the
rhythmic patterns. Since it was almost time for
dismissal we encouraged the children to share
messages with another group. Then, those receiving
could respond by using sound and rhythm. When
the dismissal bell rang, the children seemed
surprised and many were reluctant to stop.)*

Fourth Exploration

Focus: Creating sound stories

Text: "Ananse the Storyteller"

Divide: Into same groups as in previous session

Imagine: A story Ananse might tell

Create: A small story (no more than three sentences) sharing ideas in small groups
(The teacher and I visited each group to make sure the children were able to create a small story. There were a lot of spirited discussions and not a few heated arguments. The noise level rose unacceptably so we quieted the class, and asked each group to decide among themselves what was going on, and then to select one child from each group to "report out." The main problem was that there were too many ideas for one small story. Without thinking I suggested that each child write her/his story down and that we would, in turn, share all the stories. One child asked, "But who gets to be the first storyteller?" We asked for suggestions and came to the agreement that each child would write his/her name on a piece of paper, and that the papers would be picked by each member of the group from a box. The first name picked would be the first storyteller.)

Share: Small stories
(We had planned to turn the small stories into sound and rhythm patterns, but there was no time. The children were eager to share their stories and although everyone wrote a story, some chose to tell rather than read what they had written. The teacher and I suggested we talk about the differences between reading what is written and telling it. At first, the children seemed bewildered by the question until a girl said, "Even though I wrote it down, it's a story to be told. You have to hear it 'cause what I wrote doesn't have all the stuff, like the roar of the elephant." The children began to talk among themselves about why they read or told their stories. The children's conversation began to turn into an argument about which was best, reading or telling. One boy announced, "They're both good but they're different." This satisfied everyone.)

Reflect: On the process of creating sound stories
(The children were pleased with their stories. Their teacher received an enthusiastic "Yes" when she asked them if they would like to make a book of all the stories. One girl said, "If reading and telling are so different maybe we should put the reading ones in a book and the telling ones on a tape." Those who had told their stories looked unhappy. One child spoke for all of the storytellers, "But if you make a book only for the reading ones lots of us will be left out."

I said to the children, "Some words are written down but are meant to be spoken. Playwrights write their plays down so actors can read them. We can put all the stories in the book and let readers know which stories are meant to be read out loud and which are meant to be read silently." This made everyone happy, especially when their teacher agreed to type all the stories.)

Fifth Exploration

Focus: Creating sound stories

Text: "Ananse the Storyteller"

Translate: Small stories into sound and rhythm patterns
(The children drew numbers as to which story they would score first. The teacher and I went around to every group, helping them to score their small stories so they could remember what they created. Two groups decided to make one group story rather than many small ones because they had so much material they wanted to include.)

Share: Sound stories
(The children found very clever ways to create dramatic impact using primitive instruments such as tapping spoons, playing combs covered with wax paper, thumping oatmeal boxes, and blowing across jars filled with varying levels of water. The

*small stories were like tone poems, quite varied
and full of feeling.*

*One child said, "Couldn't we tell our stories as
well as play them? I'd like to know what they
mean." The children agreed and so we shared the
sound stories, adding the words that went with
them. In one group a child sang the words. In
another group, the violinist played along as the
words were spoken and sounded. The children were
quite impressed with themselves—a general
sense of achievement pervaded the room.*

*The teacher and I could barely conceal our
delight when one of the boys who had most
definitely refused to write said, "I really like these
sound stories but I'm glad we're gonna write
them into a book. Otherwise I might forget them.")*

Reflect: On ways that sounds and words affect each other
*(The children liked playing their sounds, and soon
they began to chant the words which went with
the sounds. As they gained experience, they began
to play with the connections between the sounds
and the words so that sometimes there were only
sounds and sometimes only words.)*

Sixth Exploration

Focus: Making stories from a story

Text: "Ananse the Storyteller"

Divide: Into small groups
*(The children decided to keep the groups in which
they had been working. Because two groups had
difficulty getting along, the teacher and I taught
everyone some negotiating skills. When there
were arguments, each child was allowed one
sentence to state his or her complaint. No one
could speak until each child had spoken. After a
thirty-second silence, each child was allowed one
opportunity to suggest a remedy. After another*

thirty-second silence, children voted by secret
ballot to decide which remedy to select. After doing
this a few times the children got fed up and found
their own efficient ways to settle differences such
as rotating who got to make a decision, taking
turns, and sharing why something mattered.)

Create: The story Ananse told after he had been given the
stories
(The teacher and I observed how the children
incorporated soundmaking into their stories even
though they hadn't been told to do so. The students
had so many ideas that they needed help
deciding how to include all of them into their story.
The teacher and I suggested they make a list of
ideas and then take a moment to think about all
the ideas before choosing one. We told them if
they still had trouble choosing one idea with which
to work, they could make more stories later on.
We also suggested that each child in the group have
a chance to make a contribution. There was so
much excitement that the children could not
contain their enthusiasm.

Voices rose. The teacher banged a gong and,
acting as if she were a wise woman, said, "I am
the master storyteller. You, my students, are
learning well. You have many ideas. It is as if
we are in a vegetable garden where there are more
weeds than vegetables. We must learn to weed
the garden." The children looked bewildered. She
then went on to explain how writers work,
making one draft after another until they are
satisfied with what they have written. She told
them that each person in the group was to create
one sentence and write it down on a piece of
paper. When all the sentences were read, the group
was to decide on the order of the sentences which
then became the first draft.)

Share: Stories
(The children decided to share their stories by having
each child read or tell the sentence she/he wrote. Those

who were not telling played instruments or made sounds to accompany the teller. The childen with the beautiful voices were asked by many to sing their words. The violinist got used to accompanying all the groups. At one point she grinned and said, "I'm gonna ask my mom if all this playing counts as practice time." It was wonderful to see a shy child blossom.)

Reflect: On the stories, the process of making/writing a story, and the effect of sound/music on a story
(The children discussed their stories and several children mentioned that film and television programs used music to create dramatic effects. One child wondered if they could score the stories they wrote in their book. This was the beginning of a complicated and time-consuming process, but in the end the children were very pleased with their book, Stories from Ananse.)

Exploring connections

Listen to stories with music such as Prokofiev's *Peter and the Wolf.*
Create stories after listening to a piece of music.
Create stories after making a sound/music piece.
Make instruments such as percussion instruments using ideas from other cultures.
Create communication within the classroom using musical or soundmaking instruments.
Score a story from a book the class is reading.

I have described at length the processes the teacher and I used to help the children write because not only does it show how the children changed their attitudes about writing through soundmaking and music, it also demonstrates an important idea: children, like adults, back themselves into corners. If no one helps them find a face-saving way out, many will choose to stay in the corner despite heavy costs. In the experience described above, writing was never made the issue, so the boys who didn't want to write could change their minds, as they did, in the moment of excitement. Writing became something they wanted to do for their own reasons and no one reminded them of their previous position.

Music teachers have worked with classroom teachers to explore the writing and telling of stories, using musical instruments rather than soundmaking, with equally good results. If no one pressures children to perform at a particular level, children often work at surprisingly high levels of competence, especially when every child is encouraged to explore using either soundmaking or music in his or her own way.

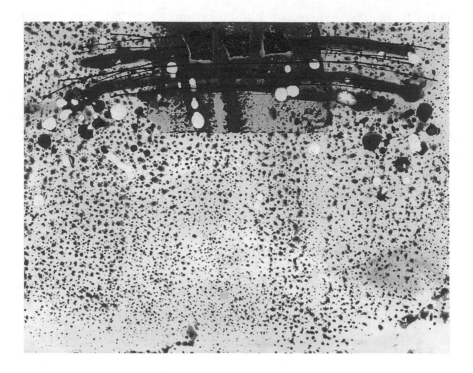

CHAPTER EIGHT

Exploring Oral Language

Oral language is the language of immediacy—a teller wants to tell something to a listener. If the listener doesn't want to hear or has to leave, there can be no telling. In earlier generations, before radio and television, storytelling was the only way an older generation could transmit the wisdom, wit, and knowledge of the culture to its younger members. The mutual act of sharing story and space helped to strengthen and deepen communal bonds, giving teller and listener a potent sense of connection.

Storytelling is a powerful act—it takes energy and imagination to collect our data and to make sense of what we know or feel, thinking and planning as we speak. Our presentation of self depends largely on what we say and how we say it. Children who develop oral fluency can "think on their feet," which boosts their self-esteem and confidence, especially when they realize they are seldom at a loss for words.

Activities exploring oral language are separated from the exploration of written language to provide children with the optimal opportunity to develop expressive fluency. Having to write down every spoken word inhibits language exploration, although children who are pleased with what they create can write down what they have said or receive help writing their words. What matters is that the exploration of oral language should not automatically include having to write. Some forms of language, such as poetry and drama, are included in oral and written language exploration so that teachers can examine a variety of ways to encourage both forms of expression.

Exploration of Storytelling

When we tell a story we create two communities: between storyteller and listener(s); and between storyteller and self. Both operate simultaneously and function differently. Storytellers telling a tale draw from disparate

159

bits and pieces of the story as they know it and the story they uncover as they tell it. Discovery, memory, and experience affect sequence, detail, feeling, accent, and shape. For the listener(s), stories create a time and space where being has magic. In the mind's eye, stories take us where we wish to be. A story that resonates within us enables us to imagine, invent, explore, and experience, safely contained by the story. Our sense of self is deepened and becomes more accessible as our understanding of the ways of the world broadens and deepens.

In the classroom, stories are usually told by the teacher and begin to disappear from most classrooms after the second or third grade. However, storytelling is an activity with as many benefits as the written transmission of stories, providing opportunities for children to improve their ability to speak in a group, expand their vocabulary, share stories, acquire poise, build community, and kindle interest in literature as a way of understanding self and other. Telling authored stories and old stories (folktales and fairy tales, myths, and legends) enables students safely to explore who they are, and what they think and feel because of the vicarious nature of the experience. In the process of hearing and telling stories from other cultures and times, students are helped to find their place in the human community, defining themselves as part of rather than apart from those whose lives differ from our own.

Stories can be one word, one sentence, one paragraph, one page, or many pages long; the length of a story is no guarantee of its importance to either the teller or the listener. I have used one-word stories to spark imagination and also spent days telling a book-length myth. What matters is the power the story has: first, to attract the attention of the storyteller; and second, to maintain the interest of the listener. In this section I share ideas about how to "grow" stories—ways to use storytelling in the classroom as a central part of teaching language arts.

The Buddy Business

In each class children select a buddy for the week. One way to do this is to have half of the class draw from a hat the name of one child from the other half of the class. Random selection stretches friendships within the class and ensures that no one feels left out or unwanted. Buddies need to work together for at least one week in order to establish good working relationships. The next week those whose names were in the hat will be the ones to draw names from the other half.

Teachers need to spend some time talking about what it means to be a buddy and what buddies do. The first task is to listen carefully, without interruption. The second task is to notice personal response: Are you interested? If so, why? If not, why not? The third task is to ask the storyteller questions with the intent of deepening and enriching the story rather than judging it. A fourth task involves sharing how the story personally affects the listener—what the story evokes in terms of feelings, memories, ideas, or dreams. Teachers can help children practice these skills by asking children to respond in these ways to stories told by teachers. As part of teaching children how to respond to stories they hear, read, and tell, it is important to point out that when we make judgments of characters or stories, we end involvement; in effect we kill the character or story. Instead of making judgments, teachers need to teach children how to ask productive questions which are fueled by curiosity and caring.

First Session: Beginning the Story

Tell: A very short folktale, drawing from cultures around the world

Paint: Each child paints, draws, or sculpts an image from the story.

Create: Each child makes a one-sentence story (using the story either to retell it or to make up a new story). Children who have the skills can write the sentence down. Partners need to be encouraged to help each other when necessary.

Share: Stories with buddy. Each partner, in turn, asks one question of the storyteller who answers in any fashion she/he chooses. Because it is best to keep the structure simple, I suggest additional questions be postponed until everyone feels comfortable with the process.

Create: Children then return to their story to add the new information supplied by addressing the question, either writing or noting key words, however they choose.

Share: Stories with another pair of buddies or, if there is time, the whole class. Each time a story is shared, listeners are encouraged to make personal associations by talking about what is evoked by the story rather than focusing on whether they like it.

Reflect: On the process as a whole class, noting what part of the experience proved especially helpful, where there are questions, and what suggestions might help storytellers with their stories.

Second Session: Developing Character

Focus: On the main character

Create: Images of this person by painting, drawing, or sculpting
(Teachers foster discussion by asking questions such as, Who is this person? What does this person look like? What does this person wear? How does this person find food? With whom does this person live or does the person live alone? The children, as a group, might suggest questions which the teacher can write on the board for the children to use as reference.)

Develop: Vocabulary lists through discussion of questions
(This is a wonderful opportunity to teach adjectives and vocabulary words. I encourage children to develop vocabulary lists in the back of their stories notebook for use when they can't think of a particular word or need a synonym.)

Buddies: Pair up and tell each other about the main character in their story. Each asks the other questions to deepen and develop the story. Children incorporate the new information into their stories, writing or noting key words and important ideas.

Share: Stories with other pairs of buddies. It is important, when possible, to leave time for children to reflect on stories and to make connections between the story and themselves.

Reflect: On how questions and vocabulary description affect storytelling

Third Session: Developing Plot

Focus: On the action in the story

Ask: Questions such as, Where is the action taking place? Why is it happening now? Who participates? Who watches? Children are encouraged to ask "where" questions, which the teacher writes on the board.

Talk: About plot development, perhaps using other stories children know to explore variety and change

Make: Images by painting, drawing, or sculpting an image of the environment in which the story takes place, placing the important characters in the setting at a particular point in the story

Share: Ideas and new information with buddy
(If skills and/or interest allow, children can write the new information into their story or note key ideas. Time permitting, children share their stories with other pairs of buddies. The more often children tell their stories, the easier they are to remember, and the more details the children will invent.

Sometimes children incorporate a television program into their story without realizing they have done so. Teachers can help them personalize the story by asking questions such as: What do you know about this character that no one else knows? How did you discover the character's secret? How is the secret discovered by other characters in the story? What happens to the character when her or his secret is discovered?)

Reflect: On the process of deepening a story—how you incorporate new ideas into the framework of an existing story

Fourth Session: Deepening the Story

Create: An image of a "peculiar incident" or a "surprise" which children then incorporate into their story. Children deepen their story by being asked to examine the incident or surprise and explore unexpected consequences.

Share: Incident or surprise with buddies. Then, skills permitting, children can use the new information to expand their story in writing or to note key ideas. *(Teachers need to encourage the active use of imagination so that children are helped to augment their ideas of what is possible. Some children don't mind having their story worked on by the whole class to demonstrate how possibilities are explored and developed. Buddies share stories with other pairs of buddies. As the stories grow in length more time will be needed for storytelling, yet the sharing provides important opportunities for the development of oral language, self-esteem, and collaborative learning.)*

Reflect: On the process of deepening a story and working collaboratively

Fifth Session: Title and Cover Design

Design: A cover and title for story

Share: Cover design and title with buddy. Encourage partners to collaborate, helping each other to smooth out rough spots, listening to each other's stories or ideas to make a final draft of the story.

Share: Stories with other pairs of buddies. Depending on time, they are shared with the class, put up on a bulletin board, or collected and printed so that everyone has a copy of each classmate's story, even if the stories are only one sentence in length.

Reflect: On the process of developing a story to tell
*(This process can be used with the class working as
a whole, which is especially effective with young
children who have not yet developed the writing
skills necessary to compose a whole story. The
teacher might begin by asking for one-sentence
stories which are then developed in ways
outlined above.)*

Although the structure of the initial story and selection of a buddy
serve as the frame, teachers can devise different points on which to
focus.

Point of View

What happens if the story is told by other characters?
How does the story change if told by a part of the environment?
How is the story shaped if the story is told by a character who
     is angry or frustrated or isolated from other characters
     in the story?

Using the Story as a Frame

Create a story from the story.
Create a story evoked by the story.
Create a story by exploring a memory or response evoked by
     the story.
Create a story by exploring what happens between one point
     in the story and the next point—the story between the
     story. What happens between one episode in the story and
     the next?
Create a story by exploring what happens after the story ends.
Create a story by exploring what happens before the story
     begins.

IN THE BEGINNING   It is useful, especially in the beginning, to use a story
or poem to initiate storytelling because it acts as a container—the
issues, ideas, and feelings evoked by the text serve as our point of
departure. For example, after telling a folktale about a time when a
husband and wife changed places for one day, I might ask my class to

imagine themselves in their families as someone or something other than who they are. If the class needs help I offer some possibilities: they can be much (exaggeration helps to stimulate imagination) larger, smaller, heavier, or skinnier; invisible; a family pet; an only child; one of twenty-seven . . . I continue to make suggestions until the group offers some ideas of their own.

MAKING IMAGES   I then ask them to select an idea of self that fascinates them. After choosing, I ask them to paint or sculpt an image of their new self, to imagine what this new existence might be like, and to title their image.

I then might ask the class to sculpt an image of this new self in relationship to their family at a particular time and place, and to think about what might have happened when they interacted with their family as their new self.

TELLING AND HEARING THE STORY   The story is practically born. All they need to do now is to tell about their experience. After we share the stories, the students and I reflect on the process of storytelling and think about ourselves as storytellers. We practice responding to each other's stories nonjudgmentally, sharing what stories make us think of, how they make us feel, and what connections we make between the stories and ourselves.

FINDING AND DEVELOPING THE STORY USING A COLLABORATIVE PROCESS   "But how do you get students to make a story when they can't find the story inside themselves?" asked a teacher to whom I was assigned to help expand her language arts program. One way is to ask people to select a character and to tell one sentence about this character.

For example, during one class period a student selected a turtle as his character and told us, "There was a turtle who lived under an old house." He had nothing more to say about this turtle. I asked the class to ask him some questions—what did they want to know about this turtle. I told them I would write their questions on the board so they could see how helpful it is to collaborate. These are some of the questions they posed to him.

How big was the turtle?
Did the turtle live all alone?
Why did the turtle live under the old house?
Did the turtle have any friends?
Did people live in the old house?

What did the turtle eat?
How did the turtle get its food?
How did the turtle spend its time?
Was the turtle a boy or a girl turtle?
What kind of turtle was it? A painted turtle? A snapping turtle?
What was the biggest adventure the turtle ever had?
Did the turtle have a family?
How did the turtle come to live under the old house?
What was most important to the turtle?
What made the turtle angry? Happy? Frustrated? Lonely?
   Excited?
What was special about this turtle?
How did this turtle come to find love?

The student didn't have to answer all these questions of course; they merely served to stimulate his thinking and to help connect the storyteller with more of the story which lives inside.

WORKING COLLABORATIVELY TO DEVELOP A STORY   Sometimes, if children have trouble thinking of a character, the class can suggest one character for everyone to use. Students can then divide into small groups and, in their groups, develop and ask questions which can be written on the board. Each group then decides which question(s) they want to explore as storytellers. The resulting stories are usually very different; the variety often stimulates further storytelling as each child particularizes the character. Once people are accustomed to asking questions as a way of helping other storytellers, they realize they can also ask themselves questions whenever they feel stuck.

USING THE FEELING OF BEING STUCK   Another way to help people get "unstuck" is to ask children to make images, either in paint or clay, of the stuck moment, the moment just before the stuck moment, and the moment just after it. Given no time to plan, students paint or sculpt without thinking ahead. The images are often vivid enough to move the storyteller to a new idea or feeling. Being stuck is often a collision between what we think should happen and what we want to happen. Our inner censor is dictating to our imagination, which never works to our creative advantage.

Sharing stories to create community has many benefits. Students build cooperative exchanges of information, and in the process, get to know each other better. They learn to ask questions to deepen stories and to focus on enhancement rather than on judgment. Students also learn to regard themselves as persons of worth—with stories to tell. Memory and listening skills improve as does the interest students take in each other's stories. If teachers incorporate the power of the dictionary and the thesaurus into the storytelling process, these books become allies, helping children to expand and to develop their expressive capacities.

While it is meaningful for teachers to talk about the importance of imagination and possibility, it is *vital* that the supporting structure of sharing stories and reflection be collaboration rather than criticism. Teaching children how to ask questions whose sole aim is to help their classmates deepen, extend, enrich, and create as an integral part of storytelling enhances the learning process for all children, regardless of their experience and expertise.

Sharing Stories in the Classroom

THE THIRTY-SECOND HOT LINE   Children love to record their uncensored views on books and stories. Tape recorders are a marvelous way to create a hot line for fellow classmates. Children read a book and then record author, title, and one or two sentences about their response to the book. The tapes can be changed weekly. Comments recorded in one classroom: "This book sucks." "It has some hard words but don't worry. The story's great." "Don't bother!" "It's a lovely book."

THE VIEW FROM HERE   In a corner of the back blackboard we hung a special cork bulletin board where students wrote the name of the book, its author, and one or two sentences about the book. In another classroom we hung individual pieces of paper with the name of a book and its author on a clothesline. Children were encouraged to write their views of the book on the paper. Each Friday, the teacher held a short session which we called the "Critic's Corner." Children shared their ideas, discussed why there were different views of a particular book, and talked about what they liked and disliked in stories. In a classroom where children wrote poorly we put up a roll of paper and asked them to paint images of the story and to write one word which either described the story or was evoked by the story. Children cut off the piece of paper and tacked it to a cork board where specific books were listed.

BUDDYING UP   Children select a partner with whom to read a book. Children read out loud to each other, deciding among themselves whether to switch after a page, paragraph, or chapter. Each pair decides how to choose a book. Sometimes each partner picks the book she or he wants to read and the pair reads two books before switching partners. Children buddy up with new partners to tell about the book they have just read.

SHOW AND TELL   In one class, one morning a week the teacher and children gather around for a fifteen-minute sharing of books. Each child is given from thirty seconds to a minute to praise, pan, and/or reflect on a book. Children may work in pairs so that shy children have support. Sometimes, they decide to focus on one aspect of a book, such as character development, in order to compare how different authors treat their subject. At times children paint favorite images of their book, which are then titled and displayed to interest other children in reading a particular book.

What guides *all* storytelling activity is the idea that sharing books and stories is pleasurable. It is a lifelong treasure and an unending source and resource for learning.

Connecting the Story to the Storyteller

We all have stories inside us—stories of our lives, stories in our imaginations—stories which comfort, educate, explain, amuse, and challenge us to become our deeper selves. However, it is one thing to be told that stories live within us and quite another to find and express them. The process of storytelling guides us, helping us to find the places inside us where our stories live. There are many ways to begin and no one way works for everyone each time. What is always required is acceptance—of ourselves and our stories. We begin where we are, with what we know, and with what we feel inside.

Exploring Connections

Create a group story beginning with a sentence that reflects the group's experience.

Create a story that begins with a personal experience and becomes fiction.

Create a story that begins with a character's experience in a story.

Create a story that begins with a feeling and is told from an imagined person's point of view.

Create a story that begins with "I wish . . ."

Create a story that reflects an adventure you would like to have.

SOURCEWORK

170 ··

Create a story for a particular person in your life.

Use a dictionary or thesaurus to augment your vocabulary.

Tape a story and send it to a friend, asking that your friend send you a story in return.

Create a drama that explores the relationship between two characters in a story.

Create a poem that explores a person, place, or theme of a story.

Create a musical composition that "tells a story."

Create a series of images that "tell a story."

Create a movement story.

Create a one-line story, and give it to a friend. Ask the friend to continue the story with his/her one-line story.

Continue giving the story to friends until you decide to stop. Each friend tells the whole story to everyone who contributes.

Exploration of Drama

Young children, especially in the beginning, generally need to work as a group with no character differentiation (each child playing a different part). In "Little Red Ridinghood," for example, all children would be Little Red Ridinghood, or the wolf, or the woodcutter, etc. As children gain experience they can begin to work in a two-person dialogue, but much depends on the interaction the class has with their teacher. When children like their teacher and feel comfortable exploring ideas and making mistakes, even first-grade children can make small plays from stories they like or from material they make up themselves. If, however, the classroom atmosphere is one of distrust, drama will be more difficult to do because showing feelings and being vulnerable is an essential part of all dramatic activity. I suggest structured ways to do drama that can help teachers to begin, even if they are inexperienced or are struggling to bring more creative approaches to their classroom teaching.

The biggest mistake inexperienced teachers make when beginning work in drama is to attempt too much at one time. Even the most basic activity can provide fruitful exploration when teachers use students' responses to make connections between self and text, self and character, and character and character. When teachers feel they don't know what to do next, it is always useful to gather children (in a circle if possible) and reflect on what has occurred, what children think might happen next, and how children feel about their work to date. I have gotten myself out of many "stuck places" by asking my students to "paint an image of myself [themselves] at this moment," and to write a few words that come to mind. Sharing their images and words helps to give me a sense of the class at this point and stimulates possibilities for what needs to come next.

I include the telling of "Little Red Ridinghood" in each structure to show where I would include the story within the activity. Once children are familiar with a common version of the story there is no need to repeat it every time. How long each structure takes, and how much time the full exploration lasts, depends on the experience and interest of teachers and their students. The sequences suggested range from simple to complex and are meant to stimulate possible ways to explore a story using drama.

Level One: For young children or those with no drama experience

Initial Exploration

Focus: Visualizing a scene or telling moment

Text: "Little Red Ridinghood"

Tell: "Little Red Ridinghood"

Paint: Image of a telling moment (powerful point) in the story that interests (angers, annoys, amazes, inspires, frightens) you

Title: Image

Share: Images and titles. Talk about why you have chosen your telling moment and how you chose your title.

Reflect: On what and how we notice and imagine when hearing a story

(Encourage a variety of points of view so that it becomes clear there is no one right or best moment. Explain that how and what we notice in a story very much depends on who we are and on our personal experiences. Because no two people are alike or have the same experience, it is quite natural for people to notice different moments in a story or to have a distinct explanation for a point also chosen by others.)

Second Exploration (with the whole class as one group)

Focus: Developing an understanding of point of view

Text: "Little Red Ridinghood"

Tell: "Little Red Ridinghood"

Select: One telling moment to explore

Share: Ideas about what the environment looks like to someone who is in the story, such as Little Red Ridinghood or the wolf

Share: Ideas about what the setting (environment) looks like to someone not in the story, such as a woodcutter or an animal
(Teachers can facilitate this discussion by talking about what setting means: Where is the play taking place? Then the discussion can explore the part setting [environment] plays in creating drama such as what happens when it is dark in the forest, or the trees are so thick Little Red Ridinghood has trouble finding her grandmother's house.
I always find it helpful, initially, to make suggestions in the form of questions. If, for example, the scene takes place in the forest, are the trees big or small? Are they close together or is there space between them? Is there a lot of sunlight

or are the trees so thick there is little sunshine?
Are there paths through the forest or do people find
their way by themselves?)

Discuss: What we mean by point of view. Who is telling the
story? How does this person's voice affect choices
in making a drama, creating characters, and
developing motivation (why people do what they
do)?

Reflect: On how point of view affects the choices, the
decisions, and the relationships we make when
creating a drama and in our own lives
(For example, if we read or hear the story after we
have had a fight with a brother or sister, our
understanding of the story might be different than
if we read or hear the story after our
grandmother has just given us the gift we have
always wanted.)

Third Exploration (with the whole class as one group)

Focus: Exploring the creation of a character

Text: "Little Red Ridinghood"

Tell: "Little Red Ridinghood"

Sculpt: An image of the character everyone agrees is most
important

Act: As if each class member is the main character in the
telling moment (everyone is Little Red
Ridinghood, the wolf, etc.). Do one action.

Sculpt: Image of your character at a particular point in the
story

Share: Images and discuss your ideas about the character as you see him, her, or it. Talk about how, or if, your sculpture changed from when you made the character the first time and when you sculpted your character at a particular point in the story.

Explore: The action of the character from the beginning to the end of the chosen moment by sharing ideas and trying out many possibilities
(Teachers can help children develop their character in an individual manner by naming possible aspects of the character or asking developmental questions. For example, if everyone is playing the wolf, the teacher might say, "The wolf is hungry. How might the wolf move? Or, the wolf has just gotten up. How might it walk if it were taking an early morning stroll?" Developmental questioning might include: How does the wolf walk if it is following Little Red Ridinghood and doesn't want to be noticed? How might the wolf initially approach the grandmother's house? Would it knock? Would it bang on the door?
By suggesting possibilities through naming potential aspects of character conception and developmental questioning, teachers help children learn what is involved in creating possibilities. When children begin to understand the process, teachers can move from direct naming and questioning to evoking possibilities, such as: How might the wolf spend a day? What might interrupt its routine?)

Reflect: On the process of how we begin to develop a character. How do group members create possibilities? How do group members make space so that participants can share ideas with the full attention of the group? How does the group decide which idea to choose?

Level Two: For children who have some experience and some writing ability

Initial Exploration

Focus: Visualizing a scene or telling moment

Text: "Little Red Ridinghood"

Tell: "Little Red Ridinghood"

Paint: Image of a telling moment (powerful point) in the story that interests you

Write: Title of image on picture

Share: Images and titles. Talk about how you chose your telling moment and title.

Reflect: On what and how we notice and imagine when hearing a story
(Consider what is involved with imagining. How is it that we are likely to conjure up different images of the same word? How do we deal with answers or ideas that cannot be supported by the text? How do we make connections between a text and what it evokes within us such as experiences or memories? How do we remain true to our vision as participants suggest many different ideas?)

Second Exploration

Focus: Developing an understanding of point of view

Text: "Little Red Ridinghood"

Tell: "Little Red Ridinghood"

Select: One telling moment to explore

Paint:	Image of the environment from the point of view of someone who is in the telling moment, such as Little Red Ridinghood, the wolf, or the grandmother
Paint:	Image of the environment from the point of view of someone who enters or works in the forest regularly, such as a woodcutter, an animal, or a schoolteacher
Share:	Images and talk about the difference in the two points of view *(What contributes to point of view? How do we develop a point of view? What might it take to change our point of view? How do we learn to live with people who have different points of view from us?)*
Reflect:	How does point of view shape choices? *(How does the environment feel [friendly, unfriendly, etc.]? What accounts for the feeling? What is most important about the environment to a particular character? For example, the woodcutter may look for the tallest trees, but these same trees may look scary to a small girl.)*

Third Exploration

Focus:	Exploring the creation of a character
Text:	"Little Red Ridinghood"
Tell:	"Little Red Ridinghood"
Select:	A telling moment and one character in your telling moment
Paint:	An image of your chosen character in the setting of your chosen telling moment
Create:	Some words to describe your character. How is your

character feeling at this time? What is your
character doing in this telling moment?
*(Teachers can help children select words by
discussing possible choices such as: Is your
character big or small? What color hair (skin) does
your character have? What might your character
have eaten for breakfast? What friends does your
character have, if any? Is your character
generally cheerful? Grumpy? Friendly? Isolated? If
so, what might cause this to be so?*

*Teachers can also help children describe their
character's action in one sentence such as: Little
Red Ridinghood is taking a basket of food to her
grandmother. The hungry wolf is looking for
something to eat. The kind mother gives her
daughter a basket of food to take to her ill
grandmother.)*

Share: Image of chosen character. Describe character, how
character is feeling, and what character is doing.

Reflect: On what we need to know in order to create a
particular character
*(Think about how who we are affects our choices.
For example, if several people choose the same
character in the same telling moment, talk about
the differences in point of view and how each
person's unique vision fits within the context of the
story.)*

Level Three: For children with experience and writing skills

Initial Exploration

Focus: Visualizing a scene or telling moment

Text: "Little Red Ridinghood"

Tell: "Little Red Ridinghood"

Paint:	Image of a telling moment in the story which interests you
Write:	Title of image on picture
Decide:	What interests you about this scene
Share:	Images, titles, and what interests you about the telling moment you have chosen. How did you come to choose the scene? Were there others you thought about choosing? If so, why didn't you choose them?
Imagine:	How your telling moment begins and ends
Share:	How you imagine your scene—people, setting, and action—with classmates in groups of four
Reflect:	On choices people have made—differences and similarities *(Consider what is involved with imagining and visualizing. How is it we conjure up different images of the same word or scene? What does it take to imagine something?)*

Second Exploration

Focus:	Developing an understanding of point of view
Text:	"Little Red Ridinghood"
Tell:	"Little Red Ridinghood"
Select:	One telling moment to explore
Select:	One character in your telling moment
Paint:	An image of the setting (environment) from the point of view of your character

Sculpt: An image of your character and place your character in the setting

Create: Some words to describe what your character thinks and feels about being in this setting. Decide what your character is doing in this setting.

Share: Images, words, and thoughts about your choices in groups of four

Paint: An image of the setting (environment) from the point of view of someone who enters or uses the forest at this particular time but is not necessarily a character in the story such as a woodcutter, an animal, a person walking in the forest.

Create: Some words to describe what this character thinks and feels about being in this setting. Decide why the character is in this setting and what the character is doing. Think about usual and unusual reasons and actions. What constitutes usual and unusual?

Share: Images, words, and thoughts about your choices in groups of four

Reflect: How does point of view affect choice? How does the environment feel (friendly, unfriendly, etc.) to a particular character? What makes your character decide this?
                (What is most important about the environment to a particular character? For example, the girl may be so happy to be free and on her own she may not even notice where she is going. The woodcutter, whose livelihood depends on finding trees to cut, might walk slowly, paying attention to where he goes and what he sees. An animal romping through the woods might see the wolf and flee. A person walking in the woods might pay more attention to where she or he is going than where he or she is in the forest.)

Third Exploration

Focus:	Exploring the creation of a character
Text:	"Little Red Ridinghood"
Tell:	"Little Red Ridinghood"
Paint:	An image of your character in the setting of your chosen image
Create:	Some words to describe your character at this particular time. How is your character feeling? Why? What is your character doing in this telling moment? Think as if you are the character, using "I" to describe your thoughts and feelings. Be specific rather than general. For example, instead of saying, "I am frightened," say, "I feel frightened in the forest because the tall trees keep the sun from shining and it is very dark, even during the day."
Share:	Images and words to describe your character's thoughts and feelings in groups of four
Create:	The sequence of actions in your telling moment, such as mother gives girl a basket to take to grandmother and girl leaves; wolf enters forest and sees little girl; little girl enters room of grandmother; girl realizes the wolf is wearing grandmother's clothes. Write down the sequence to help you remember your choices.
Choose:	Partner
Act:	Out each other's "script"
Share:	Scripts with rest of class or with other pairs
Reflect:	On process

(How does the creation of a character relate to action? How do you decide what your character will do and say at a particular time in the midst of a particular action? How can you reveal feeling through action? As an audience member, what holds your attention as you watch characters interact? How does who we are affect our choices? When we are working with a text is there any limit to the choices we can make? If so, what is this boundary? How do we make our choices? What makes a choice productive? How do we know whether a choice is supported by the text?

Teachers can help children to think about possible choices within a text by posing examples that are clearly unsupported by the text such as: the wolf really likes Little Red Ridinghood and would never hurt her; or Little Red Ridinghood wants the wolf to eat her grandmother. It is important, as an integral part of the discussion, to include "evidence" as to why a particular choice can or cannot be supported by the text. This process builds reading skills and helps children become active readers who are able to create dynamic responses to literature.)

Exploring connections:

Create internal monologue.
Create an internal monologue (what a character says to him or herself) at a particular moment in the text. For example, what might Little Red Ridinghood say to herself when her mother gives her the basket? When she sees the wolf? What might the mother say to herself as she watches Little Red Ridinghood set off with the basket? What might the wolf say to himself when he first sees Little Red Ridinghood?

Create scenes from unexplored material in a story.
For example, what happens to Little Red Ridinghood before she meets the wolf?

Create drama from real-life episodes.
For example, if a person has something difficult to
say to someone, the person and a partner
could create a role-play to explore the issue and
possible ways of responding.

*Explore how meaning is affected by how we
choose to speak a line.*
For example, let us use the sentence, "I want to go
to the store." Changing the accents changes
the meaning. Read each sentence out loud
stressing the *underlined* word. *I* want to go
to the store. I *want* to go to the store. I want to
go to the store. I want to go to the *store*.
What we are developing is subtext, the meaning
that informs the way the words are spoken.

Explore how meaning is affected by focus.
For example, discover how meaning is affected if we
look at the person with whom we are
speaking. Notice how the meaning changes if we
look away or if our back is to the person.

Explore how meaning is affected by space.
For example, what happens if we speak while keeping
our distance? Move so close we are practically
on top of someone? Keep moving toward or away
from someone as we speak? What happens if
we stand on a stool to speak or if we are sitting
or lying down while others are standing?

Teachers who use drama to explore a text sometimes do so as one
way to test how well their students understand what they have read.
No latitude is given regarding dialogue—children must use the words
that characters speak in the story whenever possible. The problem with
this approach is that it focuses attention on how well children memorize
dialogue and gives them little or no opportunity to explore what the
text means to them or how they are affected by issues raised by the
story. Children who are allowed to use the text as the point of departure—
the play is of the text but does not necessarily reproduce the text—can

still demonstrate their knowledge of the text when discussing productive choice and character motivation in relationship to the text.

When teachers structure scenes to explore a text using very focused tasks, such as exploring a telling moment or creating an internal monologue by a character at a particular moment in the text, children are taught how to use drama to deepen their understanding of the text as well as what it means to be human.

CHAPTER NINE

Exploring Written Language

Written language does not depend on immediate interaction with an audience as does oral language. The writer has time to explore, describe, and explain experiences, places, characters' thoughts, and the narrator's ideas, which readers read in their own time and place. When we write, we have time to reflect and make desired changes. We explore all we understand at any given moment knowing that tomorrow we can rework our ideas to make them clearer and more personally satisfying. I differentiate between oral and written language so that children have the opportunity to develop and extend each without having to do both at the same time. Drama is included in this section because the focus is on writing drama; the drama begins by working on scripts rather than through improvisational interaction.

When children write creatively, teachers often wonder whether to correct grammatical and spelling errors or to focus on content. Too much correction may leave children hating to write, but too little may leave children with no sense of standard form or usage. One way to solve this problem is to encourage children to consider writing as a process, with each draft focusing on a particular problem, idea, or skill. Children can be asked, "Who will read your writing?" If the child says, "No one," the writing does not have to conform to standard practice. However, if the child continues to answer in the same way, teachers can suggest the child share the writing with a buddy, a friend, a relative, or a child in another class. Once the child agrees to share writing, the teacher has the opportunity to explain and explore standard usage in a context that makes sense to the child. While this approach may not be practical all the time, it helps the child to understand the importance of writing that conforms to universal standards of spelling, grammar, and punctuation.

When looking at first drafts, teachers/readers generally need to focus on the development and deepening of ideas. When reading subsequent drafts, teachers/readers then concentrate on helping the writer to hone, shape, and clarify ideas and their expression. The more children are made part of this process, the likelier it is that they will regard suggestions and corrections as a necessary and integral part of creating personally satisfying written expression.

When I do workshops with teachers, one of their most common concerns has to do with ways to handle "mistakes," such as spelling errors, incorrect grammar, poor sentence structure, and/or a lack of compositional structure. As a way to address their concerns I evolved three levels of exploration to explain how I help children decide what to do with work that comes after spontaneous expression. I want the children to decide at which level they want to work. This method allows children to make their own choice about when and how, or if, they want to improve their work. In this way, motivation to enhance, enrich, or correct is intrinsic and self-determined, not imposed by some form of carrot-and-stick reward or punishment.

LEVEL ONE: INDIVIDUAL (ME)   Children speak to or write for themselves. No communication with others is intended. Children can make up words or write in any way they choose because they are the only person who has to understand what is said or written. This is like a whoosh of ideas, feelings, and experiences.

LEVEL TWO: PAIRS (ME AND YOU)   Children speak or write to one person. If a person cannot decipher or does not understand the writer/speaker, the person can go to the writer/speaker and question, ask for clarification, and/or ask that something written or said be repeated. Both the initiator and the receiver are in the same place at the same time and can talk to each other until understanding is achieved. Corrections or improvements are made on the basis of the receiver's questions or difficulties because the initiator wants the receiver to understand what has been said or written. Choices are made based on mutual experience and knowledge. Grammar, sentence structure, word choice, spelling, and structure may still be idiosyncratic.

LEVEL THREE: GROUP (THEY)   Children speak to an audience or write something that is read by unknown people. There is no time or place to translate idiosyncratic usage or explain intention or meaning. Word choice, grammar, spelling, and structure have to be based on standard usage.

Exploration of Poetry

To make a poem is to express the essence of an idea, experience, or feeling. Each carefully chosen word allows the poet to capture the distilled nature of what is being written. Poems are poems whether or not they rhyme, conform to a particular form (such as the sonnet), are long or short, arranged carefully on a page or splattered like drops from a shaking brush. Part of the joy of writing poetry comes from deciding how to shape the thought to the word, the word to the page, and perhaps, the word spoken to one's self or others.

For young children with minimal writing skills, poetry writing enables them to explore the meaning of their world even as older children, with more skills, strive to find the precise word or phrase that gives voice to their inner lives and experience.

Teachers who feel uncomfortable reading poetry may find it difficult to read poetry to their students. Those who think they cannot write poetry themselves, nor confidently judge the quality of the poetry their students write, may feel like avoiding teaching poetry writing. It's hard to teach what you think you can't do. Yet children derive great benefit from writing poetry—it improves their ability to identify a concept, to consider how they feel, to express what they know about the idea, and it enables them to concentrate on writing very particularly and precisely.

Focusing on process, especially for beginners, is common in the arts. Potters, for example, often talk of throwing away one hundred pots before they make one worth keeping. Authors seldom stop with a first effort, usually writing many drafts before showing their work to an editor. The act of making, whether it be a poem, story, sculpture, piece of music, or drama, is what makes knowledge possible. Each subsequent version or draft enables us to discover, learn, and acquire new ability. Although teachers help us to learn, hone our aesthetic sense, and enable us to look at our work more critically, our skills develop only as we work, practice, experience, and create. The best gift teachers can give to their students is to provide an environment where children work, learn, and explore without fear of ridicule, premature judgment, inappropriate criticism, or exploitation.

The material in this chapter focuses on poetry writing as a process that is part of the language arts curriculum and not on the poem as a product. It comes out of my experience with a newly graduated teacher who felt poorly equipped to teach a poetry unit. The second-grade children with whom we worked had been reading fairy tales, and when I asked if they had a favorite, many shouted, "Snow White and the Seven Dwarfs." I decided to use the story as the source for all the poetry activity, not only because the children liked the story, but because it provided a framework the teacher could use when working with other texts.

The structures that the teacher and I developed with the children took place over a two-week period, but readers can use the material in any way they choose—once a day, once a week, or as a unit spread out over the course of the school year. No two second grades are like the group described. Some will be more advanced, others less so. I hope teachers will read about this particular second grade's response to the poetry unit and design their own approach to teaching poetry according to the knowledge they have of their students' abilities and experiences.

Initial Exploration

Focus: Group poem

Text: "Snow White and the Seven Dwarfs"

Explore: What is a poem?
(We began by asking the children if they knew any poems. Some recited nursery rhymes, others quoted advertising jingles. When we asked them to tell us what they thought a poem was, we heard: "It rhymes." "It doesn't have to 'cause my sister writes poems and they don't rhyme." "It's short." "Oh no! My brother had to read a poem that's a whole book long." "No poem is a whole book, stupid!"

By now they were arguing with each other about what was and wasn't a poem. Finally some of the children asked for the definition of a poem. I read them the definition in Webster's New Twentieth-Century Dictionary *[unabridged second edition]:*

> *[Fr. poeme; L. poema; Gr. poiema; anything made, a poem, from posein, to make.]*
>   *1. an arrangement of words in verse; especially a rhythmical composition, sometimes rhymed, expressing facts, ideas, or*

*emotions in a style more concentrated,
imaginative, and powerful than that of
ordinary speech: some poems are in
meter, some in free verse.*
    *2. a composition, whether in verse or
prose, having beauty of thought or
language.*
    *3. anything beautiful in a way
suggesting a poem.*

*At the end of the discussion, the children decided
that a poem was like a story with all the extra
words taken out. We were ready to begin.)*

Tell: "Snow White and the Seven Dwarfs"
*(Although the children knew the story of "Snow
White," I retold it so we could all work from a
common version.)*

Think: About the story

Write: One sentence on a piece of paper, making it as short
or as long as you please
*(The only instruction we gave was that the sentence
had to be words the children wanted to have in
their version of the story.)*

Read: Your sentences out loud, in the order you want them
to be in the story
*(Many children wanted to read their sentences, so
we developed a procedure whereby each child
wanting to be next read her or his sentence. The
class decided the order of each sentence. We
repeated this process until all the sentences were
read and an order was established.)*

Sit: In a circle

Hand out: Sentences in the order in which they have been
collected

Read: Sentence you have been given, out loud, to the person on your left
(We did this to make sure each child could read the sentence easily, with no worry about mispronunciation.)

Read: The sentence out loud to the whole group

Listen: To the order of the sentences to make sure you are satisfied
(After the second reading there were a few sentences which the children agreed to rearrange. Subsequently, pieces of paper were exchanged and sentences were read again. We asked the children whether they thought this was a poem or a story, given the definition of poem *which I had read. The children were of one mind. "It's a poem," they shouted. "It's our poem."*

Their teacher collected the sentences and said she would type them on the large-print typewriter, making a copy for each child. One child sighed, "Just think, today I am a poet.")

Reflect: On process
(The children had little to say although they looked happy. The teacher told them she was very excited about their poem.)

Second Exploration

Focus: Describing place

Text: "Snow White and the Seven Dwarfs"

Paint: An image of one of the places in which the story takes place

Write: Some words to describe the place

Share: The images and words
(We asked the children to tell us why they chose as they did, and to consider what made the place

so important to them and to the story. After all the children had shared, it became evident that almost all of them had chosen one of four places: the house where Snow White lived with her father and stepmother, the forest, the house of the Seven Dwarfs, and, to our surprise, the glass coffin where Snow White lay in her poisoned sleep.)

Divide: Into four groups
(Each group chose one of the four places: the house Snow White shared with her father and stepmother, the forest, the house of the Seven Dwarfs, and the glass coffin. Although the four groups each decided to take a different place, having two or more groups work with the same place would also be interesting because the same place would have more than one group voice.)

Write: One sentence which describes your place using as many descriptive words as possible. Each child writes a sentence.
(We encouraged the children to feel free to use the thesaurus and the dictionary.)

Share: Sentences among group members and put them in the order which best represents the group's ideas and feelings

Reflect: On the process
(The teacher and I taught the children to think about the kinds of questions that stimulate writing. For example: Do we get a sense of what is special about the place in the poem? Do we have a feeling about what it might be like to be in the place we are writing about? How is the house where Snow White lives with her father and stepmother different from another house where another young girl lives? The children commented that they liked the way we were "fixing" the poems. One child said it was the first time someone said something about her writing that didn't make her feel bad. There were a lot of heads nodding in agreement.)

Third Exploration

Focus:	The voice of "place"
Text:	"Snow White and the Seven Dwarfs"
Divide:	Into working groups
Write:	One sentence in the voice of place
Place:	Sentences in the order which best represents the group's ideas
Title:	Poem sentences
Read:	Title and sentences in order to the whole group
Reflect:	On voice of place poems

(The children did not feel comfortable working without our supervision so we agreed that each group would share their sentences with the whole class. After the first group shared their sentences, one of the children noticed that some of the sentences seemed to be written by Snow White while others seemed to be by the stepmother. Their teacher asked why this mattered. The child wasn't sure but while he was thinking, another child said, "Well, Snow White feels bad about her stepmother not liking her. And the stepmother is mad because Snow White is more beautiful. That's two different stories."

In the end, after quite a lot of discussion, we decided to focus on place's point of view and ask the children in each group to pose a question which would focus their writing. The questions they decided on were: How does the house of the father and stepmother feel about what's happening within its walls? How does the forest feel about the young girl who is taken to the forest to be murdered but is freed? How does the house of the Seven Dwarfs feel about its newest inhabitant? How does the coffin feel about Snow White?

We ran out of time, so we asked the children to consider the sentence they had written and, at home, to rewrite it with their group's question in mind. Here is one example of how the sentences changed: "I have nowhere to hide from my stepmother," to "My stone walls are high and thick but I cannot help Snow White.")

Reflect: On sentences and explore reactions
(The children were very reluctant to say anything except, "That's good," or "I like it." I suggested that instead of thinking about good or bad, we think about description. Do we know how the place feels about what is happening? Does the place have one point of view or several? For example, the trees in the forest might feel sorry for Snow White while the fox in the forest thinks about what a fine dinner Snow White would make.

We decided to divide into the original groups and to work with each group's sentences as groups, rather than as individuals in the class. We had one group read its sentences and then, after each smaller group thought about suggestions they made among themselves, they were to make no more than three suggestions which might enhance the poem. Although some groups made only one or two suggestions, their advice was helpful, definitely designed to improve the work rather than critique it. The group whose work was being commented on then made their own decisions as to which suggestions they wanted to explore and incorporate.

We worked with all the groups before the poems were read again to the class. The children seemed excited about the process, and several explicitly said they were relieved they didn't have to worry about whether the poem was good.)

Fourth Exploration

Focus: Imagery and character

Text: "Snow White and the Seven Dwarfs"

Paint: An image of one of the characters in the story at a particular time in the story

Title: Your image using the present tense

Share: Images and titles
(The children were surprised at the variety of moments chosen. Even when several children had chosen the same character and moment, they had different titles and talked about the moment differently. For example, one child picked the moment when Snow White took a bite of the poisoned apple, titling his image, "The end is near." Another child titled her painting of the same point, "Snow White is fooled."
Their teacher and I talked about the importance of cherishing our own point of view. We encouraged the children to share ideas without being defensive, judgmental, or apologetic, stressing that diversity enriches life.)

Close eyes: Imagine your character at the moment you have chosen. In your mind's eye, see what she or he is wearing, where he or she is standing, sitting, or lying. Is anyone or anything else around? Is it dark or light? Is the sun shining or is it raining? How is your character feeling? What has just happened to your character?

Sculpt: An image of your character in relationship to place

Write: Four lines that come out of your imagining and your sculpture

Select: A partner

Share: Your writing with each other

Think: About the images which your partner's writing creates

Share: Any questions you might have about your partner's
writing
*(The children looked puzzled. Several asked what
we meant. One child said, "I liked his poem. Why
do I have to ask him questions?" We explained that
sometimes an idea is clearer in our mind than
it is in our writing and gave as an example, "And
the witch gave Snow White a poisoned apple."
The children were silent as if to say, "So?"*

*I asked them, "How could I make my line more
powerful?" No response. I rephrased the
question, "What would happen if I rewrote my line
so it read, 'And the witch gave Snow White a
shiny red apple, filled with poison.' "*

"That's much better," said one of the boys.

"Why?" I asked.

*"Because now I can see the apple . . . It's pretty.
But it's full of poison. It makes me feel funny."
The class murmured in agreement.*

*"So, what you're thinking about is imagery.
The question you're asking your partner has to
do with making the images in the poem so powerful,
readers can see them in their mind's eye. Do
you think you can do this?" They nodded, unsure.
"Remember, these are questions. Suppose I had
written shiny red apple and my partner asks if I
want to rewrite the line so it reads, 'beautiful,
shiny red apple.' Do you think I should do this?"*

"No," shouted several children.

"Why not?" I asked.

" 'Cause it's too much!" laughed one of the girls.

"Are you sure?" I pressed.

*She looked uncertain but then decided, "Yeah,
I'm sure."*

*"Okay," I said. "That's what it means to cherish
your vision. You are open to questions and
suggestions, and at the same time, you listen to
your own voice.")*

Reflect: On process
*(The children looked at each other as if they wanted
to say something but didn't know how. I asked*

how it felt to think of themselves as poets. They grinned shyly. One of the children said he needed more time to work on his poem. Other children agreed. We were out of time but the teacher promised she would make time later in the day for partners to look at each other's work if they chose to do so. Her casual tone of voice was exactly right, conveying the idea that the work mattered, yet exploration could be done in the children's own time and manner.

"What about the title of the poem?" asked one of the children.

"I'm using the title of my picture for the title of the poem," responded a child. There was a chorus of "me too's." And so it was.)

Fifth Exploration

Focus: From the point of view of character

Text: "Snow White and the Seven Dwarfs"

Sculpt: An image of your character at a moment in the story which to you seems very important, frightening, powerful, exciting, etc.

Write: A poem in which your character talks about how she or he is feeling at this moment
(The children had a lot of questions: How do you write dialogue? Do you have to write dialogue? How long does it have to be? Is my character talking to someone? Does my character have to talk to someone? Does it have to be a poem?

I referred back to our original discussion of what makes a poem a poem. One of the children reminded us that we had decided a poem was a story with all the extra words left out. One of the children asked, "Why do we have to write a poem? Why can't I write a story?

The teacher answered, "Because we're using poetry to explore what people in the story think and feel in a special way. They might never actually say or do what they talk about in the poem, yet when we read the poems we will know a lot about the way they feel and what they wish and hope.

"Can we make up whatever we want? Even if it wasn't in the story we heard?"

"Sure," I answered, "just as long as it can be justified by the story." The children looked blank. "Justify means to find a reason for what you're saying or doing. If we're using a text to justify a reason we have to find something in the text that supports our idea, that tells what we use to make a decision."

One of the boys started to laugh, "You mean like when I pop my stupid brother one and my mother wants to know why, so I tell her, 'Cause he hit me first?' "

"Something like that," I agreed, trying not to laugh. I asked the class to give me some examples of particular moments in the story which might make interesting poems. They offered ideas, such as when Snow White is first in the forest by herself; when she sees the shiny red apple; when she meets the seven dwarfs; when she's lying in the glass coffin.

Then one child said, "I want to write my poem about Snow White before her mother died. Can I do that even though it's not in the story?" The teacher asked the class what they thought. Somewhat hesitantly heads began to nod. They finally decided it was still part of the story, just not part of the story told.

The children worked on their poems intently, stopping to look up only when one child asked, "Can I show mine to Mary?" The teacher said they could work by themselves or with each other, resulting in a flurry of activity. She smiled at me. I smiled at her.)

Reflect: On process
(The children had obviously thought about their poetry writing. "I used to be afraid of writing poems 'cause my older sister told me it was sooo *hard," said one of the children.*

"Yeah, my brother told me it was the worst,"
said another.
    Their teacher asked them how they felt about
writing poetry now. The children enthusiastically
answered "Yes" to her suggestion that they do more
poetry writing in the future.)

Sixth Exploration

Focus: "Talking heads"

Text: "Snow White and the Seven Dwarfs"

Sculpt: An image of your character in relationship to another
character in the story at a particular moment in
the story

Title: Your sculpture, making sure we know which
characters you have sculpted. Write your title
down on a piece of paper and put it next to your
sculpture.

Arrange: Sculptures and titles so that students can look at
the sculptures and their titles

View: Sculptures by walking around, looking at the
sculptures. Note how characters are positioned
in relationship to each other.

Write: A short poem about your characters in relationship.
Consider how characters feel toward and about
each other; what they want (or don't want) from
each other; what they wish could happen; what
does happen.

Share: First draft of poems
(Almost every child put his or her hand up to share,
so the teacher asked them to divide into groups
of four. Each child read her or his poem to the
members of the small groups who then
responded to it. In the midst of the sharing one child

*announced, "I want the whole class to hear my
poem." Many children felt the same way. The
teacher agreed to make a time when they could
each read their poems to the class. I suggested that
in the meantime, they work in their small groups
to "play" with their poems, exploring ways to deepen
their imagery and clarify their ideas.*

Reflect: On process
*(The teacher asked the children to talk about the
ways they were working on their poems by
reading a line as they first wrote it and then as they
rewrote it. Several children volunteered; one
child said he had rewritten a line six times and still
wasn't sure he had it right. I asked what he
thought was the problem. "The word. I can't find
the word I'm looking for." The teacher suggested
he consult the thesaurus and offered to help him.
Immediately several children asked for similar
help. When I asked the boy if he'd ever paid attention
to words before he answered, "No, but I wasn't
writing poems before. When you write a poem you
need to be more particular. You need to find the
right word."*

*One child asked, "Can't we have time to write
poems every day? Why do we have to do it only
when it's special?"*

*Their teacher grinned and said, "I have a
present for you." The children's excitement
turned sour when she told them the present was a
poetry workbook, until she handed each child a
small handmade notebook. "Now you can write your
poems any time you want and you can add paper
whenever you need more." They had become a class
of poets.)*

Exploring Connections

Create stories from poetic imagery.
For example, one of the images the children explored
   was Snow White wandering in the forest.
   Stories could focus on: What happened to Snow

White while she was in the forest? Did she
meet anyone? How long was she in the forest?
How did she survive? How did she find her
way to the Dwarfs' house?

Create drama from poetry.
One of the recurrent images in the poems exploring
character was Snow White talking to the
animals in the forest. Drama could focus on:
Snow White's interaction with a particular
animal. A dream visit to Snow White's dead
mother. A visit with her stepmother after she
is rescued from the glass coffin. A visit with the
dwarfs after she has made a new life for
herself.

Examine poetry and meaning.
Explore how meaning is affected by word choice.
Explore how meaning is affected by the arrangement
of words on the paper.
Explore how meaning is affected by the title of a
poem.

Exploration of Storymaking

I define storymaking as the act of making stories from a story: between
incidents in a story; from a different point of view; from the way a story
resonates within us; from the way a story reminds us of an incident in
our own lives; or from the way a story might happen before or after
the actual story begins or ends.

Choosing the Story

The most important part of selecting a story to use in the classroom is
to pick one you really like, or that you think about long after you have
read or heard it. Equally important, especially with young children or
beginners, is to choose a story with clear characters, conflict or challenge, and an ending where everything is resolved. This ending resolution serves as the *container* for all storymaking activity and helps to
provide a safe boundary for all exploration.

An example of containment can be seen in the experience of a student who chose Freud's version of the story of Oedipus to explore the way the story lived in his life. Sigmund Freud stopped his retelling of the story at the point where Oedipus blinds himself and is exiled from his community. In the process of exploring the myth, the student began to examine his painful experiences of incest. His misery was compounded by his choosing an incomplete version of the story—in Freud's retelling there is no end to Oedipus's pain. Only when I was able to make the student look at the *whole* story, particularly at the part where Oedipus uses his personal agony to become wiser, learns to be of use to his community, and dies as a much respected and beloved sage (the part Freud omitted from his retelling) was the young man able to find a way to begin to heal himself. While this may be an extreme example of the way stories contain exploration, it points up the importance of choosing stories where the hero or heroine emerges more whole than he or she is at the beginning of the tale or at first meeting.

Two other factors to consider when choosing a story, especially when working with young children or beginners, are the length and accessibility of the story. Teachers need to select short stories with clearly delineated plots that can be told in less than three minutes. Yet even with older children, short stories quickly told facilitate storymaking because the story told is only the beginning of subsequent activity. If work with one story lasts for more than one session, teachers may need to create a context for the tasks by retelling the bits of the story to be used.

Make a point of choosing stories from all continents, encouraging children to notice experiences that are like, as well as unlike, their own. Motivate children to observe events, situations, and ideas without automatic judgment, or without using their own lives as the only reference point for comparison or discussion. The practice of looking at other people's lives in the context of the culture in the story helps children to examine ideas about what is "normal" or "natural." As part of the exploration of the story, children can describe what they notice without comment. This new way of thinking about people in other cultures does not come easily and requires extended experience in reading, telling, and discussing stories from cultures other than their own.

Sharing the Story

Telling a story tends to have more immediate impact on listeners than does reading a story because the teller can look at listeners and gauge their interest. Tellers use their eyes or speech to focus on those who seem less interested, encouraging them to become more involved. The best advice about how to tell stories comes from an old storyteller who says, "When the story comes from your heart, your heart tells the story." Think about what it is you want from your telling. Are you giving a performance or are you sharing a favorite story for your listeners to enjoy and use for storymaking activity? While there is nothing wrong with storytellers who perform, this cannot be the standard for teachers to use when judging their ability to tell a story. All storytellers tell by virtue of their audience's willingness to listen. If the storyteller is interested in the story, chances are the listeners will also be absorbed.

Create a space for storytelling by gathering your children around you, or by having them form a circle, sitting on the floor. Cozy seating helps to establish a "magical" space for telling stories. Starting with a formal beginning, such as "Once upon a time" or "In a place far away and a time long ago," helps students settle into listening, almost as if they are entering a special time and space. Many cultures not only have formal ways to begin the telling of stories, but also have particular ways to end a story. One example from Armenia goes like this: "Three apples fell from heaven; one for the teller of this tale, one for the listener, and one for him who heeds the teller's words." Among the Zuni, the storyteller ends with, "Thus shortens my story" or "Thus lengthens my story." Special endings not only signify the story is over, but also create a transition between the end of the story and the beginning of what is to follow.

All of the storymaking material in this section will be based on the story from Brazil, "How Hummingbird Got Its Color." This story is particularly good to use with beginners because each character has a clearly defined need and the action is easy to follow and understand. However, the story may also be used by more experienced students who are able to explore the issues of want and need with greater depth and complexity.

I include the telling of the story in each session to illustrate where I would tell the story if the class does not already know it. Sometimes, it is good to retell a story if there are a few days between sessions. Not only will we not tell the story exactly the same way each time, but listeners will not hear it the same way each time. Perhaps this is why stories are endlessly fascinating for teller and listeners alike.

The work in this section can be adapted to meet the needs of students of any age, with or without experience. With beginners, choose simple tasks and guide the discussion and reflection with more direct questions and suggestions. With more practiced students, create a complex experience by encouraging children to go deeper into the story, writing stories which explore connections between issues in the stories and those in their lives. How much time each structure takes depends upon the goals, experience, and interest of the teacher and the class.

How Hummingbird Got Its Color

Long ago, Hummingbird was a drab, gray bird who longed to be brightly colored. Whenever she looked at green leaves, blue skies, the yellow sun, red berries, or orange flowers, she sighed, wishing she too could be so pretty. Everywhere she went she asked how she might become more colorful but no one in the forest knew how to help her. Amidst all the beauty she felt dull and plain.

One day, while sipping nectar from a flower, Hummingbird heard a terrible roaring noise. Too frightened to run away as did all the other creatures, Hummingbird looked to see what was causing the commotion. She saw Panther howling with rage. After watching Panther writhe in misery, Hummingbird found the courage to fly to Panther and ask him why he was so unhappy.

"Two nights ago, I accidently stepped on Mouse's nest and killed her baby mice. Then, when I was asleep, Mouse Mother glued my eyes shut with gum and mud. Now I cannot see anything. I do not know if it is day or night. More than anything else in the world, I want to be able to see again."

Hummingbird told Panther, "I know what it is to want something badly. I want to be bright and full of color. I do not want to be drab and dull. I have asked many creatures for their advice but no one knows how to help me. Oh, I wish I knew how to exchange my gray feathers for the colors of the world."

Panther heard Hummingbird's unhappiness. "If you will peck the mud and gum from my eyes so I can see again, I will show you how to make the colors of your feathers bright and beautiful."

Although she was still afraid of Panther, Hummingbird flew to his face and gently pecked all the mud and gum from his eyes. As soon as Panther could see everything as clearly as before, he kept his promise. Joyfully, he took Hummingbird to the place where there were sands and clay of every color in the rainbow.

Panther showed Hummingbird how to mix colors of the earth, sun, moon, and stars, with strands of Spider's silk to create fine threads. Hummingbird wove the threads into a beautiful cloth of many colors, covering her whole body until there was no gray to be seen.

Panther led her to the edge of the water so she could look at herself. "Oh," was all she could say. Smiling, Panther said, "Your new dress is very beautiful." Hummingbird fluttered her wings. Panther opened and closed his eyes. The two friends parted and peacefully went on their way.

Initial Exploration

Focus: Exploring what it feels like to want to be different

Text: "How Hummingbird Got Its Color"

Tell: The first part of "How Hummingbird Got Its Color" up to the point where we know why Hummingbird is unhappy

Paint: Paint an image of Hummingbird

Write: An entry in your diary of one particular day, as if you are Hummingbird, telling what has happened on this day and how you feel about how you look (If children do not write well enough to do this, they can divide into pairs and talk to each other about their day and how they feel.)

Share: Images and diary entries (or main point of conversations)

Think: About a time when you wanted to be different. What made you feel this way? What, if anything, did you do about it? Did you begin to feel better? If not, why not? If so, why? What do you like best about yourself now?

Reflect: On what it's like to want to be different than you are

Paint: An image of yourself liking yourself

Tell: Rest of story

Reflect: On story
(To help children begin talking a teacher might need to ask questions about what makes them feel good about themselves. If children still do not respond, the teacher might recount a time when the class felt good about something they had done.)

Second Exploration

Focus: Exploring what it is like to feel helpless

Text: "How Hummingbird Got Its Color"

Tell: "How Hummingbird Got Its Color"

Paint: An image of Panther when he is feeling helpless

Write: Words that come to mind

Share: Images of helpless and words that came to mind

Imagine: You are Panther, with mud and gum in your eyes

Write: The story of an experience you have while you are
               feeling helpless
               *(If children cannot write they can divide into pairs
               and talk about their feelings as Panther.)*

Share: Stories

Reflect: On what it might be like to feel helpless
               *(Think about a time you felt helpless. What was it
               like for you? What did you do to feel better? Were
               you able to become more capable or independent?
               If children do not respond, the teacher might
               recount a time when he or she was a child and felt
               helpless, then describing how the helplessness
               was resolved in a positive way.)*

Paint: An image of yourself feeling capable or independent

Write: Words that come to mind

Share: Images and words

Reflect: On what it takes to make the transition from feeling
               helpless to feeling capable or independent
               (Think about times when you feel especially

confident and capable. Think about the qualities, skills, or resources you developed to meet challenges with confidence.)

Third Exploration

Focus:	Finding courage
Text:	"How Hummingbird Got Its Color"
Tell:	"How Hummingbird Got Its Color"
Paint:	An image of fear on the left side of the paper
Write:	Words that come to mind
Paint:	An image of courage on the right side of the paper
Write:	Words that come to mind
Share:	Images and words *(Teachers may want to put words on the board.)*
Sculpt:	An image of fear and courage in relationship to each other
Write:	One page of dialogue about what fear and courage say to each other when they talk to each other. What are fear's issues? What does courage know? Under what circumstances might they be talking with each other?
Share:	Script with a partner
Share:	Scripts with group by having partners each read one of the character's parts
Write:	On board some questions and ideas evoked by the scripts

Exploring Written Language

.... 207

Copy: Ideas and questions into a notebook for future storymaking

Write: Titles for stories you might choose to write in the future

Reflect: On questions and ideas evoked by the scripts
(The teacher might begin the discussion by asking children to look at moments in each script that seem important and how these moments reflect the children's feelings about the story and the way the issue reflects experiences in their lives. If children don't respond, the teacher might talk about what constitutes an important monent, citing examples from the class's experiences.)

Fourth Exploration

Focus: Negotiation

Text: "How Hummingbird Got Its Color"

Tell: "How Hummingbird Got Its Color"

Write: On the board all the synonyms for negotiate and negotiation that the class can think of

List: On board the skills it might take to be an effective negotiator

Sculpt: An image of negotiation

Share: Sculptures

Reflect: On questions, ideas, and issues raised
(If children are silent the teacher might stimulate thinking by asking questions such as: Have you ever negotiated or seen people negotiate? If so, under what circumstances? How do people solve problems in film and television? Why is it that guns or violence are used so much more often than

negotiation? What problems might we have in this classroom that could be addressed by negotiation?)

Choose: To be either Hummingbird or Panther

Write: A short newspaper story as Hummingbird or Panther depicting your skills as a negotiator. Describe one situation in which two parties involved in a dispute might benefit from your help. Suggest ways to help the people resolve their differences through negotiation.

Share: Newspaper stories

Reflect: On what it means to negotiate and to be a negotiator *(Examine what it means to be willing to give up something in order to get something else. How does a person negotiating know what to suggest as the terms to begin bargaining? Explore how the class might benefit from knowing how to negotiate.)*

Fifth Exploration

Focus: Getting what you want

Text: "How Hummingbird Got Its Color"

Paint: An image of unhappy on the left side of the paper

Write: Words that describe how you feel when you are unhappy

Paint: An image of happy on the right side of the paper

Write: Some words that describe how you feel when you are happy

Share: Images and words

Tell: "How Hummingbird Got Its Color"

Imagine: An animal who is very unhappy. Think about why it is unhappy.

Sculpt: An image of the unhappy animal

Write: The story of how the unhappy animal finds happiness

Share: Stories. After you share your story, sculpt your unhappy animal into a happy animal. What is it that you change?

Reflect: On what helps make us happy when we are unhappy. Are some forms of happiness longer-lasting than others? If so, why?

Sixth Exploration

Focus: The magic of color

Text: "How Hummingbird Got Its Color"

Tell: "How Hummingbird Got Its Color"

Paint: An image of dull or drab on the left side of the paper

Write: Words that come to mind

Paint: An image of the magic of color on the right side of the paper

Write: Words that come to mind

Write: One word between the two images that helps you go from drab or dull to colorful

Share: Images and words

Reflect: On issues and ideas evoked by the images and words

Imagine: You are in a land where everything is drab and dull, where there is no color. You have been told by your grandparents that once upon a time, there used to be color everywhere but one night it disappeared, never to be found again.

Select: A partner

Sculpt: An image of someone brave enough to search for the color which disappeared one night. Each partner sculpts an image.

Place: Your images in relationship to each other

Write: With your partner the story about how the two of you found color and brought it back to your land

Share: Sculptures and stories

Reflect: On what it might be like to live in a land with no color
(Why might people want to live in a land with color? What effect does color have on you? Are there colors which are special to you? If so, what are they? What makes them special? Are there people and places you associate with particular colors? If so, tell us about one person or place you associate with a particular color or colors.)

Exploring Connections

Expand vocabulary.
Learn antonyms and synonyms for words in the stories, using the dictionary and the thesaurus as sources.

Create songs or poems.
Write the song or poem of Hummingbird when she is dull and gray, longing to be different.
Write the song or poem of Panther when he is feeling helpless.
Write the song or poem of Hummingbird as she weaves and puts on her beautiful cloth.

Write the song or poem of Panther when he is once
again able to see.

Write the song or poem of Hummingbird and
Panther after they have helped each other
and become friends.

Create stories.

Write the adventure Hummingbird has just after she
leaves Panther and is now a brightly colored
bird, feeling happy and content.

Write what happens when Panther meets Mouse
Mother after he is able to see.

Create the story of what happens when
Hummingbird and Panther meet again.

Write letters to friends about Hummingbird and
Panther's experiences.

Create drama.

Turn the story into a play. Think about point of
view—will you write as if you are
Hummingbird or Panther? How do you decide?
What will you add or leave out? How do you
choose the words you decide to use? How do you
make Hummingbird and Panther into
characters who feel and think, react and act?
Some choices are productive, such as
Hummingbird's decision to help Panther even
though she is afraid of him. Some choices
lead to dead ends, such as Panther deciding to
eat Hummingbird rather than help her. How
do you make productive choices? When is a
variation a whole new story or play? What
events might you add yet still keep the same title
for the play as the story? What might you
title the play you write if you make many
changes? How do you decide?

Exploration of Drama

Although the drama exploration in this section focuses on writing and
developing scripts, we cannot effectively improve a script without reading

it out loud. Hearing one's scripts spoken by others enables the playwright to reflect on how the characters' speech and action feel and sound. Playwrights watch and listen to hear and see if the words and action are consonant. As audience members participating in the development of scripts, we want to know if the script enables us to develop a deeper understanding of who the characters are, why they do what they do, and what consequences ensue. Playwrights know that writing a play, no matter how short, is a process that takes time and interaction with those who act and those who watch. The joy of writing a play comes from seeing what was once an idea in our heads transform into life created by actors on stage.

The most difficult part of playwriting is finding an idea that is playable, for the essence of drama is action. Working from a story provides students with ways to begin, as each person connects to the part of the story which is personally moving. Folktales and myths are particularly useful because in these stories the characters are seldom well-defined or fully described. Usually the characters are known by birth order—the youngest son—or by physical attribute—the beautiful daughter, or by a special quality—the dumling (the child who isn't smart). This lack of specificity allows the playwright to use the structure of the story to create characters which may come from the story but are particularized by the writer.

The following story from Ecuador provides an interesting framework for inexperienced playwrights to begin dramatic writing. The six initial explorations suggest ways to spark interest in dramatic writing that can be used with any story that intrigues a child. In each exploration I indicate where I would tell the story if the children have not already heard the story. The second set of six explorations suggests ways to turn a story into a play with a beginning, middle, and end.

I do not have students make a play from a story just to dramatize a story, although this can be valuable in terms of learning to write in dramatic form. Rather, I want students to use the story to find their own story, to write about what the story personally stimulates within them. It is not important that students write a play which tells the same story as the told story. The point is to use the form to uncover meaning, and to let this meaning emerge, so that students write a play, having learned to create vital characters who are engaged in personally meaningful struggle.

When working with the initial six explorations, teachers need to create an effective collaborative learning environment to build support and foster quality writing among class members. Sharing work in progress is a necessary stage of development in dramatic writing and can be used to deepen all writing, regardless of the form being explored.

Although each of the second six explorations focuses on one aspect of writing, such as a monologue or a scene of meeting, work on the writing can easily extend over several sessions to include writing, reading work out loud, rewriting, reading work out loud with new listeners, rewriting, sharing work with a larger group, and rewriting, until the playwright feels satisfied that the work is either finished or represents the best she or he can do at the moment. Most playwrights come to a point in their writing when the energy of their impulse is exhausted and they have to let the work sit for a while so they can see it with "new" eyes when they once again begin to work on it.

Teachers may also want to work through the second six explorations without much rewriting to give students a sense of dramatic form and what they need to learn in order to write a play. The best advice I ever got about playwriting came from a producer friend who told me, "Don't rewrite until you have a full first draft. It's only after the play is plotted that you know who your characters will be." In fact, even in second and third drafts characters are created and discarded as the playwright's sense of the play clarifies and deepens.

Following the first and second set of explorations is a collection of theatre terms commonly used in writing and making drama. Because playwrights benefit most from seeing their work performed, suggestions are made regarding ways to stimulate, make, and perform new work, the point of which is to help playwrights see their work more clearly, rather than to perform for the sake of performance.

There is no age or grade designation for these drama activities because I have helped young students write plays, even as I struggled with older children who had fewer skills. Age and experience affect what children are able to accomplish as does student/teacher interaction, teacher enthusiasm and ability, and student curiosity. Therefore, I have designed the work in this chapter for teachers to use as a springboard, to devise the tasks that best suit their students' needs and abilities.

The Lake Where the Sky Touches the Water

Long ago there lived a ruler of the Incas who had only one son, a sickly boy whose health grew worse despite the many doctors and healers who tried to cure him. Eager to find help, the emperor sought advice from all his counselors but nothing made his son well. As time passed, the emperor grew more desperate.

One night, he made a fire in the altar and said, "Great One, I am growing old. My son is dying. Who will lead our nation? Tell me how to heal my son so he may take his place as ruler of our people."

A voice came from the fire, "There is a lake where the sky touches the water. Your son will be cured when he drinks water from this lake." As the fire burned out, the emperor found a golden flask in the ashes.

Too old to make such an arduous journey, the emperor proclaimed that whoever filled the flask with water from the lake would be richly rewarded.

Not far from the palace lived a husband and wife with two sons and a young daughter. The sons were tired of farming and persuaded their parents to let them make the journey. Although they searched everywhere, they could not find the Lake Where the Sky Touches the Water.

Discouraged, they sat down beside a brook. "What shall we do? We will never find the lake," said one.

"Perhaps there is no such lake," said the other. "We cannot keep looking. We must soon return home to help with the harvest. Let us take water from this brook and bring it to the palace. Perhaps it will cure the prince."

When the two reached the room where the prince lay, pale and weak, the emperor could not pour the water into the golden flask. The emperor's magician said, "This water is not from the Lake Where the Sky Touches the Water." Furious, the emperor threw the two young men into prison and once again sent out his messengers, pleading for someone to find the healing water.

Their little sister was tending her llamas when she heard the messengers. She begged her parents, "Please let me go, the little prince is dying." Finally her parents agreed and gave her their blessing. She harnessed her favorite llama and set out with food, water, and chicha, a drink made from crushed corn.

The little girl traveled all day and found a snug place to sleep, but during the night she heard the cries of a puma. Fearing for the life of her llama, she sent him home. The next night, sleeping in a tree, she was aroused by sparrows. "Poor little girl. She will never find the lake without our help."

"Forgive me for listening to your conversation, " she said, "but I would be grateful for your help. The emperor's son will soon die if he does not drink the healing water."

Each of the sparrows gave the girl a feather with which to make a fan. Following their directions, she put one feather on each of the fingers of her right hand. With her left hand, the little girl took the ribbon from her hair and wove it around the feathers, arranging them to make a fan. The oldest sparrow told her, "The lake is guarded by terrible creatures, each more horrible than the one before it, but if you hold the fan to your face, you will not be harmed."

A soft breeze carried the girl out of the tree, higher and higher, past huge mountains covered with snow, until it gently set her down on the shore of the Lake Where the Sky Touches the Water. As the little girl stood by the water's edge, she wondered how to carry the water. Hearing a soft thud she turned and looked. There, at the edge of the lake was a golden flask.

Just as she was about to dip the flask into the water a beast with a menacing voice said, "Go away from here or I shall eat you." The child held the fan to her face, turned away, and the beast fell asleep, gently returning to the bottom of the lake.

Dipping the flask into the water, she heard a second voice growling horribly, "Leave the lake or I will swallow you." Touching the fan to her face, the girl turned away, and the huge beast sank out of sight.

As she was filling the flask, she heard a booming, ferocious voice bubbling up from the water, "If you take one drop of my water I promise you shall not see the sun set." Holding the fan to her face, the little girl looked at the enormous beast until it too disappeared beneath the water's surface.

Quickly, the girl filled the flask and begged the wind, "Take me to the palace." Before she could say another word, she was standing at the entrance to the palace. "I must see the emperor immediately," she demanded. "I bring water from the Lake Where the Sky Touches the Water."

Hearing this, the guard hurriedly took her to the prince's room where the grieving emperor sat beside his dying son. The little girl rushed to the prince and touched his parched lips with healing water from the flask. Color returned to his face. She helped him swallow a few drops and soon he was sitting up. After a long drink, the prince said, "Father, I am well."

The grateful emperor asked the little girl what she wanted as her reward. She responded with no hesitation. "I have three wishes. Free my brothers. Return the five feathers of the magic fan to the sparrows. Grant my parents enough animals and a farm so large they will never again be poor."

"Done," commanded the emperor, smiling with joy. The little girl and her two brothers returned home where they were joyfully welcomed by their happy parents.

Creating a Framework for Writing Drama

After the story is told, most students will use the exact details of the story to write unless they are helped to expand their vision and learn how to enter into the story. However, no matter how the teacher structures the task, there will probably be a few children who will use the story as their story, with little or no development. Even when this happens, there is benefit regarding language development and expression—students must still make many decisions regarding word choice, sequence, accent, point of view, and tone.

The following activities are suggested to encourage students to explore metaphor, memory, and personal invention after the story has been told. Although they are sequenced for clarity from easiest to most complex, teachers can work with the material in any order. Though there are no suggestions regarding grade because no two groups have the same capabilities, when working with young or inexperienced children keep each task simple, putting the focus on exploring the form and developing acuity of expression.

Initial Exploration

Focus: Imagining a character in the story

Text: "The Lake Where the Sky Touches the Water"

Tell: "The Lake Where the Sky Touches the Water"

Paint: A telling moment from the story that includes at least one character

Title: Image

Write: A letter to one of the characters in the image. Tell the character how you feel about what is happening to her or him. Ask the character a question.

Collect: Letters, folding them in half. Place in box.

Select: From the box a letter to a character

Answer: Letter as if you are the character. Answer the question as part of the letter.

Read: Both letters

Reflect: On questions, answers, issues, and ideas contained in the letters. Return letter to original writer. *(What is the difference, if any, when you write to or answer as a character and when you write to someone as yourself? What might it take to create a character who makes different choices than you do?)*

Second Exploration

Focus: Inventing a character using the story as framework

Text: "The Lake Where the Sky Touches the Water"

Tell: "The Lake Where the Sky Touches the Water"

Sculpt: An image of a character from a particular point in the story in relationship to a character and situation you invent

Write: A page of dialogue between the character from the story and the character you invent

Read: Script with a partner, each helping to read the other's script

Share: Scripts with the class or in groups of six. If possible, the playwright's script should be read by other people so the playwright can hear her or his words.

Ask: Questions of playwright about issues, ideas, or characters you would like to know more about. Playwrights write down questions without answering them.

Reflect: As a class, thinking about what it takes to create a character and situation using the story as a framework. How do you invent characters who connect with a character from the story but who are not in the story? What information do you need to do this?

Third Exploration

Focus: Using the time between two incidents to create a play

Text: "The Lake Where the Sky Touches the Water"

Tell: "The Lake Where the Sky Touches the Water"

Paint:	An image of the first point in the story which is important to you
Paint:	An image of the next point in the story
Write:	The story of what happens between the two points in the story *(For example, perhaps your first image is of the girl in the air flying to the lake. Perhaps the second image is of the girl landing on the shore of the lake. The story might be about the girl's journey to the lake and might incorporate what she sees, hears, feels, thinks, and says.)*
Share:	Images and stories with a partner
Reflect:	On what it takes to imagine and create a story from a story with the whole class

Fourth Exploration

Focus:	Creating a script from your story
Text:	"The Lake Where the Sky Touches the Water"
Title:	The story you wrote in the third exploration
Create:	A one-page script from the story you have written
In fours:	Share scripts, with two people (other than playwright) reading playwright's dialogue
Share:	The invented situations with the whole class
Ask:	Questions of playwrights to stimulate their imagination and sense of possibility *(For example, suppose the script is about the girl's journey to the lake. Questions might include: How high did the girl fly? What did the wind feel like? What stops did the wind make? What did the girl see as she flew? What scary adventure did*

*she have on her way? Who did the girl meet as
she flew through the air?*

> *Playwrights need to write down the questions
without answering them because the questions
are meant to stimulate imagination and ideation.
If playwrights feel they are getting too many
questions, they can always ask the class to stop by
saying that they have enough material with
which to work.)*

Reflect: On process of inventing the detail, characters, and
action to write a play
*(Think about what helps you imagine and invent.
What gets in your way? How can you and your
classmates best help each other?)*

Fifth Exploration

Focus: Continuing a story and transforming it into a play

Text: "The Lake Where the Sky Touches the Water"

Tell: "The Lake Where the Sky Touches the Water"

Paint: An image of the girl at the end of the story

Write: Words that come to mind which describe the girl

Imagine: That while the girl is riding her llama she has an
adventure

Sculpt: An image of a person or creature she encounters

Write: A few words about the encounter

Create: A conflict between the girl and the person or creature

Write: One or two pages of dialogue exploring the conflict

Paint: An image of resolution

Write: One or two pages of dialogue which contain the climax and denouement (pronounced day-new-mon), the action in the play that follows the climax and reveals how the conflict is resolved

In fours: Read each other's scripts out loud while the playwright listens

Ask: Questions of each playwright to help develop ideas and writing

Share: Some suggestions which might help develop ideas and writing with the whole class and list them on the board for discussion

Reflect: On how imagination can be stimulated and expanded. On how ideas, characters, and situations are invented. Think about ways classmates can support and foster collaboration.

Sixth Exploration

Focus: Connecting the story and self

Text: "The Lake Where the Sky Touches the Water"

Tell: "The Lake Where the Sky Touches the Water"

Paint: An image of a point in the story which feels important to you

Think: About a time in your life which comes to mind when you think about this point

Imagine: You are a writer

Write: The story of the memory as if you were inventing a story. Create yourself as if you are a character, giving yourself a new name. Make up a pen (new) name for yourself as playwright. This helps to

give you a different perspective and can create
productive distance.

Title: Your story

Script: Your story using no more than a total of three
characters, adding any additional information or
action that comes to mind. Use your story as your
point of departure. Feel free to leave your story
and the folktale behind.

Share: Scripts in small groups so playwrights can hear their
words

Reflect: On process with the whole class
*(Think about the role of imagination and creativity
when writing a play. Consider what you need as
a playwright to imagine, invent, develop, and deepen
your work and ability. Think about ways to
create action that reveals rather than tells how a
character feels about a particular person,
experience, or idea.)*

Writing Drama

The previous explorations give students a variety of experiences which
enable them to create a new story or a script from the told story, rather
than using the story exactly as it was told. Students need to realize that
each of us, as we listen, hear our own version of the story and that this
unique response has value; our reactions help us to learn about ourselves
and what matters to us. Writing plays gives playwrights the opportunity
to explore different ideas about what it means to be human, using their
own wishes, dreams, and ideas as the lens through which they view the
world.

During the writing process, instead of focusing on judgment (good,
bad, right, or wrong) teachers and students benefit from using the
idea of *productive choice*—exploring how choice affects action and/or
development. Students examine how the choices they make further,
hinder, or even stop work in progress. Nonproductive choice closes
doors, productive choice opens them. The time for judgment occurs

only when playwrights are ready to polish their work, close to the point in creation when playwrights have written at least two or three drafts and are ready and prepared to hone their script.

Most playwrights reach a time when they feel empty—they have nothing more or new to say. When this happens it is often wise to put the play away for awhile until we have a new perspective. Teachers may want to explore a script-writing project and give students a few weeks to let their work "simmer" before looking at it again. Students can learn a lot about the creative process when they are given the time they need to learn how to make their work reflect their intentions.

Initial Exploration

Focus: Establishing the main character

Text: "The Lake Where the Sky Touches the Water"

Tell: "The Lake Where the Sky Touches the Water"

Paint: An image of the character who most interests you
*(This person does not necessarily have to be the
main character, or even a character in the story
as told—it could be the tree that the girl sleeps in.
Choose or create a character who piques your curiosity
as a playwright. The choice of main character affects
the point of view from which the play is written.
For example, if the main character is the ill prince,
the emperor, or one of the two brothers, ways
have to be found to let the character know what is
happening. A playwright can also frame the play
to suit personal interest. Perhaps the play focuses
on the emperor's search to find the way to cure
his son rather than on the cure itself. The play might
explore how the two brothers only wished to help
their parents and didn't mean to lie.)*

Write: Some words that describe the character you have
chosen

Exploring Written Language

.... 223

In pairs: Share images and words. Tell what interests you about your character. Ask questions that come to mind as you imagine who your character is, what your character wants, and what is special about your character

(When students talk about the character they choose, make sure they don't judge the character. Judgment freezes the exploration of a character, preventing further development of the character, action, and interaction. Instead, ask students to look at what their character does from the character's point of view, the circumstances under which it is done, the consequences of choice, and how the choice affects the character's feelings. This is not to say that whatever a character does is good. Rather, playwrights focus on observing, describing, and verbalizing the intentions, actions, and feelings of their chosen character. Judgment is reserved for the audience.)

Write: A monologue that your character speaks at an essential moment in the beginning of the story in your imagination

(There are two kinds of monologues: interior—*where the character speaks to him or herself; and* exterior—*where the character either talks to another person or directly to the audience. A monologue enables the character to let the audience know what she or he is thinking and feeling at a particular moment and helps intensify the audience's vicarious connection with the character.*

The first time a teacher asks students to write a monologue, the class may respond with blank stares and "Huhs?" A teacher with little practice in teaching playwriting is likely to feel that writing monologues might be a bad idea or too difficult. What students need is reassurance that they can do it, that quality is not an issue, that it is fun, and that the more they write the easier it becomes.

When working with a group of fifth graders

who looked bewildered when told to write a monologue, I asked them, "Who remembers being accused of something you didn't do?" Almost all the hands went up. "Who remembers not saying anything out loud when you were accused?" Lots of hands went up. "Who is willing to tell us what you were thinking, but not speaking, when you were being accused." Several people shared their thoughts. "Okay," I said. "What you've just told us is an interior monologue. Had you told it to a friend, it would have been an exterior monologue. Any problems?" Relieved, the class began writing.

A good way to help students begin writing a monologue is to ask them to create a precipitating circumstance, *an important event, experience, or memory, which immediately affects their character, triggering powerful thoughts, feelings and/or a need to take action.)*

In pairs: Read your monologue to your partner. Partner asks whatever questions come to mind such as: What does your character look like? What matters to your character? What is good about your character's life? What conflict does your character feel or think about? Why does this issue matter to your character now? Playwright listens, notes questions, but does not answer them. When partner has no more questions, reverse roles and repeat the process.

Share: Experience of writing and reading your monologue out loud

Reflect: With whole class on what makes a monologue interesting to hear and watch. Explore questions playwrights can use to deepen and intensify their character's expression.
(For example, it is more interesting for an audience to watch a character involved in the process of coming to a decision than it is to hear the decision. Coming to a decision is more active than is the actual decision, and allows the character to reveal

more about character identity and relationship with other people. A well-written monologue creates an opportunity for a character to grapple with an issue of great and immediate importance to the character.

This process may be repeated many times, but each time a writer rewrites, the writer learns most when she or he has a new objective or question to explore. As students become more experienced they can explore how to make a moment *[the point in the drama where the audience vicariously experiences what the actors are experiencing], and how to write with awareness of* pace *[timing],* rhythm *[variety of time within a work] and* dynamics *[overall shape of work].*

When writing a new draft, playwrights can confer with each other to determine what focus makes the most sense. Discussing ideas, painting images, and sharing bits of speeches collaboratively facilitates writing and grappling with issues.)

Second Exploration

Focus: Developing character and plot

Text: "The Lake Where the Sky touches the Water"

Tell: "The Lake Where the Sky Touches the Water"

Sculpt: An image of two characters, in relationship, meeting for the first time. One or both of the characters can be made up. Choose the specific moment which is of greatest importance to your characters.

Write: A short scene based on your sculpture
                (Consider the following question: Who are your characters? Why are they meeting? What do they want? If there is conflict, what is the problem? If there is no conflict, why are they meeting? What

are some consequences of the meeting? What might happen if the meeting never occurred?)

In threes: The playwright listens while two students read the playwright's script. Those reading may ask questions about intention, motivation, action, and resolution. In turn, all three scripts are read and questions are asked.

Rewrite: Script taking readers'/listeners' questions into consideration

In threes: Share reworked script with two new people

Share: Questions and comments about the experiences with the class as a whole. Think about what you need to know in order to continue writing.
(Consider the scripts you have heard or the one you are writing. What, if anything, stays in your mind? What impact does this material have on you? If the script were to be continued, what would you be interested in knowing? What makes you interested? If you are not interested, why do you think this is so? Share your concerns with other playwrights by asking questions which help to deepen their scripts rather than by telling them what you think is good or bad about their work.)

Reflect: On what it means to write a scene
(Think about how scenes interconnect to make a whole play. What do you know now, having written a monologue and a short scene with dialogue, that you didn't know before you started? How does hearing your work spoken by various people affect your ideas as a playwright? How do you decide to make changes in your writing? What kinds of questions or comments are particularly important in furthering your learning? How do you structure action to reveal motivation, intention, and emotion?)

Third Exploration

Focus: Creating an event in drama

Text: "The Lake Where the Sky Touches the Water"

Tell: "The Lake Where the Sky Touches the Water"

Think: About the story as you see it in your mind's eye, and what the story means to you

Paint: An image of a scene in the story which is of great importance to you. You can include a character or situation which you invent or insert into the told story

Write: Brief answers to the following questions quickly, without spending time thinking before writing: Who is in the scene? What does each person want? Why are they together now? What is the *conflict* (point of difference) or *crisis* (where the conflict is most intense)? Who is the most important person in the scene? Why? Who begins the action in the scene? How does the scene end? What questions does the action in the scene raise? For whom? Why does the scene matter to you, the playwright?

Write: A short scene with no more than three characters, based on the image you painted and your answers to the questions

In fours: Share one playwright's scene at a time—two or three people reading and the playwright listening. After each scene is read, the three people ask the playwright questions to deepen the work. Playwright writes down the questions for use when rewriting.

Share: Thoughts about the process, questions regarding the process, and general comments about the experience with the whole class. If time permits, one playwright might share a scene to help the class explore what makes a helpful question.

Reflect: On what it takes to write a compelling scene *(Depending on time, students might rework their scene once more and share it with three new people. What matters is that students have a sense of the process of playwriting and understand how to deepen their work through writing and reading the work out loud in a collaborative environment.)*

Fourth Exploration

Focus: Creating a crisis

Text: "The Lake Where the Sky Touches the Water"

Tell: "The Lake Where the Sky Touches the Water"

Sculpt: An image of a crisis in the story which feels most powerful and important to you. Feel free to invent your own crisis using information from the story. Include no more than three characters. Generally, each play has one crisis which fuels the play and informs each scene. Within each scene there may be conflict which arises from the difficulties characters have trying to accomplish their goals or satisfy their needs.

Write: A scene which explores this crisis including no more than three characters. To end a scene, particularly a powerful scene, the playwright has to present enough information so the audience knows what the problem is, but not so much information that the audience feels the problem is solved.

In fours: Share each playwright's scene in turn, reading the scenes out loud. Readers/listeners ask the playwright questions which the playwright writes down for later use in rewriting.

Share: Thoughts about process, questions regarding the process, and general comments about creating and writing a scene which reveals the crisis of the play. If time permits, one playwright might share a scene to help the class learn how to ask effective questions, to explore how one knows how and when to start and stop a scene that explores and defines the crisis of the play.

Reflect: On what it takes to decide on the crisis of the play, how one writes it, and ways to start and stop the scene
(Students benefit from reworking and sharing their scene with three new people. Stressing process rather than product establishes the importance and benefits of collaboration.)

Fifth Exploration

Focus: Creating a climax

Text: "The Lake Where the Sky Touches the Water"

Tell: "The Lake Where the Sky Touches the Water"

Paint: An image of the climax (where the plot begins to be resolved). Feel free to invent your own climax based on how the story resonates within you.

Sculpt: The characters (no more than three) who are in the scene and place them in relationship to each other at the most important point in the scene

Write: A scene where the plot begins to be resolved
(To focus the writing of the scene, students might briefly outline the events of the scene that need to be included. The climax should not be confused with the denouement, which is the action that resolves issues remaining after the climax has been reached.)

In fours: Share scene with three others, each playwright in turn hearing their scene read aloud. Readers/

SOURCEWORK

230 ···

listeners ask questions which the playwright writes
down but does not attempt to answer.
*(Make sure students do not defend, justify, or even
explain their writing at this point, for the work
is just beginning.)*

Share: Thoughts about the process, questions about how
to decide which point in the play is the crisis,
how to resolve it, and how to start and stop a scene

Reflect: As a class, on how a playwright decides what
constitutes a climax and how it relates to scenes
that come before and after
*(Students profit from discussing their work with
other playwrights and from having many
opportunities to write, hear their work read, and to
rewrite. It is important, if the rewriting is to be
a genuine exploration, that playwrights undertake
each rewriting with new ideas to explore,
whether they be about character, action, plot
development, or language. As students learn to
ask effective questions, they can be of enormous
help to each other. Teachers might want to label
the time students use to write plays in class as the
"Playwrights' Collaborative," thus stressing the
special nature of the work. Theatre is always a
collaborative art—many people are needed to
transform the work from words on a page to live
actors creating characters on the stage. This is
a fine time for students to experience the struggle
and joy of working collaboratively.)*

Sixth Exploration

Focus: Writing a short play

Text: "The Lake Where the Sky Touches the Water"
*(This activity may take place over several sessions
and students may write in and out of class. Each
session has to have a clear task so that students
know exactly what to focus on in their writing.*

I highly recommend that each session end with sharing and reflection, with classmates, parents, and/or friends, so that writers have some sense of what they have done, and how they think and feel about their work. If sharing and reflection take place out of class, students need to know the importance of structuring the feedback so that it is helpful rather than hindering or hurtful. Using the question mode [where writers write down the question without answering] helps to focus the readers'/listeners' responses beneficially.)

Tell: "The Lake Where the Sky Touches the Water"

Paint: Images of all the scenes you want to have in your play (no more than three). Feel free to invent scenes and characters which are not in the told story but which interest you.
(The number of characters in each scene and the number of scenes in the play is purposely limited so that beginning writers are not overwhelmed by too much complexity.)

Write: For each image: Who is in the scene? What brings them together at this time? What does each person want? What action takes place during this scene? How does the scene begin? How does the scene end? What questions are answered by the scene? What questions remain unresolved?
(If the session ends here, students share their ideas with a partner and focus on whether the sequence of scenes seems complete. Questions by partner examine the sequence logic, character development, and the way the action reveals character feeling, motivation, and intention.

Reflection by the group focuses on how a playwright decides which are the important and necessary scenes, what information needs to be known about each scene, and how characters grow and/or change as the play unfolds.)

Write: The play
(For each scene written the playwright must decide: Who is in the scene [no more than three characters]? What does each character want? What is the central conflict? Why are the characters together at this time? What are the consequences of their meeting? How does the end of this scene lead into the next scene? How is the conflict eventually resolved or the play ended?)

In fours: Share work. Students can share their writing scene by scene or as a whole play. The readers'/listeners' task is to ask questions which help the playwright deepen and enhance the writing. If the group has difficulties, it helps to write down questions or concerns to share with the larger group when the class meets as a whole.

Share: As a class, the experiences of writing, reading, and/ or hearing a play or scenes from a play. Put questions and concerns on the blackboard for group to discuss when reflecting on the process of writing scenes which make a whole play.

Reflect: On questions and concerns arising from writing a play, having the play read, rewriting the play, etc., until the playwright is ready to have the play performed, *script in hand*. This is the stage of playwriting where the playwright, or a person designated as director, works with actors who read the parts and play the action to give the playwright a sense of flow, word choice, character motivation, action, and resolution. This "performance" enables the playwright to sense the worth of the play as actors take the words from the page and move them onto the stage, creating in real time and real space.

Exploring Connections

Create movement.
Create the movement of each of the three beasts.
Create the making of the fan in movement.
Create a movement journey for the girl.

Create songs or poems.
Write a song or poem for each character as his or
her introduction to the audience.
Write a song or poem that sets the tone for the play.
Write a song or poem that all the characters speak
to end the play.

Expand vocabulary.
Find new words which are appropriate for the
characters to use.
Use the dictionary and thesaurus to find antonyms
and synonyms.

Improve reading fluency.
Read scripts to improve reading comprehension.
Read stories to develop ideas for new plays.

Improve self-esteem.
Work with others to produce a new play through
collaboration and cooperation.
Learn to negotiate and resolve conflicts without
violence or bullying.

Create stories.
Make up new stories based on ideas evoked from
plays.
Work in pairs or small groups to create ideas for
new plays.

Develop language.
Select a pen pal from the class. Write to each other
as if you are characters in the same play.
Discuss what is happening to each of you as these
characters. Collect the letters and make them
into a book as part of a series, *Letters from
Famous Characters*.
Write a prologue to introduce the play or an epilogue
as an afterword to the play.
Write a monologue that a character might speak
within the play that is not part of the script.
Write a letter the girl might write to her
grandchildren about her experiences when
she was a young girl.

Create a dialogue between the girl and a character of your choosing which takes place ten years after the story ends.

Selected Theatre Vocabulary

- *Blocking:*   The pattern of movement which actors follow in order to underscore what they are saying and feeling
- *Climax:*   The point at which the conflict begins to be resolved
- *Conflict:*   The problem or issue which motivates the play
- *Crisis:*   The point at which the conflict is most intense and cannot be ignored or denied by the characters
- *Denouement:*   The action following the climax where unresolved issues are resolved
- *Dynamics:*   The overall rhythmic pattern of scenes and play
- *Emotional projection:*   The intensity with which actors speak and move, allowing the audience to feel what the actor is feeling. The larger the space, the more an actor has to project.
- *Exposition:*   The writing that explains what an audience needs to know about characters, setting, conflict, and action
- *Focus:*   What the director does to make sure the stage picture enhances and is consonant with what actors are saying and doing
- *Intention:*   What a character aims to do
- *Moment:*   The instance of impact where the audience feels what the actor is feeling. A moment is made when good writing, good acting, correct timing, and focus all come together.
- *Motivation:*   The ideas, feelings, experiences, and actions that cause characters to feel, speak, act, and interact
- *Nonverbal communication:*   What actors do through the use of movement, vocal tone, tension level, and eye contact to show what their character is feeling and thinking
- *Pace:*   The timing with which actors speak and move
- *Point of view:*   The person whose perception informs the action of the play. Also, the chosen focus of the director.
- *Projection:*   The volume at which actors speak in order to be heard
- *Props:*   Objects that actors use to create characters' lives on stage
- *Rhythm:*   The variety in timing with which actors speak and move

- *Through line:*   The central idea, conflict, or action which is the spine or core of the play, and which motivates all dialogue and action in each scene.
- *Set:*   The environment in which the actors play the play
- *Stage geography:*   From the actors' point of view (facing the audience): stage right, stage left, upstage (the back), downstage (the front), center stage. House refers to where the audience sits.
- *Willing suspension of disbelief:*   A believable reality created by the playwright, where action and setting is consistent and acceptable to the audience

Some Questions to Consider When Looking at a Script

- What information does the script provide to help actors build their characters?
- What information does the actor have to invent? What are the parameters which guide the actor? What are some productive choices, justified by the script, actors might consider when building a character? What information in the script helps actors choose between various productive choices?
- How is the conflict played out in each scene?
- What is the crisis?
- Where is the climax?
- Where is the moment in each scene?
- What do we need to know about the play, characters, conflict, and action, in order to make the moment happen for the audience? What script information do we need in order to design the blocking, nonverbal communication, action, and emotional projection in order to make a moment?
- Does the language of the play reflect character, create a believable reality, and further the playwright's intention?
- Has the playwright created a script where there is variety in feeling and action? For example, if the script contains a lot of scenes where people are tense, angry, and/or frightened, the audience may begin to laugh in inappropriate places because the playwright has not provided audience release. This is why Shakespeare always included comic relief, even in his darkest tragedies.
- Does the script contain complete information for a director to direct the play without consulting the playwright?

Playing the Play: Script in Hand

The performance experiences in this section have to do with helping playwrights hear and see their work, a vital part of the playwriting process. Therefore, all that is required for these performances are scripts for each actor, a director to help the actors play the play, and a few people to watch the work and share their responses with the playwright and actors.

FIRST READ-THROUGH   The director is in charge of the reading and assigns roles, before reading when possible. Each actor has her or his own script. It is best if actors receive scripts before read through to facilitate a fluent reading without interruption. Stage directions are best read by a person not reading a role. The playwright listens and makes notes on script regarding problems and the nature of the problem. The discussion after the reading centers on how the script works in terms of believable characterization and action, conflict, and resolution. Suggestions for the playwright are best made in question form and are written down by the playwright for future use. Encourage playwrights to listen openly, without defensiveness, to enjoy the exchange of ideas and responses.

SECOND READ-THROUGH   Director assigns roles. Playwright listens and takes notes. Discussion centers on what the playwright needs to consider before script is performed.

REHEARSALS   When working on a new script there are always rough spots, either in the writing or in the action of the script, so it is important for the playwright to be present at all rehearsals. The director is in charge of rehearsals and the performance. If a playwright has questions or disagrees with the director, these matters are discussed after the rehearsal with the director.

Because the scripts are being performed to give playwrights a chance to see and hear their work, it is beneficial for actors to play the play with their scripts in hand rather than taking time to memorize the script. This serves two functions: first, playwrights are able to make changes in the script up until the performance; second, actors can focus on creating their characters and playing their action, speaking the playwright's exact words, without having to worry about memorizing the script. The latter is especially important for new playwrights because when actors are struggling to remember lines they usually invent their own, thus depriving playwrights of the opportunity to hear their script as they wrote it.

After roles have been assigned, the cast and director read the play together, with the actors on their feet, each actor paying attention to how her or his character behaves, what the character wants, and how the character does or does not get this. Before each rehearsal begins, directors focus the rehearsal by telling actors what will be explored, whether it is blocking, character development, fluency of speaking, or emotional projection.

At the first rehearsal after the read through, the director blocks the play, working with the actors to develop a plan so that actors know when to move, why, and with what intention and result. All movement connotes something. If actors move away from each other this may suggest that there is disagreement. If actors stand very close to each other the audience may conclude that they like each other or at least feel comfortable with one another. Although some directors tell actors what to do, a collaborative approach provides the most learning for everyone involved.

For example, suppose an actor unconsciously moves toward another actor while she is reading, suggesting to the director that this movement is organic to the life of the scene. The astute director will bring this to the actor's attention so the actor can make what was unconscious, conscious. Blocking also prevents traffic jams on stage, which is especially important if actors are working in small spaces.

After actors know where and when to move, they focus on how. They think about what informs their action and behavior—what it is they want from the other characters in the situation. This is also the time that actors and directors make sure there is emotional projection, that actors are able to show their characters' feelings. The smaller the acting space and distance between actors and audience, the easier it is for inexperienced actors to show their feelings. Conversely, too large a space, especially for beginning actors, will make it difficult for them to fill the space, thus depriving playwrights of important information regarding the emotional life of their play.

The next step is to make sure actors can be seen and heard by the audience. During rehearsals directors usually sit in various parts of the house to make sure there is visibility and audibility, and to check that all props and/or furniture are safe for the actors to use—no pointy edges, unbalanced boxes, or unsafe ladders.

Actors, director, and playwright can decide what costumes or props (if any) they want to use. These should be kept to a minimum so as not to distract from the main focus, allowing playwrights to see and hear their words in action. Because there are many plays being worked on in a class, students might wish to create a set using common "furniture," such as wooden crates from a supermarket and simple props like scarves, hats, aprons, etc., to suggest character. When I staged a play festival for new scripts, all the plays were played on a bare stage with one or two common bits of furniture. It was fascinating to see how the actors created different worlds through their speech and action and one or two props unique to their character.

In a class of twenty-seven it is possible to have four groups rehearsing simultaneously—three actors, one director, one playwright, and two or three observers to give feedback to the actors and the director as to what they see and hear. After each rehearsal, especially when several groups are rehearsing at the same time, the class benefits from meeting as a whole for a few minutes to discuss what has happened and to reflect on the work in progress. This not only accentuates the collaborative nature of the theatre process, but also encourages students to ask questions and explore "stuck places," making it possible for the group to suggest new approaches. Generally, three or four rehearsals allow playwrights to make necessary changes in their scripts and give the actors time to familiarize themselves with their characters' words and actions.

PERFORMANCE   Performance is exciting, even in a classroom where actors may be playing in a small space emptied of chairs and desks. What makes theatre special is not fancy costumes, bright lights, and special effects, but the world the actors create through their involvement in the action, taking place in real time and real space. What differentiates live theatre from television and movies is that no matter how or what actors have rehearsed, nothing can be taken for granted. The audience experiences only what happens at each performance—actors playing in the present in real time and real space.

POST-PERFORMANCE DISCUSSION   All performances of new scripts are works in progress. If there is an invited audience (people other than class members), they too become part of the exploratory process by participating in a discussion with the playwright, director, actors, and class after the performance. Because the invited audience members may not be familiar with the method of asking questions to deepen and enhance a script, the teacher needs to explain conversation guidelines and suggest beneficial ways of responding to the play before the discussion begins. The teacher directs the discussion to protect participants from unwanted and unnecessary judgment and criticism.

After the discussion with the audience, the original groups of actors, playwright, director, and observers benefit from meeting and talking about the performance experience. At this time playwrights may decide to make final changes in their script, based on their experience of the play, the groups' assessment of the script, and the performance. Care must be taken not to let negative feelings influence the discussion. Once a person blames, defensive reactions begin. I find it useful to lay out the parameters of the discussion: What issues are we looking at? What do we want to learn? How do we reflect on our experience? What do we know now that we didn't know before? What can we take from this experience to use when we write or perform our next play?

SCRIPT LIBRARY   After each play has been performed, the script can be typed in appropriate form, bound, copied (one for the playwright), and kept in a "script library" in the classroom or school library. This not only makes the work of the class visible, but also serves as material for reading and future writing. Playwrights might want to write sequels or create a new play about one of the characters not fully explored or issues which were evoked by the original play.

FESTIVAL OF NEW PLAYS   Students who have worked hard at playwriting may find it enjoyable to perform all the scripts written during the year in a festival of new plays, inviting other students, parents, and/or friends. This not only provides a new opportunity for playwrights to see their scripts performed, but also creates an occasion for classmates to demonstrate the benefits of collaborative learning as students change roles— playwrights become actors, actors become directors, and observers become actors.

Collaborative storymaking

In groups of four, create a story about what happens to one of the characters in the story that is not part of the told story. For instance, write an incident that happens to the prince when he is well. Write an incident that happens to the two brothers while they are in prison. Write an incident that happens to the emperor while his son is sick and the girl is on her journey. Write an incident in the emperor's life when his son is healthy and strong.

List possibilities for storymaking on the blackboard. Encourage wild ideas. Suggest questions to develop ideas into stories. Divide into small groups, each group working on the same story idea, to explore each group's notion of the story idea.

Make a book of story ideas that anyone in the class can add to or use to make a story. Leave space for students to write questions or suggest ideas for story development.

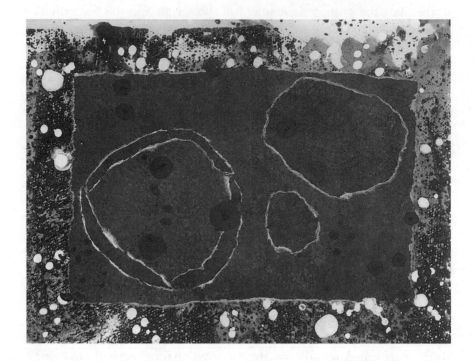

CHAPTER TEN

Reflection and Assessment

A long time ago there lived a young farmer in Southern Africa who worked hard tending his farm. One evening, when he went to milk the cows he could not squeeze a drop of milk from their udders. He wondered how this happened.

The next evening, when he went to milk the cows, he found that once again, he could not squeeze a bit of milk from the cows. The third evening, he went to the barn earlier than usual and hid, waiting to see what would happen. At milking time, a delicate ladder dropped down, and from it stepped a beautiful young woman holding a basket. She deftly milked the cows, climbed up the ladder, and disappeared.

The next evening, when the ladder descended, the young farmer took the woman by her hand and asked her to stay and be his wife. She consented, with one condition. He was never to look in her basket. The young man readily agreed. They were married and lived contentedly for many years.

One day, while his wife was working in the fields, the husband came home for a tool and stumbled over the basket. Curious, he opened the basket and stared inside. He picked it up and looked inside. Seeing nothing, he was about to put it back when he saw his wife.

"You gave me your promise you would not look inside my basket."

"This is true," said the man, "but so what? There is nothing in your basket."

"Are you sure?" asked the woman. The man nodded. "Look again dear husband," pleaded his wife.

"I see nothing," said the man. "There is nothing to be seen."

"Oh," said his wife, "if you see nothing in my basket I must leave." With that, the ladder descended and she returned to her family in the stars.

How one reflects on one's experience—what one sees and hears—depends very much on the one who looks. Previous experience, vantage point, mood, agenda—all affect the way we look and how we see. It isn't so much a matter of right and wrong as it is a function of perspective. Who we are, what we want and need, and how we feel, all affect the way we view a situation. Nowhere is this truer than when we make decisions about the assessment of school programs. Students, teachers, administrators, parents, and community all look at education through different lenses. Yet teachers are the ones who are fundamentally held answerable for what happens in the classroom.

Part of the difficulty in devising adequate assessment programs is that there is no common definition of the word. For some, assessment equals testing. For others, assessment constitutes a view of work which involves all aspects of learning—basic exploration and development of skills; problem identification; investigation of possible solutions; and selection, justification, and reflection of solution.

In this chapter I suggest ways for teachers to consider the process of assessment, not only of their students, but also of themselves—how a teacher teaches greatly influences how students learn.

Establishing Priorities

Children need to be able to take in information, explore its ramifications, process possibilities, and design ways to use what they have read, heard, or seen. Therefore, teachers need to define clearly the language arts skills children have to have in order to use language effectively. I think these skills include the ability to

- Be a passionate reader, a confident writer, and an assured speaker
- Image and enter into the world of the imagination to create new possibilities
- Translate inner imagery into outer action and expression
- Ask questions which lead to productive choices
- Explore diverse ideas without prejudice or premature judgment
- Use suggestions and questions to deepen one's own work and the work of others
- Enter into the world of the text and explore the life of the characters, their situations, ideas, and experiences, establishing connections between self and text
- Create narratives which reflect real and imagined experience and feeling
- Use language precisely, imaginatively, and accurately so that it reflects writers' intentions, ideas, feelings, and perspective
- Use drama to explore vicariously the world of the imagination—

Reflection and Assessment

.... 243

to create character, explore role, and act as if the invented
world is real

More often than not, what stops teachers from exploring new ways
of teaching language arts is the problem of accountability. How do we
evaluate new programs if there are no existing guides, measures, or
tests? How can we be responsible for programs we have never attempted
and cannot be sure will meet our goals? Do we have the right to subject
our students to material we think is good but have not tried? What do
we need to know in order to use new methods with some degree of
confidence and capability? What assessment tools are appropriate for
particular areas of learning? How do we assess what is not quantifiable?
What part, if any, does assessment of the teacher play in the assessment
of the class and of each child?

The work in reflection and assessment in this book is guided by
two fundamental principles. The first is that children learn best when
they are genuinely interested in what they are being asked to do, though
this is not to say children ought to do only what and as they choose.
The second principle, integrally connected to the first, is that we learn
most effectively when we are motivated by internal needs, wonders, and
curiosities, rather than by external rewards or punishments, which
generally work only for a short time.

We can all agree that children need to develop and improve their
ability to read, write, and speak fluently and articulately so that they
can function in the world. The question is how best to make this happen.
I believe we need to pay more attention to the power of the inner voice
that activates curiosity and wonder and less attention to external rewards.
I do not find the carrot-and-stick method of external reward and punishment very effective in the long run because children learn to focus on
pleasing others rather than on becoming self-assured learners.

Intrinsic motivation is both unique and particular to each child.
Although all children want to feel successful, some may want to be the
best in math or reading; others may want to paint or write well. If
teachers help children to connect what is personally important to them
with what is being asked of them at any given moment, many children
will accept a task and do it as well as they can, knowing they will have
the opportunity to do what really matters to them. They may also find
they are very good at tasks they didn't know they could do so successfully.
Intrinsic motivation is not only about what it takes to make us want
to learn and feel good about what we are doing, it also has to do with
how we learn best. Some children want to figure out a problem all
by themselves, without having a teacher or parent give unasked-for

information, while others learn best with step-by-step supervision until they know they can complete an assigned task. Yet both groups can feel equally satisfied when they achieve mastery. By teaching children to be sensitive to what motivates them, we also empower them to become self-directed learners, aware of the satisfaction involved in learning or achieving what is personally important. We help them comprehend the joy and delight of discovery.

As teachers, we understand that while we must provide opportunities for children to learn effectively, we also have to prove to administrators, parents, and community that our chosen methods are effective. The process of being accountable, even when one wants to examine new approaches, requires that teachers connect reflection and assessment with daily experience so that they can examine and explain their educational techniques when asked to do so.

All reflection and assessment takes place in context. We have to ask, "What were the children's skill levels before the new activity, and what are they now?" Although teachers select appropriate and important categories and levels of skill development for children's continuing growth, they must also meet standardized requirements and test scores while they generally play no part in developing or in choosing whether their students will take a particular test. Because classroom management affects all classroom experience and activity, I emphasize the importance of collaborative learning as an integral aspect of reflection and assessment. Repeatedly, I have discovered, after working in a great variety of classrooms, that this way of teaching and learning creates the environment in which children are most likely to feel safe and respected for who they are and how they need to learn. I continue to notice that the amount of involvement children have in their learning is directly proportional to the way the teacher structures the learning environment.

A Framework with Which to Begin

Administrative and parental support, or lack thereof, affects the way teachers explore new ways to reflect on and assess students' work. The questions and ideas in this chapter are resource rather than prescription, designed to assist readers to devise programs that creatively meet their individual needs and situations.

Part of the reason I have been successful in creating and implementing innovative teaching and learning programs at a variety of institutions is the recognition that as a teacher, I often feel as if I speak a language very different from my supervisors and administrators, even though we use the same words and think we use them in similar ways. I take it as my responsibility not only to devise teaching and learning techniques which meet my supervisors' and administrators' definitions of appropriate, responsible, and well-thought-through, but also to have the means to prove these programs are effective.

Always, the bottom line seems to be, How do you know your ideas will work? How will you measure your program's educational value? Answering these questions well often means the difference between death and life for a program. I have found that when I demonstrate what makes my programs work well, administrators and supervisors are more willing to give me the necessary space and time to explore possibilities. I have also learned that if the "product" seems like a good idea, administrators are sometimes willing to help me make the program a reality.

For example, a teacher of first graders asked me to help her devise interesting ways to increase the number of books her children volunteered to read. As preparation, we asked each child to keep a log of books (title, author, and one-sentence reaction) read in class during allotted reading periods for two weeks. We explicitly worded the description so there was no hint that more was better. I suggested we get three cheap tape recorders for children to record their impressions of the books they were reading. Any child could play a tape to find out what was "hot." She had one tape recorder and I lent her mine so we started with two. The children loved recording their comments and pretty soon the number of books checked out of the classroom library began to increase. We asked the principal to come to the classroom to watch the children use the recorders. He was so impressed that he asked the PTA to buy several recorders for the school and suggested the teacher share her idea and results with other teachers.

During the subsequent teachers' meeting one of the teachers asked, "But how do you know the children are reading the books? Maybe they're just making up what they say they've read."

Her response was, "I thought that might happen and I think it did because I heard two students arguing. One complained, 'You said . . . was a good book and it stinks. How come you said it was good?' The other child said, 'Well, I only read the first part but that part was good.' The second child responded, 'Then you should say the first part is good, not the whole book.'"

Students cheat if they want to, regardless of the system used to prevent it. I devise learning strategies to make cheating irrelevant. For example, teachers give tests to know if or how well students have read the assigned text. But I ascertain how well my students have read a text by using a variety of techniques, such as asking students to paint an image of a telling passage and to write some words that come to mind about what the passage evokes and how the passage reflects their understanding of the text. We share the images, word ideas, and passages with the class. After this, we talk about our choices, what we notice, and how our experience informs our reading. We might share the words a character uses to describe what's happening at a point of crisis or explore how a character changes in the course of the text by reading passages out loud to reference our ideas. Students know they cannot participate if they haven't read the text, so they do their reading. They quickly learn there is no way to cheat; either they've read the book or they haven't. In the course of working with the text—making connections between who they are and what they read—students often discover how much they enjoy reading when they read for themselves, rather than with a "teacher on their shoulder."

Often, teachers' ideas about cheating while participating in activities other than tests reflects the teacher's attitude more than the students'. If sharing ideas is the equivalent of cheating, how can children explore ideas without being punished? If cheating is the primary or only concern as to whether an activity is worth trying, few programs will be given the time they require for the chance to succeed. In my experience, even if children make up information or lie about what they claim to have read, peer pressure and peer curiosity usually prevail in the end, especially if *all* books are valued rather than those which are long or have big words. Teachers may worry that children will read only trash if left to their own devices, yet in my experience, when children have easy access to good books, they often turn to them after the trash has left them feeling unsatisfied. However, if control is the hidden agenda— who determines what I read—the good books often remain unread as a way of establishing personal sovereignty.

Because many children are used to being punished or rewarded by external responses, it takes a fair amount of time and clearly supportive teacher attitudes for students to learn to feel the pleasure of accomplishment for its own sake. Why not give intrinsic incentive a chance to work? We have everything to gain and a lot to lose if we continue to graduate students who can't or hate to read, write, and/or speak.

To establish a productive framework for reflection and assessment teachers first need to decide what is most important to them about how and what students learn and to set their educational goals accordingly. Second, teachers need to know what goals have been set for them by administrators, school boards, and national or state tests. Third, teachers have to figure out ways to help children want to learn so they can experience the pleasure of learning even as they take tests and submit to other forms of measurement.

Reflection and Assessment

.... 247

Assessment Strategies to Encourage Learning

Making Space for Children to Share in Planning

When children want to learn, the classroom is a joyful place; teachers work with energy and zest, children buzz with curiosity and purpose. One way to encourage this process is to include children in designing some aspects of their educational experience. This participation doesn't always have to be planned ahead of time—teachers who are open to the moment sometimes discover wonderful opportunities to allow children to modify what has been devised.

As part of a drama-in-education program, I brought fifteen books to a second grade whose teacher had asked me to help her find ways to encourage the children to want to read. I had asked the children to suggest ways to help make reading more enjoyable and designed sessions where children would not only read books together, but also share thoughts and feelings about their reading. I intended to have the children role-play favorite parts as one way to assess their reading progress because in order to create characters from the books the children needed to read with some understanding.

After placing the books all around the room, I asked the children to find a partner and walk around the room, browsing among the books until they found a book both partners wanted to read. The children dutifully followed instructions, looking at books, at me, at their teacher, waiting. We smiled to encourage them but gave no further directions. We wanted them to become intrigued by a book of their own accord. One pair stopped and began to look at a book. A boy walked up to them, took the book out of their hands and said, "We're supposed to keep walking."

One of the pair grabbed the book back and said, "Who says?"

"Teacher says."

"Oh yeah?"

"Yeah."

By this time everyone was watching, waiting for the fight to begin. The teacher said quietly, "If you find a book that interests you and your partner, find a place to sit and read." After a time, all but one pair had found books and were reading. The boy who had grabbed the book continued to walk, even though his partner kept trying to interest him in a book she liked. I went up to him and asked, "Have you found a book you like?"

"No! They're all dumb."

"What makes them dumb?"

"They're boring."

"What makes them boring?" He shrugged. I was working with the class for the first time and did not know how well the boy could read, or if he could read at all. Not wanting him to lose face I asked, "Would the two of you like to write your own book?" He looked startled, she looked fearful.

I got some paper and sat down on the floor with them, snuggled in a corner for coziness and privacy. "What do you want your story to be about?"

"Murder," said the boy.

"Friends," said the girl.

Groaning inwardly—murder is not my favorite subject—I began to ask each of them questions, one at a time. "Who is the story about?"

"A boy," he said.

"A girl," she said.

"How old are they?"

"Ten," answered the boy.

"Eight," answered the girl.

After a series of questions and some compromise, they determined that the two characters, a ten-year-old boy and an eight-year-old girl, were friends vacationing at a beach resort with their parents. The pair could not agree on who was murdered or why. The time we set aside was quickly coming to an end so I asked, with more than a little desperation, "What if it wasn't a person who was murdered? What if it was a school of fish that got murdered by a company dumping toxic waste into the ocean even though it's illegal?" Both children became excited, shouting suggestions back and forth, too fast for me to write down. I had an idea.

"We have the beginning and a bit of the middle of a story. Would you mind sharing your story with the rest of the class?" They nodded happily. "Would it be okay if the class plays with your ideas?" They agreed and took turns sharing their story with the class. Each pair was asked to decide what came next, writing one or two sentences. We suggested that those needing help with writing or coming up with ideas seek help from their neighbors. In about ten minutes we sat the children in a circle and asked them to share what they had come up with, in the order they felt was appropriate to the development of the story. Their teacher and I took turns writing down what was said or read on separate pieces of paper for ease of shuffling. We ordered their bits of story according to the children's sense of order. Although we spent more time than we planned on helping the children negotiate an order they could all live with, we continued because their teacher felt what they were learning was too important to stop or for us to arbitrarily impose an order.

By the time the class finished sharing and ordering each contribution, we had all but the ending. The boy who wanted the story to be about murder stood up and said, "Me and Annie should finish the story 'cause we started it." No one objected. The two of them talked together, while the class listened, and rather quickly came up with a mutually satisfactory ending. After the whole story was read I asked, "Who is the author?"

"Me and Annie," he said.

"But we helped," complained some of the children.

"Yeah, that's not fair," said others.

"Well, it was our idea," said the boy. Shouting filled the room.

The teacher said to him, "How about if we list you and Annie first, and then write, with the help of . . . and list all the other names?" Agreed.

The teacher promised to type the story on the big-letter typewriter during her lunch break. I offered to get copies made on mine. At the end of the school day, each child had a copy of the story to take home. What was their homework? To read the story the class had written to someone.

The next day, I thought we would proceed with the original plan, having children read books in pairs followed by drama, but the children had other ideas. When we asked pairs to find books to read, several children complained, "Why can't we write our own story, like Felix and Annie did?"

"How come they get to make their own story and we don't?"

Why indeed? New plan, born out of action and reaction. Because the reason for my being in the classroom was to encourage reading through drama, I proposed that each pair find a book that appealed to them, read it, and decide what made it appealing. I gave each pair small notebooks in which they could write down the books they read, the name of the author, and what it was that made the story interesting to them. The pairs did not have to agree on anything except the chosen book. After the book was read, each pair was to find something "unfinished" in the story that they wanted to "finish, to make a new story." The children wanted to know how long the story had to be. Any length. How to decide what was "unfinished." Whatever makes you curious. What happens if one person doesn't write so good? Partners help each other. What if the story is dumb? A story is a story—all stories have value.

At the end of my stay, each child had read at least five books, each pair had written four stories by themselves and helped to write the fifth. Children had learned to list the books they read using standard bibliographic notation and to write about what caught their interest. The last day, I asked the children to tell me about their least and most favorite books and to give me reasons for their choices. Luck was with us. As we were in the middle of the discussion, the principal walked in and asked if he could visit for awhile. The children hardly missed a beat, sharing their responses to the books. Most fun was when children disagreed with each other about a book they had read, arguing for their favorite with passion and eloquence. Later, the principal commended the teacher for creating an environment where children cared so much about reading.

What about the drama? The teacher and I designed a series of activities based on the stories the children wrote. To improve oral expression, we asked the children to decide on a topic either from the books they read or from the stories they wrote, to pick one of the characters they had created, and to talk about the topic as if they were their character. Each discussion centered on a new topic chosen by the children who always participated in role, both interviewing and responding. To assess improvement in oral expression, for a week before the drama program, the teacher made a check mark next to each child's name every time a child volunteered to speak. She repeated this the week of the drama program, as well as the week following the drama work. There was substantial improvement in the number of checks, more in the week of the drama program than in the week after, but more after than before the drama work. Because she found this system productive, she decided to incorporate phenomenological assessment as a regular part of her classroom language arts activity evaluation. Eventually, we extended assessment activity to enable children to devise ways to keep track of their progress in reading, writing, and speaking. Such measures included logs, story books, taped speeches, and learning journals.

Motivation

In school, children are usually punished for bad work or behavior and rewarded for success. Most methods depend on extrinsic motivation. If you anger the teacher, you stay after school or go to the principal's office. Please the teacher and you get a gold star. While these strategies may result in "good" behavior in the short run, they do little or nothing to develop a lifelong interest in learning, nor do they empower children to reflect on their experiences or encourage them to love to learn. In fact, I think reliance on extrinsic punishment and reward destroys the joy most children feel about learning when they first start school.

Shifting emphasis from extrinsic to intrinsic rewards and responses takes time, but the results are well worth the effort. Even with young children, shifting from external to internal control can bring about unexpected results. For example, I don't tolerate chaos very well, and when I approached my first Head Start session and saw fifteen children running and screaming, my heart sank. I wondered how I would survive.

I managed to gather and quiet the children and tell them, "I have little capacity for chaos." The children stared at me.

One child said, "Too bad," and they all laughed. When I asked them if they knew what capacity and chaos meant they shook their heads. I explained that I needed order in the classroom to be a good teacher, and that we would have to work together to create an environment that allowed all of us to function best. They solemnly agreed. During the first activity, building with blocks, every child who built a tower had it knocked down before it was finished. There were tears, hitting, scratching, and cursing.

I sat them down and asked, "Who likes to knock down towers?" Every hand went up; they all laughed delightedly at the thought of knocking down people's creations. Then I asked, "Who likes to have their towers knocked down?" Not a hand went up. Silence. "Well," I said, "I think we have a problem. Everyone wants to knock down towers but no one wants to have their tower knocked down. What are we going to do?"

We had a surprisingly good conversation as children suggested ways to accommodate both the builders and destroyers. We decided to try all the ideas before making any decision as to which idea worked best. I told them that what we were doing was called experimenting, as part of research to find a solution, and that when you experiment, you also have to evaluate how well the experiment works. I asked them how they might know which idea worked best. One child suggested, "If you build your tower and no one knocks it down."

"If people ask can they knock your tower down."

"If people help you."

In contrast to the first time when children built and knocked down with no regard to anyone, this time they worked self-consciously. Some children began to build while others watched. No one rushed to knock down a tower. When three children said they were finished, a few children ran menacingly toward the builders, stopping at the last minute to ask if they could knock them down. The answer was a resounding, "No. Build your own." Eventually, after a lot of group discussion and trial and error, we worked out ways for the children to build and knock down their creations that worked surprisingly well most of the time.

Image Journals

Images made from paint, clay, crayons, or magic markers record feelings as well as ideas and provide useful information, especially when children want to reflect on what a text, unit, or project means to them, in terms of both what they have learned and how they react to the experience.

Images made with fingerpaint work well because the medium is primitive, helping to reinforce the idea that the imagemaking is about knowing and not about making art. The images are made as children work with a text, recording ideas from and about the text as well as personal reactions to the text. Students date images and write a few words about the text and the image for later reflection. Images kept in a looseleaf notebook provide a record of what has been read and what the reader thought and felt about the text. Similar image journals can be kept for work in science, math, social studies, or any other subject. Images can be made and notated in less than a minute. In the beginning, children may need help deciding what to write, but I continually suggest they write whatever comes to mind. I want children to learn to pay attention to their own ideas, attitudes, feelings, and experiences.

Reading Logs

One of the easiest ways for teachers to assess learning is to compare behavior—before, during, and after a particular activity. Although keeping track of twenty-five to thirty children can be problematic and tiresome, difficulties are minimized when teachers enlist the help of the students. When I suggest this to teachers their first objection is always about cheating. Notwithstanding the fact that cheating can and will take place when children are given the opportunity to record their progress, I have found that this is mostly a transitory phenomenon, especially when a variety of methods are used to explore what the children claim to have done.

Children learn how to make a bibliography when they keep reading logs in which they use standard bibliographic notation to record title, author, publisher, place, and date of publishing. They write two to five sentences (depending on ability of child) describing the main characters and plot, dating each entry. Leaving a space for second or third opinions, they can change their mind about the book or write in more detail about some aspect evoked by their reading.

The logs are kept in the classroom and students who want to find a good book can look at anyone's reading logs for ideas or suggestions. Once a week, children can gather in small groups for "book talk," telling something about a book they have read recently, discussing what they think and feel about the text and why, or reading brief passages from the book as part of their sharing. Group members are then encouraged to ask questions—if a child says a book is boring or stupid, others will ask to hear more about why it is boring or stupid. They are taught to cite passages or quote character responses as evidence to support their findings. Once every two weeks the class gathers as a whole to create a "Best Books/Worst Books" list.

Although initially children sometimes make up entries, this behavior sharply decreases after a while. Teachers with whom I spoke thought it had to do with a shift in emphasis. They found ways to let the children know that although it was nice to have many entries, it was just as important to be able to talk about each book in some depth, at a moment's notice. Teachers developed strategies to spot-check children's lists by picking up a log, reading an entry, and spontaneously asking a child, "Tell me about this book." Other teachers devised "walk abouts" where children went around the room asking each other about books listed in the logs. When parents or administrators came into the classroom children were encouraged to share their logs and to talk about memorable books. What children seem to like most about keeping reading logs is that in June they take their log home, having a record of all the books they read during the school year as well as what they thought about them.

Learning Journals

In traditional patterns of education students receive information, take tests, are given grades, and then move to (or are held back in) the next grade. Except for a report card, many children have little or nothing to show for their year in school. One way to address this problem is to have children make learning journals which can be made with looseleaf folders, file boxes, or large envelopes. During the course of the school year children select sample pieces of work to put into their file and keep regular entries about what they learned, what happened of significance, or what they are feeling about a classroom event. Some teachers provide a few minutes at the end of the day for children to record their entry. Children are encouraged to keep their journals in the classroom to avoid losing or not having them when they want to record in them.

Teachers with whom I have worked say that helping children keep learning journals is worth the time and effort that it takes to teach children how to write in their journals. At the end of a particular period of time (lesson, day, unit, project, marking period) children paint or draw how they are feeling and write a bit about what they have learned and/or what they want or need to learn. Each journal entry is dated and kept in chronological order. Teachers set guidelines for an appropriate journal entry and discuss why and when they will periodically look at the journals to evaluate how children are notating experience. If a child is not writing much, the teacher usually has a conference to discover what might free the child to write more often or more personally. If a child appears to be worried or anxious, or refuses to write, the teacher talks with the child to explore what is happening. Journals are kept in school until the end of the school year and remain the property of the child. Any child who can write, even a little, can keep a learning journal— the less the child can write, the more the child can make images. What matters is that children become accustomed to reflecting on their classroom experiences.

Like reading logs, learning journals provide tangible evidence of what the child has learned during a year. Both documents enhance a child's self-esteem and serve as testimony that the child is a person who can learn and who knows what it means to struggle with the unknown. Unlike reading logs, journals record the child's unique experience of all aspects of their education. Learning journals also help to document how a child learns by the way learning experiences are recorded. Some children need multisensory modes in order to learn—to listen, feel, and read information before they process it. For others, single modes such as listening or reading suffice. If children know how they best learn, they may be less likely to fail or to be totally at the mercy of the teacher teaching them at any given moment.

Student Portfolios

Student portfolios, containing a wide variety of written work and projects, document student work in the classroom for a period of time, usually one school year. Properly executed, the portfolio provides a comprehensive developmental assessment of students' work. Portfolios best serve students when they include a wide range of work that demonstrates failures and successes, records growth and development, and shows finished products. An initial math test with a failing grade followed by tests with better grades highlights the student's progress and also records initial problems that were later solved. Similarly, the portfolio needs to include initial and subsequent drafts of papers to demonstrate what the student has been able to accomplish through multiple revisions of writing. I encourage children to include images made in the service of writing a paper, recording responses to a book, or developing a character in drama. Unlike portfolios developed to prove expertise in professional and adult situations, student portfolios are best used to chronicle the student's learning journey and as such, need to be carefully structured.

When teachers decide to institute student portfolios, there are several issues to be addressed. How and where will the data be kept?

Who has access to the material? How will the contents be selected? How will the portfolio be assessed during and at the end of the year? To whom does the portfolio belong? Do students pick none, some, or all of the work to be included? According to what criteria? If students take their portfolios home at the end of the year, should copies be made of selected work to serve as part of students' permanent record? If so, who decides the basis on which papers, tests, and/or projects are selected?

Students who participate in the portfolio process learn to reflect on their work in progress and assess what they have learned when they compare drafts to final product. If they help to develop assessment questions they also learn to consider what is involved in evaluating an educational experience, realizing that learning involves more than knowing the right answer. Some questions students might want to answer periodically include: How do you define failure and success? What did you want to learn when you wrote this paper, completed this project, or took this test? How did your experience (writing a paper, designing a project, doing research, taking a test) hinder or help you to learn? Whose help, collaboration, or advice did you seek or were you given? What difficulties, if any, did you experience when you engaged in this activity? How did you deal with them? Now that this paper, project, or test is completed, what did you learn? How will this learning help you the next time you undertake a similar activity?

Periodic reviews, done quarterly, semi-yearly, and/or annually, most appropriately focus on a comprehensive assessment of progress and include references to earlier evaluations so that students become aware of particular weaknesses and strengths in their classwork and of the ways these have been affected by previous work. Teachers and students find it useful to evaluate the contents of portfolios on a regular basis, usually four times a year, to cull the contents, keeping the work that best demonstrates the child's learning and development.

Teachers who use portfolios have to create assignments that allow students to show their skills. Although this takes time, the change in assessment techniques enables students to demonstrate knowledge acquired over time rather than to depend solely on how well they do on a particular test on a given day. Teachers can identify skills that will be tested on standardized tests yet teach in ways that foster their students' ability to analyze, synthesize, and think critically. Using the portfolio system, normally intelligent children who generally do badly on tests, and as a result feel stupid, benefit from the opportunity to demonstrate competence over time rather than be dependent on one tester's notion of what constitutes excellence.

To test reading using the portfolio system, teachers might assign essays with questions designed to encourage students to demonstrate depth of understanding and writing competence. Professional writers write as many drafts as they need until their work is finished. Why not allow students the same opportunity? To test math competencies teachers might assign a survey with students selecting an issue that interests them, asking students to draw graphs to illustrate their findings. To test knowledge in science students might be asked to select a topic about which they are curious and to find ways to get the information they require or to design a test which might reveal what they want to know. Such assignments not only test what students know, but also how well students think and how much they know about where to go to find requisite information.

Teachers may still want to test students as a check on the usefulness of the portfolio, but if a child consistently spells correctly when writing papers, what need is there to give spelling tests? If teachers want to know how well a student understands a text, students can be asked to write a response paper, create a drama based on the text, write monologues, and so on. Once teachers decide that portfolios are valuable, lessons can be designed to demonstrate student knowledge and understanding of process through projects, research, papers, and presentations.

Assessing Creative Work

When my students design projects, make drama, paint a series of images to explore an idea, write poems or songs, or compose a piece of music, their creations must be assessed as part of their course work. Each student, regardless of the medium, begins with a personally important question of great concern, and does a minimum of two drafts. Questions for the first draft focus on evoking ideas, connecting the maker to the question and to the work, and include

> What is the question which motivates your work?
> What questions, if any, does your chosen question evoke? If you have new questions, do they affect or relate to your work? If so, how?
> What makes you choose this particular medium?
> How have you explored your question—what ideas have you considered, rejected, used? Why?
> How do you feel about your working experience and your work?
> What was your primary focus when creating this piece?
> What problems or unresolved issues remain for you? Why?

What aspects of the work most please you? Why?
How can I (the class) help you deepen your work?
How does presenting your work affect the material you decide
    to share and how you share it?

Questions for subsequent and final drafts focus on shaping, honing, and
polishing, and include

How do you feel about your work?
What ideas seem most important?
What are you learning (have your learned) from making this
    piece?
What questions do you have about your work (in progress)?
How does your initial question spur your exploration?
How does your initial question relate to where you are now?
What have you learned about what you need or want to learn?
What might you do were you to continue working on this piece?

Questions I ask myself about the final or completed work include

How well was the student able to articulate a personally
    meaningful question? If the question changed, what stimulated
    the change? What new learning resulted from the change
    of questions?
How well was the student able to develop a way to explore his/
    her question in personally meaningful ways?
How well was the student able to use questions and suggestions
    from the class and others to deepen her/his work? Using
    what criteria?
How well was the student able to satisfy or to learn more about
    his/her initial question? Using what criteria?
How well has the student used what was learned in class to
    explore and extend knowledge as she/he worked on the
    piece? Using what criteria?
How does the final piece reflect originality, creativity, and depth
    of exploration?
How well does the final presentation "speak for itself"?

Benefits from using logs, journals, and portfolios as a form of assessment:

Students who are able to document their learning through
    journals, logs, and portfolios leave school each year with a

concrete sense of their own achievement. They know they are persons who can learn. Their self-confidence is based on tangible evidence which they can continue to look at long after the school year has passed.

Grades occasionally reflect teacher-student relationships, which, when difficult, may affect how teachers assess students. Under the portfolio system, parents can take the child's portfolio to the school and show what the child was able to accomplish under the guidance of a previous teacher with whom the child had a good relationship. Similarly, if a child who has been doing well in school begins to fail, parents can use the portfolio to help explore the nature of current difficulties.

When children transfer from one school to another, portfolios give teachers and administrators at the new school a personal and comprehensive look at what a student knows and how the student learns.

Taxpayers in the community might be less likely to complain about the cost of education if they are invited to browse through journals, logs, and portfolios to see what students are accomplishing.

How well we learn is, in large measure, dependent on how well we think we can learn. Cumulative, well-documented evidence of our ability to learn, collected over a substantial period of time, nurtures our self-esteem and confidence. We are more likely to think we can learn if we have proof that in the past, we were able to master new skills and develop new abilities.

Because the success of new teaching methods is directly connected to how well they can be assessed, I have devised categories which I think are important, both to evaluate children's work and to empower children to reflect and evaluate their own learning. When I begin to devise new programs, I ask myself questions, not so much to find specific answers, but to discover the parameters of my concerns and the issues that are most crucial to designing an effective program. Therefore, within each category I have listed questions that occurred to me as I wrote this chapter. I include them to show the way I work and to create a framework for reflection and assessment in language arts development and practice. All questions are fueled by the general question, "How do I know?"

"Love of Learning" and "Educational Development" contain questions teachers might ask themselves. "Incentives and Rewards," "Exploring Connections Between Teaching Methods and Assessment," and "Lifelong Development" contain questions of interest to teachers, administrators, parents, and school board members. The last group of questions are those which learners might ask themselves.

Love of Learning

Are children becoming more enthusiastic about reading, writing, and/ or speaking? Do they approach language arts activities with interest and eagerness? Do they know how to ask for help from other students and the teacher without feeling they have failed if they do so? Do children have enough confidence in their ability to learn so they can try new activities with a fair amount of self-esteem? Have class members learned to share skills with each other so that asking what a word means or what a book is like constitutes normal and expected behavior rather than cheating? Are children excited about sharing their work and discoveries with others? Do children love to read? To learn new words? To share ideas with the whole class as well as smaller groups within the class? To write letters? To make poems? To work cooperatively in a collaborative learning environment to produce work they are proud of and pleased with? How can I help my students to transform nonproductive choices into those which are productive? To use "failure" and "mistakes" as learning experiences in the service of becoming more knowledgeable? Have children learned to say "I think" or "I feel" or "I want," to take responsibility for their ideas? To articulate their needs, wants, and wishes clearly, comfortably, and without defensiveness or apprehension? If not, how can I help them to learn this so they are able to take responsibility for their actions and expression?

Educational Development

QUANTITY   Are children reading, writing, and/or speaking more than they did before the project started? If so, how do I know? If not, why not? Because it is important to collect samples of children's writing and speaking before formal instruction begins, how do I determine and isolate particular skills involved in storytelling, storymaking, drama, and poetry writing? What might it take for children to improve the amount of reading, writing, and speaking they do "on their own time," that is, without specific direction to read, write, or speak? Do I document the nature of each child's learning involvement? If not why not? If so, what is the nature of my documentation?

QUALITY   How do I decide on the quality of children's reading, writing, and speaking? What makes for quality experience and response? How do I share my knowledge with my students so they know how to recognize quality work, whether their own or the work of classmates? How is children's progress communicated to parents and administrators on a regular, noncrisis basis?

ABILITY TO TAKE RISKS   Are children willing to take risks when asked to learn, especially in a new way? How do I know this? If I haven't considered risk taking to be important, how do I decide what steps a child needs to take in order to learn a particular skill or bit of knowledge? How do I create an environment in which children consider risk taking to be a normal part of learning? How do I help children to identify aspects of learning that may be personally difficult so they are aware of how and when to ask for help?

Incentives and Rewards

How are children punished or rewarded in the classroom? Are children primarily motivated by extrinsic factors (teachers, administrators, peers, and/or community) or by intrinsic factors (self-fulfillment, self-discovery, self-satisfaction)? What is the nature of these punishments and rewards? Who chose them? Under what circumstances? How were or are they evaluated? Is a "carrot-stick" system operative? (Do it badly, you are punished; do it well, you are rewarded.) If so, who decides what constitutes a "stick" or a "carrot"? What was/is the teacher's experience as a learner regarding punishment and/or rewards? How does the teacher's experience as a learner affect choices made as a teacher? How important is the issue of student empowerment—to the teacher, to the administration, to parents, to the community? What role, if any, does student empowerment have in structuring punishments or rewards? What role, if any, do students play in determining classroom punishments and rewards? If students do help to choose deterrents and incentives, how are their choices evaluated? By whom? How often? Under what circumstances?

Exploring Connections Between Teaching Methods and Assessment

Does the teacher's philosophy of teaching include a process that begins with methods of helping students to learn and ends with reflection and assessment? If not, why not? If so, how? What role, if any, do students play in setting goals for learning and in designing ways to evaluate outcomes? How important is student participation? Who decides? On what basis? To what purpose? What support, if any, do administrators give to help teachers design methods of reflection and assessment that are consonant with individual teacher's views and ideas about the nature of good teaching?

Lifelong Development

How are educational objectives set and focused in terms of time period? What role, if any, does lifelong development play in the goals teachers set for themselves and their students? What constitutes a lifelong goal? Who decides whether lifelong development is crucial? In what context? If lifelong development is deemed important, how is this choice manifested in methods used to reflect on and assess learning? How important is the development and nurturance of nonacademic qualities such as self-confidence, self-esteem, a sense of personal competence? How do teachers help students learn to structure a variety of ways to accomplish goals and tasks, both those they set for themselves as well as those set by others?

Questions Which Empower Children to Become Active Learners

How do I think about myself as a learner? How do I measure my progress? What can I do to show my progress to concerned others? What helps me to learn? What prevents or hinders my learning? How do I feel if I have to ask for help? What helps me to feel safe enough to say, "I don't know?" What are some ways I can help others to learn? What kind of teacher helps me want to learn? How do I build my self-confidence when learning new skills or trying new methods? How do I problem solve? How do I look at my work: At the beginning? When I have some experience? When I know what I'm doing? What, if anything, makes me want to come to school? What hinders or helps me become an active learner? How might I contribute to creating a good learning environment? What skills do I need to negotiate or resolve conflicts when it comes to my learning and me as a learner? What helps me to feel good about myself as a learner?

No matter what questions are asked or how they are explored, the process of asking questions enables the questioner to become more aware of issues affecting the design and implementation of assessment strategies.

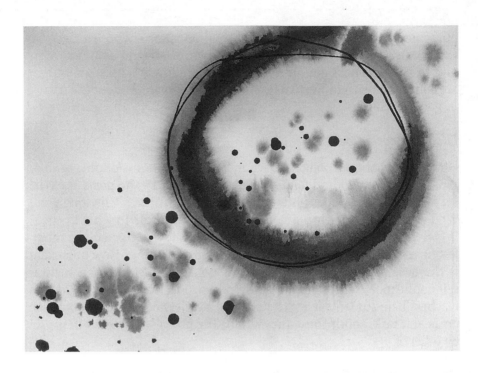

Afterword

Stories speak to me in every state and struggle. When I need to know what's going on inside me I read stories until I find one that that makes a connection to who I am and what I am feeling. It's as if a light goes on inside me and I'm able to see, whereas before the story, there was only darkness. When I thought about how to end this book, this story found me.

A Bargain Is a Bargain (Central Asia)

Once upon a time a young girl and her father, a penniless woodcutter, lived in a bare and meager hut. The father had only a small ax, a lame horse, and an old mule with which to earn money. One day, he told his nine-year-old daughter that he was going to market with a load of wood. As he was leaving she said to him, "Be careful father, at the market, one man's loss is another man's gain."

The woodcutter arrived at the market and stood beside his horse who carried the load of wood. For a long time no one came to buy. Then, at dusk, a rich bai (merchant) walked over to him and said, "I'll give you one kanga if you will sell your wood exactly as it is." The woodcutter agreed and led the horse to the bai's mansion where he unloaded the wood. As the woodman started to take his horse away the bai shouted, "Stop! I bought the wood 'exactly as it is,' which means the horse that carried the wood is my horse now. If you are not content let us go before the judge."

After hearing the story the judge decreed, "Woodcutter, you agreed to the terms. The horse belongs to the bai." Exhausted and unhappy, the poor man returned to his daughter and told her of the strange bargain and the judge's ruling.

"Never mind father. Tomorrow I shall take the mule and go to market. Perhaps I will be lucky and sell our wood for a good price."

Early the next morning the little girl put the load of wood on the mule and set off. After arriving at the market, she stood all day beside the mule with the load of wood on its back, with no customers, until the same bai came by. He offered her two kangas for the wood, "Exactly as it is."

The little girl agreed saying, "I will sell my wood exactly as it is, if you will pay your money exactly as it is." The bai agreed and led her to his mansion.

Giving her the two coins, the bai prepared to take the mule but the little girl said, "Sir, you have my mule with the wood, exactly as it is. Now you have to pay my price, exactly as it is. Give me your arm which was attached to the money." The bai roared with anger but the little girl stood her ground. Finally, they went before the judge.

After hearing the story the judge said, "A bargain is a bargain. If you will not give the girl your arm you must pay its worth in gold." With some of the money, the little girl bought a new horse and returned to her father who laughed and cried when she told her tale.

And so it is said, "A wise head is worth more than a full purse."

References

The books listed here have been personally useful in my learning, growth, and development.

The Arts

Berger, John. 1977. *Ways Of Seeing*. New York: Penguin.

Coe, Ralph, cat. 1976. *Sacred Circles: Two Thousand Years of North American Art*. London: Arts Council of Great Britain.

Csaky, Mick, ed. 1979. *How Does it Feel? Exploring the World of Your Senses*. New York: Harmony.

Duncan, David Douglas. 1978. *Magic Worlds of Fantasy*. New York: Harcourt Brace Jovanovich.

Feng, Gia-fu, and Jane English. 1972. *Lao Tsu: Tao Te Ching*. New York: Vintage.

Green, Gerald. 1969. *The Artists of Terezin*. New York: Hawthorn.

King, Nancy. 1971. *Theatre Movement: The Actor and His Space*. New York: Drama Book Publishers.

———. 1975. *Giving Form to Feeling*. New York: Drama Book Specialists.

———. 1981. *A Movement Approach to Acting*. Englewood Cliffs, NJ: Prentice-Hall.

———. 1981. "From Literature to Drama to Life." In *Children and Drama*, 2nd. ed. Ed. Nellie McCaslin. New York: Longman.

Miller, Alice. 1986. *Pictures of a Childhood*. New York: Farrar, Straus & Giroux.

Morse, John D., ed. 1972. *Ben Shahn*. New York: Praeger.

Novitch, Miriam, Lucy Dawidowicz, and Tom Freudenheim. 1981. *Spiritual Resistance: Art from Concentration Camps* 1940–1945. New York: Union of American Hebrew Congregations.

Reiser, Dolf. 1972. *Art and Science*. London: Studio Vista.

Rockefeller, David Jr., ed. 1977. *Coming to Our Senses*. New York: McGraw-Hill.

Rubin, William, ed. 1984. *Primitivism in 20th Century Art: Affinity of the Tribal and the Modern*. Vols. 1 & 2. New York: Museum of Modern Art.

Samuels, Mike and Nancy. 1975. *Seeing with the Mind's Eye*. New York: Random House.

Thorndike, Joseph J. 1979. *Discovery of Lost Worlds*. New York: American Heritage Publishing Co.

Witkin, Robert. 1974. *The Intelligence of Feeling*. London: Heinemann.

Wolff, Robert. 1971. *On Art and Learning*. New York: Grossman.

Psychology

Bettelheim, Bruno. 1977. *The Uses of Enchantment.* New York: Vintage.

Brandon, David. 1976. *Zen in the Art of Helping.* London: Routledge & Kegan Paul.

Dieckmann, Hans. 1978. *Twice Told Tales: The Psychological Use of Fairy Tales.* Wilmette, IL: Chiron.

Fabry, Joseph B. 1968. *The Pursuit of Meaning.* Boston: Beacon Press.

Freud, Anna. 1968. *Ego and the Mechanisms of Defense.* New York: International University Press.

Gardner, Howard. 1980. *Frames of Mind: The Theory of Multiple Intelligences.* New York: Basic Books.

Gendlin, Eugene T. 1981. *Focusing.* New York: A Bernard Geis Associates Book.

Goleman, Daniel. 1985. *Vital Lies Simple Truths.* New York: Simon & Schuster.

Gordon, David. 1978. *Therapeutic Metaphors.* Cupertino, CA: META.

Harding, Esther. 1971. *Womens's Mysteries, Ancient and Modern.* New York: C. G. Jung Foundation.

Jung, C. G. 1972. *Four Archetypes: Mother, Rebirth, Spirit, Trickster.* London: Routledge & Kegan Paul.

Jung, C. G. 1971. *The Portable Jung.* Ed. Joseph Campbell. New York: Penguin.

Keyes, Margaret. 1974. *The Inward Journey.* Berkeley, CA: Celestial Arts.

Kornfield, Jack. 1993. *A Path with Heart.* New York: Bantam Books.

Lazarus, Arnold. 1977. *In The Mind's Eye.* New York and London: The Guilford Press.

Luke, Helen M. 1982. *The Way of Woman.* Three Rivers, MI: Apple Farm.

Luthi, Max. 1970. *Once Upon a Time: On the Nature of Fairy Tales.* Bloomington, IN: Indiana University Press.

Maslow, Abraham. 1962. *Toward a Psychology of Being.* Princeton, NJ: Van Nostrand.

May, Rollo. 1975. *The Courage to Create.* New York: Bantam.

Miller, Alice. 1986. *Thou Shalt Not Be Aware: Society's Betrayal of Children.* New York: New American Library.

Moon, Sheila. 1970. *A Magic Dwells.* Wesleyan, CT: Wesleyan University Press.

Moustakas, Clark, ed. 1956. *The Self: Explorations in Personal Growth.* New York: Harper Colophon.

Neumann, Erich. 1954. *The Origins and History of Consciousness.* Princeton, NJ: Bollingen Series.

———. 1956. *Amor and Psyche.* Princeton, NJ: Bollingen Series.

———. 1972. *The Great Mother.* Princeton, NJ: Bollingen Series.

Ornstein, Robert E. 1977. *The Psychology of Consciousness.* 2d ed. New York: Harcourt Brace Jovanovich.

Ouspensky, P. D. 1974. *The Psychology of Man's Possible Evolution.* New York: Vintage.

Peck, M. Scott. 1983. *People of the Lie: The Hope for Healing Human Evil.* New York: Simon & Schuster.

Reynolds, David. 1988. *Water Bears No Scars: Japanese Lifeways for Personal Growth.* New York: William Morrow.

Sale, Roger. 1978. *Fairy Tales and After.* Cambridge, MA: Harvard University Press.

Schachtel, Ernest. *Metamorphosis.* New York: Basic Books.

Spence, Donald P. 1982. *Narrative Truth and Historical Truth.* New York and London: W. W. Norton.

Sternberg, Robert J. 1988. *The Triarchic Mind.* New York: Viking.

References

.... 267

Watkins, Mary. 1976. *Waking Dreams*. New York: Harper Colophon.

White, John, ed. 1972. *The Highest State of Consciousness*. Garden City, NY: Doubleday/ Anchor.

Zolla, Elemire. 1981. *Archetypes*. London: Allen & Unwin.

Myths and Tales

Abrahams, Roger. 1983. *African Folktales*. New York: Pantheon.

Albert, Mary. 1983. *How the Birds Got Their Colours: An Aboriginal Story*. Sydney: Ashton Scholastic.

Asbjornsen, Peter Christen, and Jorgen Moe. 1960. *Norwegian Folktales*. New York: Pantheon.

Aung, Maung Htin, and Helen G. Trager. 1968. *A Kingdom Lost for a Drop of Honey and Other Burmese Folktales*. New York: Parents Magazine Press.

Ausubel, Nathan. 1952. *A Treasury of Jewish Folklore*. New York: Crown.

Benardete, Seth, ed. 1965. *Larousse Greek and Roman Mythology*. New York: McGraw-Hill.

Biebuyck, Daniel, and Kahombo C. Mateene, eds. and trans. 1971. *The Mwindo Epic*. Berkeley and Los Angeles, CA: University of California Press.

Bierhorst, John. 1983. *The Sacred Path: Spells Prayers and Power Songs of the American Indians*. New York: William Morrow.

Black Elk. 1953. *The Sacred Pipe*. Ed. Joseph Epes Brown. Baltimore, MD: Penguin.

Booss, Claire, ed. 1984. *Scandinavian Folk and Fairy Tales: Tales from Norway, Sweden, Denmark, Finland, Iceland*. New York: Avenel Books.

Buber, Martin. 1947. *Tales of the Hasidim: The Early Masters*. New York: Schocken.

———. 1948. *Tales of the Hasidim: Later Masters*. New York: Schocken.

Calvino, Italo. 1956. *Italian Folktales*. New York: Pantheon.

Carey, George. 1971. *Maryland Folk Legends and Folksongs*. Cambridge, MA: Tidewater.

Chalk, Gary. 1984. *Tales of Ancient China*. London: Frederick Muller.

Chandler, Robert. 1979. *The Magic Ring and Other Russian Folktales*. London: Faber & Faber.

Christie, Anthony. 1968. *Chinese Mythology*. London: Hamlyn.

Cole, Joanna, ed. 1983. *Best Loved Folktales of the World*. Garden City, NY: Anchor Books/Doubleday.

Courlander, Harold, and George Herzog. 1947. *The Cow-Tail Switch and Other West African Stories*. New York: Henry Holt.

Crossley-Holland, Kevin. 1980. *The Norse Myths*. New York: Penguin.

Davidson, H. R. Ellis. 1969. *Scandinavian Mythology*. London: Hamlyn.

Degh, Linda, ed. 1965. *Folktales of Hungary*. Chicago, IL: University of Chicago Press.

DePaola, Tomie. 1983. *The Legend of the Bluebonnet*. New York: G. P. Putnam's Sons.

de Valera, Sinead. 1973. *Irish Fairytales*. London: Piccolo.

———. 1979. *More Irish Fairytales*. London: Piccolo.

Dorson, Richard M., ed. 1975. *Folktales Told Around the World*. Chicago, IL: University of Chicago Press.

Downing, Charles. 1956. *Russian Tales and Legends*. London: Oxford University Press.

Drake-Brockman H., ed. 1953. *Australian Legendary Tales*. Sydney: Angus and Robertson.

Feldmann, Susan, ed. 1963. *African Myths and Tales*. New York: Dell.

Fisher, Sally. 1980. *The Shining Princess*. New York: Metropolitan Museum of Art (A Studio Book), and Viking.

Gantz, Jeffrey. 1981. *Early Irish Myths and Sagas*. New York: Dorset.

Garfield, Leon, and Edward Blishen. 1970. *The God Beneath the Sea*. London: Kestrel Books.

——. 1974. *The Golden Shadow*. London: Carousel.

Garner, Alan. 1975. *The Guizer: A Book of Fools*. London: Hamish Hamilton.

Goodrich, Norma Lorre. 1960. *Ancient Myths*. New York: Mentor Books.

——. 1977. *Medieval Myths*. New York: Mentor Books.

Graves, Robert, and Raphael Patai. 1983. *Hebrew Myths: The Book of Genesis*. New York: Greenwich House.

Gray, John. 1969. *Near Eastern Mythology*. London: Hamlyn.

Green, Roger Lancelyn. 1967. *Tales of Ancient Egypt*. London: The Bodley Head.

Grundtvig, Svend. 1928. *The Emerald Fairy Book*. London: John F. Shaw & Co.

Haile, Berard, O. F. M. 1979. *Waterway*. Flagstaff, AZ: Museum of Northern Arizona Press.

Haviland, Virginia. 1973. *Told in India*. Toronto: Little, Brown.

Highwater, Jamake. 1986. *Anpao: An American Indian Odyssey*. New York: Harper Torchbook.

Hillerman, Tony. 1972. *The Boy Who Made Dragonfly*. New York: Harper & Row.

Hooke, S. H. 1963. *Middle Eastern Mythology*. London: Pelican.

Hyde-Chambers, Frederick and Audrey. 1981. *Tibetan Folktales*. Boulder, CO, and London: Shambhala.

In-Sob, Zong, ed. and trans. 1979. *Folktales from Korea*. New York: Grove Press.

Isaacs, Jennifer, ed. 1980. *Australian Dreaming: 40,000 Years of Aborignal History*. Sydney: Lansdowne.

Jameson, Cynthia. 1975. *Tales from the Steppes*. New York: Coward, McCann & Geoghegan.

Jewett, Eleanore M. 1953. *Which Was Witch? Tales of Ghosts and Magic from Korea*. New York: Viking.

Jones, Gwyn. 1955. *Welsh Legends and Folktales*. London: Puffin.

Jordan, A. C. 1979. *Tales from Southern Africa*. Berkeley and Los Angeles, CA: University of California Press.

Kendall, Carol and Yao-wen Li. 1978. *Sweet and Sour: Tales from China*. London: The Bodley Head.

Killip, Kathleen. 1980. *Twisting the Rope and Other Folktales from the Isle of Man*. London: Hodder and Stoughton.

Knappert, Jan. 1977. *Myths and Legends of Indonesia*. Hong Kong: Heinemann Educational Books (Asia).

——. 1980. *Malay Myths and Legends*. Hong Kong: Heinemann Educational Books (Asia).

Kramer, Samuel Noah, ed. 1961. *Mythologies of the Ancient World*. Garden City, NY: Anchor Books/Doubleday.

Lee, F. H. 1932. *Folktales of All Nations*. New York: Coward-McCann.

Levin, Meyer. 1931. *Classic Hassidic Tales*. New York: Dorset.

Lopez, Barry Holstun. 1977. *Giving Birth to Thunder, Sleeping with His Daughter*. New York: Avon Books.

Mackenzie, Donald. 1985. *German Myths and Legends*. New York: Avenel Books, Crown Publishers.

Maclagan, David. 1977. *Creation Myths*. London: Thames and Hudson.

Macmillan, Cyrus. 1974. *Canadian Wonder Tales*. London: The Bodley Head.

Manning-Sanders, Ruth. 1976. *Scottish Folktales*. London: Methuen.

Marriott, Alice, and Carol K. Rachlin. 1968. *American Indian Mythology*. New York: Mentor Books.

———. 1975. *Plains Indian Mythology*. New York: Mentor Books.

Marshall, Alan. 1952. *People of the Dreamtime*. Melbourne: Hyland House.

Massola, Aldo. 1968. *Bunjil's Cave*. Melbourne: Lansdowne Press.

McAlpine, Helen and William. 1958. *Japanese Tales and Legends*. London: Oxford University Press.

Megas, Georgios, ed. 1970. *Folktales of Greece*. Chicago, IL: University of Chicago Press.

Mercatante, Anthony S. 1978. *Good and Evil: Mythology and Folklore*. New York: Harper & Row.

Mercer, John. 1982. *The Stories of Vanishing Peoples*. London: Allison & Busby.

Miller, Olive Beaupre, ed. 1926. *Tales Told in Holland*. Chicago, IL: Book House for Children.

Minatoya, Lydia. 1992. *Talking to High Monks in the Snow*. New York: HarperCollins.

Monaghan, Patricia. 1981. *The Book of Goddesses and Heroines*. New York: E. P. Dutton.

Mullett, G. M. 1980. *Spider Woman Stories*. Tucson, AZ: University of Arizona Press.

Neihardt, J. 1961. *Black Elk Speaks*. Lincoln, NE: University of Nebraska Press.

Nicholson, Irene. 1967. *Mexican and Central American Mythology*. New York: Hamlyn.

Opie, Iona and Peter. 1974. *The Classic Fairy Tales*. London: Oxford University Press.

Pascheles, Wolff. n.d. *Jewish Legends of the Middle Ages*. London: Shapiro Vallentine.

Petrovitch, Woislav. 1927. *Hero Tales and Legends of the Serbians*. London: George G. Harrap.

Pino-Saavedra, Yolando. 1968. *Folktales of Chile*. London: Routledge & Kegan Paul.

Polsky, Howard W., and Yaella Wozner. 1989. *Everyday Miracles: The Healing Wisdom of Hasidic Stories*. London: Jason Aronson.

Power, Rhoda. 1969. *Stories from Everywhere*. London: Dennis Dobson.

Qoyawayma, Elizabeth. 1928. *The Sun Girl*. Flagstaff, AZ: Museum of Northern Arizona Press.

Radin, Paul. 1972. *The Trickster*. New York: Shocken.

Randolph, Vance. 1976. *Pissing in the Snow and Other Ozark Folktales*. New York: A Bard Book.

Ransome, Arthur. 1916. *Old Peter's Russian Tales*. London: Nelson.

Riordan, James. 1985. *The Woman in the Moon*. New York: Dial.

Roberts, Moss. 1979. *Chinese Fairytales and Fantasies*. New York: Pantheon.

Robinson, Gail. 1981. *Raven the Trickster*. London: Chatto & Windus.

Robinson, Gail, and Douglas Hill. 1975. *Coyote the Trickster*. London: Piccolo.

Salkey, Andrew, ed. 1980. *Caribbean Folktales and Legends*. London: Bogle-L'Ouverture Publications.

Schwartz, Howard. 1983. *Elijah's Violin and Other Jewish Fairytales*. New York: Harper & Row.

Shah, Idries, ed. 1979. *World Tales*. New York: Harcourt Brace Jovanovich.

Sherlock, Philip. 1986. *West Indian Folktales*. Oxford: Oxford University Press.

Simpson, Jacqueline. 1972. *Icelandic Folktales and Legends*. Berkeley and Los Angeles, CA: University of California Press.

Sleigh, Barbara. 1979. *Winged Magic*. London: Hodder and Stoughton.

Spence, Lewis. 1920. *The Myths of Mexico and Peru*. London: George G. Harrap.

Sproul, Barbara C. 1979. *Primal Myths*. London: Rider.

Stephens, James. 1920. *Irish Fairytales*. New York: Macmillan.

Stuchl, Vladimir, ed. 1979. *American Fairytales.* London: Octopus Books.
Sun, Ruth Q. 1967. *Land of Seagull and Fox: Folktales of Vietnam.* Rutland, VT: Charles E. Tuttle.
Tedlock, Dennis, trans. 1985. *Popol Vuh.* New York: Simon & Schuster.
Toor, Frances. 1985. *A Treasury of Mexican Folkways.* New York: Bonanza Books.
Turner, Frederic, ed. 1977. *The Portable North American* Indian *Reader.* New York: Penguin.
Uchida, Yoshiko. 1955. *The Magic Listening Cap: More Folktales from Japan.* Harcourt, Brace & World.
Underhill, Ruth M., Donald M. Bahr, Baptisto Lopez, Jose Pancho, and David Lopez. *Rainhouse and Ocean: Speeches for the Papago Year.* Flagstaff, AZ: Museum of Northern Arizona Press.
Van Over, Raymond, ed. 1980. *Sun Songs.* New York: Mentor Books.
Van Woerkom, Dorothy. 1975. *The Queen Who Couldn't Bake Gingerbread.* New York: Alfred A. Knopf.
Von Franz, Marie-Louise. 1972. *Creation Myths.* Zurich: Spring Publications.
Vyas, Chiman. 1972. *Folktales of Zambia.* Lusaka, Zambia: Neczam.
Waley, Arthur. 1973. *Dear Monkey.* New York: Bobbs-Merrill.
Waters, Frank. 1969. *Book of the Hopi.* New York: Ballantine.
Wenig, Adolf. 1923. *Beyond the Giant Mountains: Tales from Bohemia.* Boston: Houghton Mifflin.
Williams-Ellis, Amabel. 1981. *The Story Spirits: Tales from the Far East, Africa and the Caribbean.* London: Piccolo.
Wister, A.L. 1907. *Enchanted and Enchanting.* Boston: J. B. Lippincott.
Wolkstein, Diane, and Samuel N. Kramer. 1983. *Inanna.* New York: Harper Colophon.
Yagawa, Sumiko. 1979. *The Crane Wife.* New York: Mulberry Books.
Yolen, Jane, ed. 1986. *Favorite Folktales from Around the World.* New York: Pantheon.
Zimmerman, J. E. 1974. *A Dictionary of Classical Mythology.* New York: Bantam.

Creativity and Education

Abbs, Peter, ed. n.d. *Myth and Symbol in Education.* London: Tract/Cockpit Publications.
Ashton-Warner, Sylvia. 1964. *Teacher.* New York: Bantam.
Brown, George Isaac. 1971. *Human Teaching for Human Learning.* New York: Viking.
Bruner, Jerome. 1973. *Beyond the Information Given.* New York: W. W. Norton.
———. 1979. *On Knowing: Essays for the Left Hand.* Cambridge, MA: Belknap Press of Harvard University Press.
———. 1986. *Actual Minds, Possible Worlds.* Cambridge, MA: Harvard University Press.
Cox, Harvey. 1969. *The Feast of Fools.* Cambridge, MA: Harvard University Press.
deBono, Edward. 1970. *Lateral Thinking.* New York: Penguin.
Dewey, John. 1938. *Experience and Education.* New York: Collier.
Edwards, Betty. 1979. *Drawing on the Right Side of the Brain.* Los Angeles, CA: J. P. Tarcher.
Eisner, Elliot, ed. 1985. *Learning and Teaching the Ways of Knowing.* Chicago, IL: University of Chicago Press.
Fish, Stanley. 1980. *Is There a Text in the Class?* Cambridge, MA, and London: Harvard University Press.
Friere, Paul. 1973. *Education for Critical Consciousness.* New York: Seabury Press.
Ghiselin, Brewster, ed. 1955. *The Creative Process.* New York: Mentor Books.

Goldberg, Philip. 1983. *The Intuitive Edge*. Los Angeles, CA: J. P. Tarcher.

Gowan, J. C., J. Khatena, and E. P. Torrance. 1981. *Creativity: Educational Implications*. Dubuque, IA: Kendall/Hunt.

Gray, Farnum, and George C. Mager. 1973. *Liberating Education*. Berkeley, CA: McCutchan.

Greeley, Andrew. 1974. *Ecstasy—A Way of Knowing*. Englewood Cliffs, NJ: Prentice-Hall.

Holtz, Barry, ed. 1984. *Back to the Sources: Reading Classic Jewish Texts*. New York: Summit Books.

Houston, Jean. 1982. *The Possible Human*. Los Angeles, CA: J. P. Tarcher.

Huizinga, J. 1950. *Homo Ludens*. Boston, MA: Beacon Press.

John-Steiner, Vera. 1987. *Notebooks of the Mind*. New York: Harper & Row.

Jones, Richard M. 1968. *Fantasy and Feeling in Education*. New York: New York University Press.

Kagan, Jerome, ed. 1967. *Creativity and Learning*. Boston, MA: Beacon Press.

Karl, Frederick R., and Leo Hamalian. 1963. *The Existential Imagination*. Greenwich, CT: Fawcett.

King, Nancy, and Marianne Nikolov. 1992. "Storymaking and Drama with Two Groups of Hungarian Children." *Modern English Teacher* 1(2).

Koestler, Arthur. 1964. *The Act of Creation*. New York: Dell.

Kurfiss, Joanne G. 1988. *Critical Thinking: Theory, Research, Practice and Possibilities*. College Station, TX: Association for the Study of Higher Education.

Le Shan, Lawrence. 1975. *How to Meditate*. New York: Bantam.

Pfeiffer, John. 1982. *The Creative Explosion*. New York: Harper & Row.

Reimer, Bennett, and Ralph A. Smith, eds. 1992. *The Arts, Education, and Aesthetic Knowing*. Chicago, IL: University of Chicago Press.

Richards, M. C. 1973. *The Crossing Point*. Middletown, CT: Wesleyan University Press.

Rothenberg, Albert. 1979. *The Emerging Goddess: The Creative Process in Art, Science, and Other Fields*. Chicago, IL, and London: University of Chicago Press.

Rothenberg, Albert, and Carl R. Hausman, eds. 1976. *The Creativity Question*. Durham, NC: Duke University Press.

Ruitenbeck, Hendrik, ed. 1965. *The Creative Imagination*. Chicago, IL: Quadrangle.

Samples, Bob. 1976. *The Metaphoric Mind*. Reading, MA: Addison-Wesley.

Shor, Ira. 1980. *Critical Teaching and Everyday Life*. Boston, MA: South End Press.

Singer, Jerome. 1975. *The Inner World of Daydreaming*. New York: Harper & Row.

Staude, John-Raphael, ed. 1977. *Consciousness and Creativity*. Berkeley, CA: Ross Books.

Suzuki, Shunryu. 1970. *Zen Mind Beginner's Mind*. New York and Tokyo: Weatherhill.

Torrance, E. Paul. 1963. *Creativity*. Washington, D.C.: National Education Association.

Vernon, P. E., ed. 1970. *Creativity*. London: Penguin Books.

Williams, Linda Verlee. 1983. *Teaching for the Two-Sided Mind*. New York: Touchstone Book, Simon & Schuster.

Willis, George, and William H. Schubert, eds. 1991. *Reflections from the Heart of Educational Inquiry*. New York: State University of New York Press.

Storymaking

Gersie, Alida, and Nancy King. 1990. *Storymaking in Education and Therapy*. Stockholm: Stockholm Institute of Education, and London: Jessica Kingsley Press.

Heilbrun, Carolyn G. 1988. *Writing a Woman's Life*. New York: W. W. Norton.

Keen, Sam, and Anne Valley-Fox. 1974. *Telling Your Story.* New York: New American Library.

King, Nancy. 1993. *Storymaking and Drama: An Approach to Teaching Language and Literature at the Secondary and Post-secondary Levels.* Portsmouth, NH: Heinemann.

Mellon, Nancy. 1992. *Storytelling and the Art of the Imagination.* Rockport, MA: Element.

Stone, Elizabeth. 1988. *Black Sheep and Kissing Cousins.* New York: Penguin.

Index

academic inquiry, acknowledging feelings in, 10–11
accomplishment, sense of, 76
accountability, 243
action, in stories, developing, 163–64
actions, as component of learning, 97
active learning, 67–68, 96
    questions for children, 261
    value of, 69
activities, as component of learning, 97
"Anase the Storyteller," 146, 148–56
anger, acknowledging, 10
"Ant and the Elephant, The," 86–87
arms, warm-up activities, 115
arts
    assessment of, 256–61
    decision-making in, 8
    materials, 14–15, 120, 122–23
    value of, 2, 8–9, 69–72
assessment, 243–61, See also evaluation
    context for, 244
    of creative work, 256–61
    of educational development, 259–60
    encouraging learning through, 247–56
    framework for, 244–46
    image journals, 251–52
    involving children in, 247–50
    journals, 252–53
    learning journals, 253–54
    lifelong development and, 261
    love of learning, 59
    motivation, 250–51
    principles for, 243
    student portfolios, 254–56
    teaching methods and, 260–61
at-risk students, encouraging participation by, 27–33

attention, creativity and, 44–45
audience, for dramatic performance, 238
"Author's Corner," 53

balloons, movement activities about, 130–36
"Bargain Is a Bargain, A," 263–64
beginnings, of stories, 161–62, 202
Bettelheim, Bruno, 90
bibliographies, reading logs, 252
blocking, in dramatic performance, 234, 237
bobbing, as warm-up, 114
body movement. See movement
body sounds, 116
book reports, using movement, 56
book reviews, by children, 168, 169, 245, 252–53
brainstorming, 41
buddies, 160–61
    developing stories with, 161–65
    exploring imaginative movement with, 142–43
    reading with, 168–69

centering, as relaxation activity, 116
chants, 63–64
characters
    creating, 143–45, 173–74, 176–77, 180–81, 217
    developing, 162–63, 225–26
    for drama, 222–26
    exploring through sculpture, 125–26
    main, 162–63, 222–25
    in poetry, 194–98
    point of view of, 196–98
    in relation to other characters, 198–200
    through movement, 143–45
    visualizing, 123–24

273

characters (*cont.*)
  writing letters to, 216
  writing monologues for, 223–24
cheating, by students, 245–46, 252
child abuse, revealed in personal stories, 128
children. *See* students
choices
  making, 42
  productive, 221–22
  reflecting on, 42
"Cinderella," 27–33, 104
classroom activities
  encouraging participation in, 110–16
  framework for designing, 109–17
  grade levels for, 130
  organization of, 109–10
  participation in, 110–13
  program design components, 109
  relaxation, 116–17
  warm-up, 114–16
classroom management, 67–105
  collaborative learning and, 91–96, 244
  components of learning, 96–98
  creating community, 84–91
  discipline, 76–80
  engagement, 72–76
  imagination, creativity, and expression,
    80–84
  process-centered learning, 98–104
  response-tasks, 104–5
  restructuring, 14
clay, 120, 122–23, *See also* sculpting
climax, in drama, 229–30, 234
collaborative learning, 91–96, *See also* groups
  in drama, 230
  storymaking through, 166–67, 239
  value of, 96, 244
collapsing, as warm-up, 115
color, images of, 209–10
comfort levels, 111, 113
commentary, guidelines for, 113
communication. *See* language arts;
  nonverbal communication; oral language;
    written language
community
  between storytellers and listeners, 159–60
  between storytellers and self, 159–60
  creating in classroom, 84–91
  creating through sharing stories, 167–68
  nurturing, 90–91

competition, 91
conflict, in drama, 227, 234
connections, exploring, 127
containment, in storymaking, 200–201
control, fear of loss of, 69
convergent thinking, 68
cooperation, for collaborative learning, 91–96
costumes, 237–38
covers, for stories, 164
"Coyote and His Name," 63–64
creative work, assessing, 256–59
creativity
  classroom management and, 80–84
  ideas for exploring, 45–47
  loss of, 80
  regaining access to, 44–45
  stifling, 7
  suggestions for, 45
crisis, in drama, 227, 228–29, 234
"Critic's Corner," 168

dance, 55, *See also* movement
decision-making, *See also* problem-solving
  in creative projects, 8
Delaware, University of, Honor Program, 1
denouement, defined, 234
description of place, for poetry, 190–91
dialogue, memorizing, 182–83
diaries, 54, 204
differentiation, 68–69
directors, 236–37
disbelief, willing suspension of, 235
discipline, inner, 76–80
discomfort levels, 111, 113
discussion
  of images, 121–22
  vs. violence, 90
disruption, *See also* problem students
  planning for, 112–13
divergent thinking, 68
drafts, 155
  rewriting, 213
  spelling and grammatical errors in, 185–86
drama, 23–33, 49, 58–61, *See also* playwriting;
    plot; scenes; scripts
  conflict in, 227
  costumes for, 237–38
  directors, 236–37
  exploring, 49, 64–65, 170–83
  festivals of new plays, 239

memorization of lines, 182–83
movement, 56–57
performance, 236–39
points of view in, 172–73, 175–76, 178–79
props for, 237–38
teacher expectations for, 170–71
theatre vocabulary, 234–35
value of, 50, 69–71
visualizing scenes and telling moments, 171–72, 175, 177–78
dramatizing, dramamaking vs., 101–2
drumming, storytelling through, 146
dynamics, defined, 234

educational development, 259–60
Einstein, Albert, 119
emotional projection, defined, 234
empowerment, through sound names, 150–51
endings, of stories, 202
engagement, 72–76
evaluation, *See also* assessment
  as component of learning, 97–98
  scripts, 235
events
  between incidents in stories, writing about, 217–18
  creating in drama, 227–28
  exploring effects on relationships, 126–27
experimenting, 251
Exploring Connections, 110
  connecting stories to storytellers, 169–70
  creating characters through movement, 144–45
  creating and releasing tension, 138
  drama, 181–82
  imagemaking, 127
  imaginative movement, 139–40, 142–43
  interdependence, 137–38
  kinesthetic cues, 140
  movement, 136
  playwriting, 232–34
  poetic imagery, 199–200
  precise movement, 141–42
  sound stories, 156
  storymaking, 210–11
exposition, defined, 234
expression
  classroom management and, 80–84
  learning through, 11–13
  meaning and, 182

exterior monologues, 223
extrinsic motivation, 250

feelings
  acknowledging, 9–11
  exploring effects on perception, 127–28
  learning through, 11–13
  writing about, for storymaking, 204–7, 208–9
feet, warm-up activities, 115–16
festivals, of new plays, 239
fingerpainting, *See also* images and imagemaking
  choosing images for, 122
  encouraging engagement with, 72–76
  exploring imagination and creativity through, 45–46
  materials for, 14–15, 120
  for problem-solving, 39–40
  purpose of, 120
  student refusal, 121
flexibility, encouraging, 40
focus, 110
  meaning and, 182
  through dramatic play, 80
focus (theatre), defined, 234
follow-the-leader, 139–40
Freud, Sigmund, 201

gibberish, as relaxation activity, 117
grade levels, 130
grading, 258
Graham, Martha, 8
grammatical errors, 185–86
group bounce, 130
group follow-the-leader, 130
group poetry, 188–90
groups, *See also* collaborative learning
  community in, 84–91
  movement in, 133–34
  well-being of, 84

habitual behavior, 37–40
head, warm-up activities, 115
history, studying through drama, 58–61
"How Hummingbird Got Its Color," 202–11

image journals, 51, 90, 120, 251–52
images and imagemaking, 49, 50–52
  ability and, 69

images and imagemaking (*cont.*)
  of characters in drama, 222
  of characters in poetry, 193–96
  of characters in relation to other characters,
    198–200
  of characters in stories, 216
  choosing, 122
  color, 209–10
  creating stories from, 166, 199–200
  of ease, as relaxation activity, 116–17
  encouraging engagement with, 72–76
  exploring, 49, 64–65, 119–29
  of feelings, 204–7
  of invented characters, 217
  of negotiation, 207–8
  vs. painting, 50
  responses to, 121–22
  sharing ideas through, 52
  stimulating with movement, 134
  time allowed for, 50
  of time between incidents in stories, 217–
    18
  titles of, 194
  value of, 69–71, 119
imagination
  classroom management and, 80–84
  encouraging, 74
  ideas for exploring, 45–47
  invoking, 68
  regaining access to, 43–44
incentives, 260–61
incest, 201
inner discipline, developing through dramatic
  play, 76–80
inner resources, 40, 83–84
intention, defined, 234
interdependence, 137–38
interior monologues, 223
internal monologue, 181
intrinsic motivation, 243–44, 246
  shifting to, 250–51

"Jack and the Beanstalk," 85, 99, 123–27
journals, 257–58
  image, 51, 90, 120, 251–52
  learning, 253–54, 257–58
"Journey of the Stream, The," 91–92
judgment
  avoiding, 85, 121–22
  during playwriting, 221–22, 223

kinesthetic cues, 140
kinesthetic sense, 131
Korea, 37

labeling, by teachers, 99
"Lake Where the Sky Touches the Water, The,"
  213–32
language arts, *See also* nonverbal
  communication; oral language; tools
  for
  teaching language arts; written language
  developing through drama, 233
  establishing priorities for, 242–44
  tools for teaching, 49–65
laughter, inappropriate, 111
learning, *See also* collaborative learning
  components of, 96–98
  encouraging through assessment, 247–56
  love of, 22–23, 259
  process-centered, 98–104
  through expressing feelings, 11–13
learning journals, 253–54, 257–58
legs, warm-up activities, 115–16
letter-writing, to characters, 216
lifelong development, 261
listening skills, 85, 161
"Little Red Riding Hood," 53–54, 142, 143,
  170–81
logs, reading, 252–53, 257–58

main characters, 162–63, 222–25., *See also*
  characters
math, 13
  imagemaking, 71
  movement, 56
  storymaking, 54, 95–96
meaning
  focus and, 182
  space and, 182
  through verbal expression, 182
memories, writing as a script, 220–21
memorization
  of lines of dialogue, 182–83
  retention and, 80
  of scripts, 236
Minatoya, Lydia, 3
mirroring, 141–42
moment, defined, 234
"Momotaro the Peach Boy," 3
monologues

exterior, 223
interior, 223
internal, 181
for main characters, 223–24
reading out loud, 224–25
motivation
defined, 234
extrinsic, 250
incentives and rewards, 260–61
intrinsic, 243–44, 246, 250–51
movement, 49, 55–58
benefits of, 129–30
as a common image, 132–33
creating characters through, 143–45
in drama, 232, 237
exploring, 49, 64–65, 129–45
follow-the-leader activities, 139–40
imaginative, 139–40, 142–43
as nonverbal communication, 135
precise, 141–42
in small groups, 133–34
sound and, 133
stimulating imagery with, 134
vocabulary, 135–36
music, 49, 61–64
chants, 63–64
exploring, 145–57
new words for songs, 62–63

names
sound, 147–48
sound and rhythm, 147–48, 150
Native American stories, 59–61
negotiation, images of, 207–8
newspaper stories, 208
nonverbal communication, 119–57
defined, 234
imagemaking, 119–29
imaginative, 142–43
movement, 129–45
signals, 113
soundmaking and music, 145–55
notebooks, for image journals, 51, 90, 120,
251–52

observation
of patterns, 38–39
by teachers, 12–14, 38–39
Oedipus, 201
one-word stories, 81–83

oral language, 159–83, *See also* language arts
drama, 170–83
encouraging through movement, 57
encouraging through nonverbal
communication, 119
power of, 159
storytelling, 159–70
organization, of activities, 109

pace, defined, 234
painting, *See also* fingerpainting; images and
imagemaking
vs. imagemaking, 50
as tool for teaching, 49
participation, 110–16
disruption and, 112–13
self-consciousness and, 110–11
student refusal, 121
warming up for, 114–16
partners
buddies, 160–61
creating images with, 131–32
interdependence with, 137–38
kinesthetic cues with, 140
nonverbal communication with, 142–43
patterns
describing, 39–40
observing, 38–39
sound and rhythm, 150–51
perception, effects of feelings on, 127–28
performance, 236–39
audience for, 238
discussion following, 238–39
rehearsals for, 236–38
personal stories
creating drama from, 182
memories, 220–21
sharing, 128
place
describing, 190–91
point of view and, 179
voice of, 192–93
planning, involving students in, 247–50
playwriting, 23–33, 211–39, *See also* drama;
plot; scenes; scripts
character development, 173–74, 176–77,
180–81, 225–26
vs. dramatizing, 101–2
encouraging creativity in, 215–16
events, 227–28

playwriting (*cont.*)
    framework for, 215–21
    from poetry, 200
    from real-life episodes, 182
    from stories, 211, 212–13, 218–20
    ideas for, 212
    productive choice in, 221–22
    reading scripts out loud, 211–12
    reflection during, 232
    rewriting, 230
    sharing and reflection prior to, 231
    short play, 230–32
    telling moments, 172–73, 175–76, 178–79,
        180
    with young children, 170–71
plot, *See also* drama; playwriting
    climax in, 229–30
    conflict in, 227
    crisis in, 227, 228–29
    deepening, 164
    developing, 163, 225–26
poetry, 187–200
    attitudes toward, 187, 197–98, 199
    benefits of, 187
    character point of view in, 196–98
    character relationships in, 198–200
    defining, 188–89, 196–97
    in drama, 233
    group, 188–90
    imagery in, 193–96
    place description in, 190–91
    responding to, 193, 195
    titles for, 196
    voice of place in, 192–93
    writing drama from, 200
    writing from stories, 199, 210–11
    writing stories from, 199–200
point of view
    of characters, in poetry, 196–98
    cherishing, 194, 195
    developing understanding of, 165, 172–73,
        175–76, 178–79
    expressed in image titles, 194
    of place, in poetry, 192–93
    retelling stories from, 101–3
    in theatre, 234
    uniqueness of, 221
"Poor Tailor, The," 67
portfolios, student, 254–56, 257–58
potential, working toward, 83–84

precise movement, 141–42
preparation, by teachers, 13–15, 37–47, 109
priorities, establishing, 242–44
problem-solving
    choosing solutions, 42
    exploring possibilities, 40–42
    reflecting on choice and process, 42
    through brainstorming, 41
    through breaking habitual patterns, 39
problem students
    disruption by, 112–13
    process-centered learning and, 98–104
    working with, 23–27
process-centered learning, 98–104
    suggestions for, 103–4
productive choice, in playwriting, 221–22
projection, defined, 234
props, 234, 237–38

"Queen Who Couldn't Bake Gingerbread, The"
        (Van Woerkom), 93
questions, 110
    for active learning, 261
    stifling, 7
    as stimulation for storytelling, 166–67
quick release, as relaxation activity, 116

reading
    with buddies, 168–69
    encouraging, 245–46
    improving fluency through drama, 233
reading logs, 252–53, 257–58
reading out loud
    monologues, 224–25
    scripts, 211–12
    storytelling vs., 201–2
real-life episodes, creating drama from, 182
recording, as component of learning, 98
reflection, 110
    context for, 244
    during playwriting, 232
    principles for, 243
    prior to playwriting, 231
rehearsals, 236–38
relationships
    in drama, 225–26
    effects of events on, 126–27
    images of, 198, 225
relaxation activities, 116–17
resourcefulness, 40, 83–84

response
  by listeners, 161
  nonjudgmental, 85, 121–22
  to poetry, 193, 195
response-tasks, 104–5
revision
  as component of learning, 97
  of drafts, 213
rewards, 260–61
rhythm, 61, 62, 64
  sound and rhythm names, 147–48, 150
rhythm (theatre), 234
risk-taking, 260
role-playing, 58–61

scenes
  planning, 231
  visualizing, 171–72, 175, 177–78
  writing, 225–26
science, 13
  movement, 56
  storymaking, 54
script library, 239
scripts, *See also* drama; playwriting
  about memories, 220–21
  evaluating, 235
  first read-through, 236
  from stories, 218–20
  memorizing, 236
  performance, 236–39
  reading out loud, 211–12
  rehearsals, 236–38
  second read-through, 236
sculpting, *See also* clay
  characters in relationships, 198, 225
  choosing images for, 122
  for creating characters, 173–74
  for exploring characters, 125–26
  for exploring imagination and creativity,
    45–46
  for problem-solving, 39–40
  purpose of, 120
  as tool for teaching, 49
"Seeing Is Believing," 37–38
self, connecting stories to, 220–21
self-confidence, 19, 20
self-consciousness, 110–11
self-discovery
  through expression, 12–13
  through image-making, 119

self-esteem
  building through play-writing, 23–33
  improving through drama, 233
  teacher's influence on, 17
sentences, for group poem, 189–90
set, defined, 235
setting. See place
sharing, 110, 231
shoulders, warm-up activities, 115
show and tell, 169
silence, productive, 121
"slow learners," sound and music for, 62
"Snow White and the Seven Dwarfs," 187–200
songs
  in drama, 233
  writing from stories, 210–11
  writing new words for, 62–63
soundmaking, 49, 61–64
  defined, 145
  exploration of, 145–57
  movement and, 133
  as warm-up activity, 116
sound names, 147–48
sound and rhythm names, 147–48, 150
sound and rhythm patterns, 150–51
sound stories, 148–49
  creating, 151–54
  from stories, 154–56
  vocabulary, 150–51
sound words, 147–48
space
  exploring as a common image, 130
  meaning and, 182
spelling errors, 185–86
stage geography, 235
"Stone Soup," 83
stories
  beginning, 161–62, 202
  books of images about, 90
  choosing for storymaking, 200–201, 202
  connecting to self, 220–21
  connecting to storytellers, 169–70
  covers for, 164
  drafts of, 155
  drama from vs. dramatizing, 101–2
  encouraging confidence through, 18–19
  endings for, 202
  exploring through imagery, 125
  as frames, 165
  from poetic images, 199–200

stories (*cont.*)
  healing effects of, 90
  individual interpretations of, 89–90
  influence of, 17–33
  inspiration for, 165–66, 169–70
  as inspiration for poetry, 199
  length of, 160, 201
  repetition of, 90
  sharing, 168–69, 201–3
  sound, 148–56
  student reviews of, 168
  titles for, 164
  value of, 2
Stories Project, 1, 12, 72
storymaking, 49, 52–55, 165, 200–211
  collaborative, 166–67, 239
  containment in, 200–201
  defined, 200
  diaries, 54, 204
  enjoyment of, 52–53, 75–76
  exploring, 49, 64–65
  feelings in, 204–7, 208–9
  from different viewpoints, 101–3
  from one word, 81–83
  getting unstuck, 167
  for math and science problems, 54
  origins of, 83
  for problem-solving, 40
  questions for, 166–67
  sharing stories, 201–3
  stories for, 53–54, 154–56, 165, 200–201,
    202
  written, 200–211
storytellers, 169–70
storytelling, 159–70
  exploring imagination and creativity
    through, 46–47
  power of, 159
  vs. reading a story, 201–2
  response by listeners, 161
  space for, 202
  in storymaking process, 166
  through drumming, 146
stretching, as warm-up, 114
striking, as warm-up, 114–15
stuck moments, getting unstuck, 167
student portfolios, 254–56, 257–58
students
  book reviews by, 245–46
  cheating by, 245–46

community among, 84–91
disruption by, 112–13
involving in planning, 247–50
labeled as non-achievers, 27–33
labeled as trouble-makers, 23–26
self-consciousness of, 110–11
teaching to function in school setting,
  26–27
stumbling blocks, identifying, 111
suspension of disbelief, defined, 235
swinging, as warm-up, 114
symbolization, 68

talking, vs. violence, 90
talking drums, 146
tape recorders, for student book reviews, 168,
  245
teachers
  accountability concerns, 243
  art demonstrations by, 49
  benefits of collaborative learning for, 96
  concerns about cheating, 246
  discomfort with poetry in, 187
  expectations of, 170–71
  as facilitators, 68
  fear of loss of control by, 69
  labeling of students by, 23–33
  observation by, 12–14, 38–39
  preparation by, 13–15, 37–47, 109
  restructuring classroom practice, 14
  self-consciousness of, 110–11
teaching methods, assessment and, 260–61
television programs, incorporated into plot
  development, 163
telling moments
  exploring, 172–73, 175–76, 178–79, 180
  visualizing, 124–25, 171–72, 175, 177–
    78
tension, creating and releasing, 138
testing, 256
text, 110
theatre vocabulary, 234–35
thinking time, 121
through line, 235
time constraints, for imagemaking, 50
titles
  of images, 194
  for poetry, 196
  of sculptures, 198
  for stories, 164

tools for teaching language arts, 49–65
  defined, 49
  drama, 49, 58–61, 64–65
  ideas for exploring, 64–65
  imagemaking, 49, 50–52, 64–65
  movement, 49, 55–58, 64–65
  sound and music, 49, 61–64
  storymaking, 49, 52–55, 64–65
torso, warm-up activities, 115
trickster stories, 112
troubled students. *See* problem students
two-person scenes, exploring movement
    through, 144–45

Van Woerkom, Dorothy, 93
verbal communication. *See* oral language
vibrating, as warm-up, 115
viewpoints. *See* points of view
violence, talking vs., 90
vision, faithfulness to, 121–22
visualizing, 69
  characters, 123–24
  scenes and telling moments, 171–72, 175,
    177–78
  telling moments, 124–25
vocabulary
  expanding through playwriting, 233

expanding through storymaking, 210
related to movement, 135–36
sound stories, 150–51
theatre, 234–35
vocabulary lists, 162
voice of place, in poetry, 192–93

"walkabouts," 253
warm-up activities, 114–16
  parts of body, 115–16
  types of, 114–15
West African folktales, 146
willing suspension of disbelief, defined, 235
wind sounds, 88, 116
words, sound, 147–48
wrists, warm-up activities, 115
writing
  exploring imagination and creativity
    through, 46–47
  new words for old songs, 62–63
written language, 185–239, *See also* language
    arts
  drama, 211–39
  levels of, 186
  poetry, 187–200
  spelling and grammatical errors in, 185–86
  storymaking, 200–211